CAPABILITIES AND SOCIAL JUSTICE

This is probably the best introduction to the capability approach in social sciences ever written. Emphasis is laid on the philosophical background of the capability approach. The author compares the theories of Sen and Nussbaum to welfarism, Rawlsian and rights-based approaches. The merits and weaknesses of consequentialist and deontological versions are clearly explained. Capability theorists will be particularly interested in John Alexander's argument that the capability approach is closer to republicanism than to mainstream liberalism. Throughout the text, the practical relevance of philosophical debates for development issues is made clear. Arguments are carefully devised in a highly readable text.
Antoon Vandevelde, University of Leuven, Belgium and editor of
Gifts and Interests, Peeters, 2000

John Alexander's work is a very good study of one of the leading approaches to social justice in contemporary political theory. It shows a very strong grasp of the authors discussed and is completely up-to-date on the relevant literature. It is very well written – very clear throughout, well-structured, and easy to follow. The lines of argument in the work are always on the mark and are challenging and original. As a whole, the book makes an important contribution to the literature on social justice and is particularly strong on bringing together traditions that are often seen as rivals.
John Baker, University College Dublin, Ireland and author of
Arguing for Equality, Verso, 1987 and co-author of *Equality: From Theory to Action*, Palgrave, 2004

This is a very helpful discussion of the main issues connected with the capability approach to social justice associated with Amartya Sen and Martha Nussbaum. John Alexander is very well versed in recent discussions of social justice and in addition to giving a lucid account of the capability approach brings it into fruitful dialogue with the main strands of that recent discussion. He writes with intelligence and lucidity, and brings his work together in a well-argued text that engages and enlightens the reader.
William Desmond, University of Leuven, Belgium and author of many books
including *Hegel's God* (Ashgate), *Ethics and the Between* (SUNY) and
God and the Between (Blackwell)

Capabilities and Social Justice
The Political Philosophy of Amartya Sen and Martha Nussbaum

JOHN M. ALEXANDER
University of Leuven, Belgium

ASHGATE

© John M. Alexander 2008

Published by
Ashgate Publishing Limited
Wey Court East
Union Street
Farnham
Surrey GU9 7PT
England

Ashgate Publishing Company
Suite 420
101 Cherry Street
Burlington, VT 05401-4405
USA

Ashgate website: http://www.ashgate.com

British Library Cataloguing in Publication Data
Alexander, John M.
Capabilities and social justice: the political philosophy of Amartya Sen and Martha Nussbaum
1. Sen, Amartya Kumar – Political and social views 2. Nussbaum, Martha Craven, 1947 – Political and social views 3. Social justice 4. Political science – Philosophy
I. Title
320.5'13'0922

Library of Congress Cataloging-in-Publication Data
Alexander, John M.
Capabilities and social justice: the political philosophy of Amartya Sen and Martha Nussbaum / John M. Alexander.
    p. cm.
Includes bibliographical references.
  ISBN 978-0-7546-6187-0 (hardback: alk. paper) 1. Distributive justice. 2. Social justice.
3. Social choice. 4. Merit (Ethics) 5. Resource allocation–Political aspects. 6. Sen, Amartya Kumar. 7. Nussbaum, Martha Craven, 1947- I. Title.
HB523.A43 2007
320.01–dc22

2007013124

ISBN 978-0-7546-6187-0

Reprinted 2009

Printed and bound in Great Britain by TJI Digital, Padstow, Cornwall.

*To Nancy, Vincy, and
my beloved parents, Michael and Anthoniammal*

Contents

Acknowledgements

As I complete this work and look back in retrospect, what even to my own amazement stands out is the magnitude of indebtedness that I have accumulated over the years; I begin to wonder whether I would ever be able to repay for all the inspiration, encouragement and support I have received from so many people. In the first place I deeply appreciate the kindness of Antoon Vandevelde who offered me the opportunity to work on this research project and has been very supportive throughout. His critical remarks and suggestions on different versions of the text have played a great role in improving the line of reasoning and arguments. I admire his keen intellect, philosophical wisdom and kind-heartedness. John Baker, Erik Schokkaert, Luc Van Liedekerke, Philippe Van Parijs, André Van de Putte, Herman De Dijn, Yvonne Denier, Jane Buckingham, Joe Arun, S.G. Selvam, Ronald Tinnevelt, Roger Burggraeve, Koen Decancq, Kurt Devooght, Bart Engelen, Stijn Neuteleers, Thomas Nys, Sylvie Loriaux, Jos Philips and Stefan Rummens have all been kind enough to read different parts of the book at various stages and give their valuable comments.

The Research Council of the University of Leuven, Belgium has generously supported this research project including my research visits to the University of Cambridge, UK, Harvard University, US and WIDER, United Nations University, Finland. I owe a special thanks to P. Christie SJ, Director of Loyola Institute of Business Administration for his unwavering support and encouragement, and to Camillus Fernando, Stanislaus Swamikannu, Bellarmine Fernando and other salesians of Don Bosco, Tamil Nadu, India and their counterparts in Flanders, Belgium particularly Piet Palmans and Jos Claes for giving me the opportunity, hospitality and the most conducive atmosphere to embark on this research venture.

Starting from December 2001, I have had the occasion to present different parts of this work at the conferences organized by the Human Development and Capability Association (HDCA) and the UK Association for Social and Legal Philosophy. I have greatly benefited from the reactions and cordiality of the participants and organizers of these events particularly Ingrid Robeyns, Enrica Chiappero, Flavio Comim, Des Gasper, Gideon Calder and Ananda Duraiappah.

For some years now, I have been trying to express my views and concerns on different issues of social justice. I wish to express my gratitude to Mr N. Ram, Editor-in-Chief of India's national newspaper *The Hindu* and fortnightly *Frontline* and his editorial staff particularly R. Vijaya Sankar for providing me with a forum to write for a wider readership. I appreciate very much the help of Claire Dawson for meticulously reading and correcting the manuscript, and Maria Alphonse, Gerard Saverimuttu and Cyriac Thayil for assisting me with technical details. I cherish with fondness the support and affection that I have received during these years from the families and friends of Rita Dedobbeleer, Rudi Huwaert, Bart Baele, Caroline and Ludo Meyvis, Kathy and Eric Goethals, Jochim Lourduswamy and Renilde Van de Velde.

And finally, both Amartya Sen and Martha Nussbaum have made my work a challenging and rewarding experience. In the winter of 2004, Sen was gracious to invite me to Harvard to be a visiting researcher under his guidance. Nussbaum offered me valuable comments when I presented parts of my research at the HDCA international conferences. I thank them for their kindness and encouragement in these and other moments. Their work which combines a passion for justice with the richness of philosophical reasoning is a great source of insight and inspiration for me. I would be more than content if this book is able to offer even a glimpse of that combination.

J.M. Alexander
31 January 2008, the 120th death anniversary of
Don Bosco – the philosopher and friend of youth

Introduction

How should we assess a person's well-being and quality of life? In what sense, as a matter of justice, should a person be judged as equal or unequal in society? These are two distinct questions demanding different levels of inquiry. We can for example, consider a wide range of things to be valuable for a person's well-being – from a life of bare survival to scientific and social achievements to leisure, luxury, emotional maturity and spiritual realization. Yet we might not find all of them to be relevant to judge whether or not the person's standing in society is equal. A theory of justice cannot be tantamount to a theory of well-being. Judgments regarding claims of justice invariably require not only identifying and delineating certain aspects of well-being, but also finding the appropriate normative principles by which to treat people as equals in society. Even though the capability approach, advocated by Amartya Sen and Martha Nussbaum, originated as providing a unique answer to the first question, the question about well-being and the quality of life particularly in the context of poverty and deprivation, it is also now envisaged by extension as a distinct approach to issues of social justice.

I have two main motivations for undertaking this treatise on human capabilities and justice. One is to develop a systematic philosophical study of the capability approach, focusing particularly on those claims and characteristics which can provide justification for it as an approach to social justice. The other is my discomfort with the way some capability theorists and others tend to draw the capability approach exclusively within a liberal paradigm. I try to show that when carefully studied and interpreted, the capability approach offers valuable resources for a critique of the liberal conception of justice.

I shall briefly delve into each of these motivations before turning to the point of how these have inspired and shaped the arguments and structure of the book. In recent years, Sen and Nussbaum's collaborative work on the capability approach has come to play a major role in normative economics, social ethics and political philosophy. It has received a warm reception from many academics as well as a wider support among international agencies and non-governmental organizations. Unfortunately, most of the theoretical discussions so far have been somewhat narrow, concentrating either on the doctrinal differences between Sen and Nussbaum or on the conceptual and policy superiority of their approaches. With a view to building further upon the valuable contributions these discussions have made in situating the capability approach in the ongoing conversations and debates in social sciences and development discourse in particular, the primary aim of the book is to broaden and turn the course of these discussions towards the intellectual structure and philosophical underpinnings of the capability approach. As it is construed, elucidated and critically scrutinized here, the fundamental intent of a capability theorist is to defend the idea that social justice consists in creating the greatest possible condition for the realization of basic capabilities for all. Readers who are familiar with the capability approach literature would know that the pioneers of the approach themselves do not articulate their objectives exactly along these lines. Nonetheless such an ecumenical formulation captures most of what they intend to achieve. The ideal of realizing basic capabilities for all is a central impetus in the works of Nussbaum and Elizabeth Anderson who explicitly endorse a list of basic capabilities, although Nussbaum advocates a comparatively more elaborate list than Anderson. This is also the guiding principle for Sen who, without committing himself to a definite list of basic capabilities, envisions the approach as a plural and public conception of justice intimately tied to democracy and public reasoning.

Strictly speaking, the ideal of realizing basic capabilities for all citizens so that people would have the required economic, social and political freedoms to lead the type of life they have reason to value need not necessarily be viewed as a social justice claim. It can very well be the consequence of a judgement that certain absolute forms of poverty and capability deprivation are bad and even scandalous, and that no decent society should tolerate them, particularly when it has the material and human resources to overcome them. What then makes it precisely a social justice claim? If it is a social justice claim, how should we respond? The aspiration of realizing basic capabilities for all can be justified to be a justice claim when it flows from the moral judgement that all capability inequalities in life prospects meted out to people by the basic structure of society and for which they are not responsible are *prima facie* unjust. Hence as a response, the focus of the capability approach as a theory of justice is not to level down or even out people's differences in talents, capacities and potentialities, but to design society's economic and political institutions in such a way that adequate material and social resources are available to everyone in order to possess and exercise a set of basic capabilities that go to make up a decent life. At the same time, it is of supreme importance to be aware that social justice is not a canonical profession in a single principle, but an aspiration to realize certain human and institutional conditions embodying a plurality of principles and balancing their demands in a coherent way. This implies that depending on the kind of basic capability at stake, some principles and patterns of distribution more than others become relevant for social justice to obtain in the society in question. For example, when it concerns capabilities such as being adequately nourished (nutrition), being sufficiently educated (basic education) or the ability to avoid common and preventable illness (primary health care), it would be social responsibility rather than merely individual merit and achievement which should be stressed. As a result, realizing these capabilities for all citizens would require a social safety net in the form of unemployment benefits, minimum-wage legislation, primary health insurance, pension provisions, affirmative policies, etc – although there are likely to be disagreements with regard to how tight the safety net should be and what level of social minimum it should guarantee. These institutional expressions of social responsibility and solidarity can be justified only to the extent that they are meant not to replace or undermine agency and personal responsibility but to facilitate them. On the other hand, when it concerns more complex capabilities relating to social positions, jobs, careers, honours, recognition and political participation, other considerations such as efficiency, desert or fair equality of opportunity will come to the fore. In all these, the key point to bear in mind is that the realization of the ideal of basic capabilities for all will involve a plurality of equally valuable principles and complex institutional structures.

Moreover, the understanding of the term 'basic' embodied in the ideal of 'basic capabilities for all' assumes a special connotation. Sen was indeed perceptive to point out that poverty is relative in terms of resources and absolute in terms of capabilities for the reason that depending on the context different amounts of resources might be required to achieve the same functioning. Yet when we want to spell out the different capabilities that should exert a normative pull, it turns out that what might be deemed as 'basic' – or even analogous concepts such as 'urgent' and 'decent' – is relative to culture, history and the level of a country's economic prosperity and political maturity. The things which may be stated as basic and vital in one place might be considered as nonessential and a luxury in another context. An everyday or a commonsense reading that is likely to be shared by most societies is the idea that basic capabilities are those whose absence would foreclose the exercise and development of many other capabilities. Adequate nutrition and good health, we might say, open the door for education, learning and creativity, just as literacy and appropriate levels of formal and public education facilitate informed social interaction and political participation. Experience has, however, shown that the everyday understanding can be biased, less generous and not up to the mark. One possible way to overcome the potential arbitrariness and inadequacy is to flesh out the content and to come up with a list of basic capabilities that could be endorsed for political purposes – as Nussbaum and Anderson have proposed to do. Such an approach has to face the problems of paternalism and justification but in principle, these incriminations can be somewhat tempered by pointing out that the list is open-ended and that the abstract and vague character of the items on the list permits multiple specifications according to contexts through subsequent legislative, executive and judicial procedures. Another possible choice is to relativize the importance of making a list and appeal more to fair processes of public reasoning and democratic institutions. It is true that a list of basic capabilities can play a pertinent role in informing and counterchecking our intuitions regarding social justice, as it is with the Universal Declaration of Human Rights or the list of fundamental entitlements embodied in a country's constitutions. However, they cannot be a proxy for the larger process of value construction through public debate and discussion. Most societies do have some operative understanding of principles and policies pertaining to justice, implicitly acknowledged as part of the social ethos and interpretative social dialogue or explicitly invoked in public discussion and political justification. Philosophical conceptions of justice do not have to exactly mirror public conceptions, but they cannot be completely remote from them, either.

The second motivation of this treatise is to illustrate how the capability approach breaks with certain forms of liberalism at key points. 'Liberalism' means different things to different people and includes various great philosophers such as Locke, Rousseau, Kant, Mill, Berlin, Rawls, Dworkin and many others. Nonetheless, one prototypical idea that has remained central to the liberal tradition is the moral equality of each individual. Human beings are ends in themselves and must be treated with dignity and respect irrespective of their class, caste, creed and gender. The capability theorists are in strong agreement with this liberal tenet. However, along with the idea of moral equality, liberalism has also bequeathed an accompanying idea, the idea of freedom as non-interference: individuals are said to be free only when there is no interference from others – the state, the law or fellow citizens. This is central to *laissez-faire* liberalism, but its residue can be found to varying degrees in other camps as well.

The capability theorists disagree with this presupposition. Freedom is not merely the absence of interference, but also the possession of different capabilities to achieve valuable human functionings. A person who is poor, uneducated, unemployed, afflicted by a preventable disease or socially excluded might encounter no interference from the state or fellow citizens, but he or she certainly lacks the required capacities and opportunities to live a life of freedom. This being the stark reality in most of our contemporary capitalist liberal democracies, it is important to emphasize the idea that a society fails to treat some of its members as equals not only when it restricts or interferes with them, but also when it permits them to grow up in poverty and suffer various forms of capability shortfalls and deprivation. Hence, the capability theorists, as it is argued here, are not against interferences *per se*. It is well within the spirit of the capability approach to tolerate certain qualified forms of 'interferences' for redistributive purposes and for the provision of public goods so that maximum conditions for basic capabilities can be realized for all citizens. Particularly when these interventions are capabilities-promoting for everyone and are stipulated to take place under the purview of a fair rule of law and in compliance with human rights, they can hardly be considered as interferences in the negative sense of the term.

Coming as they are from different cultural, intellectual and academic backgrounds, Sen and Nussbaum have developed the central intuitions of the capability approach with different emphases and in somewhat different directions. While Sen defines the relevant concepts and indicates the possibility of an alternative paradigm of justice supported by a broad consequentialist ethics, Nussbaum strengthens the theoretical edifice of the capability approach by showing its connection to Aristotle's ethics and political philosophy and by developing a hybrid theory of capabilities that blends Aristotelian philosophy with certain liberal doctrines. Sen pioneered the idea in welfare economics and political philosophy that people's well-being and their standing in society should be assessed not merely in terms of resources available to them or the psychological sensations generated by the utilization of those resources, but rather on the basis of 'functionings' and 'capability to valuable human functionings'. The conceptual forerunner to this idea can be traced back to the concept of 'entitlements' that emerged in the context of Sen's study of famines. Contrary to the conventional Malthusian wisdom that attributed famines to the shortage of food supply, Sen's political economy of famines illustrates a bitter truth: millions of people die during famines not mainly because there is any significant decline of food available in the region, but because they lose their entitlements – abilities and purchasing power to acquire food and to achieve health and nourishment. Therefore, the fight against famines, poverty and other major societal failures can be more effectively won by protecting and promoting people's entitlements and by recognizing the interconnections of economic and political forces that cause these failures.

Nussbaum must be accredited for having philosophized the capability approach particularly by indicating how Sen's insight revisits some of the key Aristotelian ideas. Aristotle rejects hedonism, and characterizes people who focus only on pleasure, money and wealth as those lacking depth. The good life, according to Aristotle, consists in identifying and organizing one's life in accordance with a set of 'valuable human functions'. Aristotle also proposes an allied political philosophy whose main concern is to design appropriate political principles and institutions which would facilitate the good life of the citizens. The metaphor of 'the thick vague conception' of human flourishing that the earlier Nussbaum deployed in order to derive the universal list of capabilities is indicative of her dissatisfaction with dominant liberal theories and throws much light on her own objective to take the frontiers of political philosophy in the footsteps of Aristotle. Yet Nussbaum is also a critical and judicious reader of Aristotle. Although Aristotle thought that the good life should consist in striving for valuable human functions and excellence, he also entertained the idea that certain categories of people such as the slaves, craftsmen, foreign residents and women did not qualify for a fuller social and political participation. The lack of the idea of equal human dignity is a major deficit in Aristotle's thinking. Nussbaum's hybrid theory of capabilities reconstructs Aristotle filling up this lacuna. Just as much of contemporary liberal apathy towards people's capability failures and deprivation can be exorcized by confronting it with the Aristotelian capabilities-oriented reasoning, a revival of Aristotle's philosophy for contemporary purposes would also have to rework and correct its underlying hierarchical and elitist propensities.

Bearing in mind the two purposes of this project spelled out thus far, the arguments of the book are arranged into seven successive chapters, divided into two parts. The reader, I hope, finds this to be a plausible and defensible interpretation of the capability approach to social justice. In Chapters 1 to 3 in Part I, the basic insights and concepts of the capability approach are introduced in discussion with two other influential theories in contemporary political philosophy: utilitarianism and Rawls's justice as fairness theory. I try to show how the limitations of these theories serve as points of departure for a capabilities-oriented understanding of justice. Attention is also paid to the specific contributions of Sen, Nussbaum and Anderson and to some of the key objections that have come up in the recent philosophical literature. Even though the capability approach has its own unique difficulties and ambivalences to resolve at the level of both theory and practice, the three chapters of Part I argue for the conclusion that a capabilities-based understanding of justice emerges as a persuasive non-utilitarian approach.

Chapters 4 to 7 in Part II examine in depth and in some detail the underlying ethical and political principles as well as the philosophical traditions involved in the capability approach. Having identified the theory of broad consequentialism, the issue of individual responsibility and Nussbaum's hybrid theory of capabilities to be the major philosophical foundations for a capabilities-based theory of social justice, I discuss the problems and issues involved in each of these areas. In the seventh and final chapter, I try to give an overall view of the capability approach, focusing particularly on the way the capability approach can be elevated as a political conception. Here two conclusions are suggested. First, it is argued that the capability approach has the potential to offer a critique of the liberal conception of justice, since it seeks to embody the ideal of realizing basic capabilities for everyone in positive freedom and public reasoning. Second, it is pointed out that a capabilities-based critique of the liberal conception of justice can be much more radicalized by extending the theoretical framework of the capability approach so as to incorporate the republican notion of freedom as non-domination.

PART I
The Capability Approach
in Perspective

Chapter 1

Sen's Critique of Utilitarianism

Considerable evidence suggests that if we use an increase in our incomes, as many of us do, simply to buy bigger houses and more expensive cars, then we do not end up any happier than before. But if we use an increase in our incomes to buy more of certain *inconspicuous* goods – such as freedom from a long commute or a stressful job – then the evidence paints a different picture. The less we spend on conspicuous goods, the better we can afford to alleviate congestion; and the more time we can devote to family and friends, to exercise and sleep, travel and other restorative activities. On the best available evidence, reallocating our time and money in these and other similar ways would result in healthier, longer – and happier – lives.

Robert H. Frank, 'How Not to Buy Happiness'

How can you measure Progress if you don't know what it costs and who has paid for it? How can the 'market' put a price on things – food, clothes, electricity, running water – when it doesn't take into account the *real* cost of production?

Arundhati Roy, *The Algebra of Infinite Justice*

From the late eighteenth century, utilitarianism has been a prominent moral theory particularly in the sphere of public philosophy, even though some of its defenders have advocated it as a comprehensive theory suitable both for personal and public morality. The main intention of these theorists was to search for a *single* criterion or principle based on which individual actions as well as social policies and institutions can be evaluated. There are different varieties of utilitarianism depending on whether one takes utility to be some psychological states of pleasure or happiness, or whether one takes utility to be the satisfaction of 'actual' or 'rational' preferences. Nonetheless the fundamental tenet of utilitarianism is that one should do whatever maximizes total or average utility. Sen has often developed the theoretical foundations of the capability approach in response to the limitations of the various forms of utilitarianism and envisages a capabilities-based understanding of justice as an alternative non-utilitarian approach.

One of Sen's crucial objections to utilitarianism is that it is a subjective approach to well-being which requires us to maximize utility or welfare construed as pleasure, happiness or preference-satisfaction. Sen does not advocate a dictatorial or paternalistic approach by which governments, policymakers and interested third parties would pursue or promote people's well-being against their own will and consent. Yet he thinks that an approach to social justice should search for certain non-subjective criteria as the basis for claims of justice. Sen's critique of utilitarianism, as discussed in what follows, shares a number of common features with those of

Rawls, Dworkin, Williams, Elster and Scanlon. However, Sen also takes up issues with different forms of utilitarianism with applying his own unique economic and philosophical insights and viewpoints. While some of them are reminiscent of Aristotle's admonition of hedonism, others try to revive Adam Smith's appreciation for the complexity of moral sentiments and human motivations. Sen's (1980) criticism has generally made use of two lines of approach. The first one, which Sen calls the 'prior-principle critique', consists in appealing to general principles such as freedom, human rights, equity and commitment which at a more fundamental level conflict with the principle of utility. The second one known as the 'case-implication critique' exposes the inconsistencies present in various forms of utilitarianism by constructing examples of special cases that counter-check our moral intuitions. Moreover, Sen finds the consequentialist ethics (§1.2) espoused by utilitarianism and the anthropological vision of *homo economicus* (§1.3) underlying the standard economic explanation of motivation and rationality to be reductionist.

1.1 Forms of Utilitarianism

a) Hedonism

Jeremy Bentham (1748-1832), generally considered the father of utilitarianism, advocated that 'the greatest happiness of the greatest number' should be the criterion of assessment for social policies and individual actions. By this he meant that the sum total of human happiness should be made as large as possible over the long run. Furthermore, he construed 'happiness' in terms of mental states of pleasure and pain: a life is said to be going well to the extent it contained a balance of pleasurable sensations over painful ones (Bentham 1970). Bentham envisaged utilitarianism to be a 'democratic' theory in the sense that everyone *a priori* should be treated as equally important: 'everybody is to count for one, and nobody for more than one'. This principle implies that each person's interests and preferences should be given equal consideration and that no one has the right to either change them, or in instances of social choices, assign them more or less weight than those of others. It is important to note that Bentham conceived of the utilitarian criterion of maximizing happiness as a *rival* to individual rights as the criterion of social justice. According to Bentham, positive rights specified by the existing legislations and institutions might either be a hindrance or helpful to the maximization of utility and hence, the worth of individual rights (including moral and human rights) should be judged according to the standard of utility.

From the standpoint of Sen's capability approach, the Benthamite utilitarianism is a hedonistic view of human well-being. There is indeed something attractive about the idea that individuals should pursue happiness and avoid pain and suffering. Perhaps this is the reason why utilitarianism has for so long remained an appealing theory in public philosophy. But to reduce happiness to psychological states of pleasurable sensations and to advocate pleasure as the sole criterion of well-being is problematic. It is nothing other than inadequate judgement to assess people's quality of life purely on the basis of their feelings of pleasure. Pleasurable sensation cannot be the only good that people seek in life. There are many other things that people find valuable to pursue even when they involve considerable discomfort and pain. Therefore, as an alternative approach it seems more appropriate to evaluate people's lives on the basis of different and heterogeneous 'doings' and 'beings' which Sen technically calls 'functionings' such as nutrition, health, education, social recognition and political participation. These functionings may contribute to different mental states including pleasure and happiness, but nevertheless they are quite distinct from the psychological sensations they induce.

Moreover, when we apply Sen's prior-principle critique, the hedonistic species of utilitarianism turns out to be a false egalitarian doctrine for it assumes that persons are nothing but a sum of their pleasure. As an implication of the utilitarian maxim 'everybody is to count for one, nobody for more than one', it is true that every person is treated as equal or of equal worth irrespective of whether one is a man or woman, Muslim or Christian, black or white. But this is in effect not an equal treatment because the items of worth or elements of value are not persons as such, but rather experiences of pleasure or satisfaction which persons have. Even though from a moral point of view people's interests matter equally, it does not follow that the best way of giving form to that idea is to give the desire of each person the same weight without regard for the 'content' of those desires and the impact they are likely to have on others (Hart 1979: 829-830; Kymlicka 1990: 26). If people get pleasure from inflicting harm on others, should that be counted? As Sen insists, egalitarian judgements should take into account not just utility information concerning people's pleasurable experiences, but whether they conflict with non-utility factors such as people's human rights and commitments. Also, from the case-implication point of view, Sen (1997a: 16-20) finds utilitarianism to be morally counter-intuitive. He considers the example of a handicapped person who needs extra money to be mobile and another person, a pleasure-wizard, who derives a great deal of satisfaction from every dollar that he is able to spend. Equalizing marginal utility between the two requires giving more money to the latter and less to the really needy, the handicapped person.

The philosophical basis for Sen's criticism of hedonism and his proposal to view human well-being in terms of what people are *actually* able to do and be can be embedded in a long tradition going back to Aristotle, whereby 'pleasure' was to be distinguished from 'happiness'. As sketched out in his *Ethics*, Book I, for Aristotle happiness (*eudaimonia*) consists in pursuing worthwhile *activities* of excellence and character rather than pleasurable amusements. He also argued that these valuable activities are varied and plural: art and science, love and friendship, ethical and political excellence and so on. Aristotle never suggests that pleasure is something bad or something that should be avoided. What he uncompromisingly rejects is the identification of happiness with a life of pleasure. Pleasure, he believed, is something that usually accompanies an unobstructed performance and accomplishment of the activities that constitute happiness. A life of pure pleasure, for Aristotle, is something meant for cattle and not for human beings (*Ethics* I, 5: 68).[1] As Arendt (1958: 175ff.)

---

1   Henceforth, Aristotle's writings will be referred to in the following sequence: title of the work (*Ethics*, *Politics* or *On Rhetoric*), Book number, Chapter number and finally the relevant page numbers of the editions found in the bibliography.

has illuminatingly demonstrated, not only for Aristotle, but generally in the Greek tradition, it was common to make a distinction between *praxis* and *poiésis*, between action and work. For the Greeks, action was superior to just fabrication of things for use and consumption. The former belongs to the sphere of freedom because through action and speech, argument and discussion, people can participate in the public realm both as equals to others and at the same time distinguish themselves from others by creativity and excellence. The latter belongs to the sphere of necessity and routine where the producer often has to conform and cater to the tastes of the consumer. In the Greek paradigm then, it is not the one who produces the violin, but the one who plays it who appreciates its real worth. Hedonism is, in a way, incapable of making this distinction because it regards the relation between actions and happiness as cause to effect: actions do not have an intrinsic importance and independent value; they are instrumentally valued in function of experiences they produce.

b) Utilitarian Liberalism

John Stuart Mill (1806-1873) is a more complex philosopher than other utilitarian thinkers. He professes allegiance to utilitarianism as well as to liberal values, both vying with each other for equal consideration. Mill holds an important place in moral philosophy not because he suggested a non-utilitarian approach to public philosophy, in fact he remained a strong advocate of utilitarianism, but because his philosophy genuinely exhibits the tension of having to be a *utilitarian* and *liberal* at the same time (Lyons 1977; Annas 1977). Mill refines and broadens the content of utility: 'I regard utility as the ultimate appeal on all ethical questions; but it must be utility in the largest sense, grounded on the permanent interests of man as a progressive being' (Mill 1995: 81). Accordingly, Mill's conception of happiness includes not merely 'quantitative' but also 'qualitative' experiences and associates happiness with 'self-development'. A happy person, according to Mill, is one who refines his tastes, increases his sympathies and pays close attention to his character and standards of excellence. In this sense Mill, in his definition of happiness, is much closer to Aristotle than to his utilitarian guru Bentham.

Furthermore, on the societal level, Mill advances a number of liberal tenets. In *On Liberty* (1995), he advocates anti-paternalism as a general social policy and argues for the 'liberty principle', namely the only good reason to restrict an adult individual's liberty is to prevent harm to others. In his writings on political economy (Mill 1965), he favours economic competition and free exchange, but he also envisages a role for the state in providing public goods, which otherwise would not be provided by an unregulated capitalist economy. In his political writings (Mill 1974a; 1980), he defends equal rights for women and argues for representative democracy with universal suffrage, although qualified by a sort of plural ballot scheme that gives extra votes to better-educated voters. However, Mill (1974b) holds the view that these various liberal claims are consistent with the general aim of utilitarianism in the sense that more utility would be generated and maximum happiness can be achieved by adherence to these liberal principles.

Mill's justification of democratic rights on grounds of utilitarianism has provoked the criticism that individual rights such as citizenship, the right to vote, free speech, and political participation are simple demands of justice which have their own intrinsic importance regardless of whether or not they would favourably contribute to general welfare. A firm commitment to individual rights, as Mill claims, need not always be consistent with the recommendation to undertake actions or policies that would maximize the sum of happiness. In this regard, as some feminist thinkers point out, Mill's support for the liberation of women embodies a confused mixture of a 'reformist approach' founded on utilitarian concerns and a 'radical approach' which upholds women's equality on its own terms (Annas 1977). Entrenched unfairness and inequalities against women cannot be overcome by an approach that takes people's (women's as well as men's) preferences as they are and then suggest changes that would merely produce the maximum satisfaction of desires. On the contrary, we require a non-utilitarian approach that not only takes existing preferences, attitudes and institutions as part of the problem, but also envisages circumstances of equality where women, just like men, would be respected as sources of certain inviolable claims.[2]

Sen's own views on the intrinsic value of liberal and democratic rights (more fully discussed in Chapter 7) are an important corrective to those of Mill which try to justify such rights on utilitarian grounds of maximizing social utility. Sen advocates the idea that democracy – understood both in a fundamental sense of free and fair elections, a functioning democratic government, vibrant opposition parties, free and critical press, etc and in a broader sense of public reasoning and discussion – positively contributes towards many socially desirable goals such as overcoming famines and achieving equity. But democratic rights do not only have *derivative* importance in terms of what they contribute to social goals, but rather they have their *intrinsic* importance. Democratic rights are non-negotiable claims which cannot be subjected to the calculation of utility maximization.

c) Actual and Rational Preferences

Unlike Bentham or Mill, modern utilitarians do not characterize utility as experiences of pleasure or happiness, but as satisfaction of preferences. Preference theories, as distinguished from experiential or desire theories inspired by Bentham or Mill, hold

---

2   The importance of valuing certain democratic rights intrinsically rather than merely instrumentally justifying them in terms of general welfare as Mill tried to do has been axiomatically demonstrated by Sen's 'liberal paradox', which is formally referred to as 'the Impossibility of a Paretian Liberal' (Sen 1970; 1979). The paradox demonstrates that there is a fundamental conflict between the traditional welfare approaches and the value of freedom. Until recently, most economists have reasoned within the framework that accepted the Pareto criterion as a necessary, although not a sufficient, condition for economic justice (Schokkaert 1992: 70ff.). Sen's liberal paradox has now shown that even on a purely abstract level the Pareto criterion can be in tension with liberalism, particularly when liberalism is understood as a view that individuals should have a private sphere in which they can do things as they please without social constraint. For a survey of the vast amount of literature that Sen's liberal paradox has generated, see Hausman and McPherson (1996: 174ff.), Schokkaert (1992), and Sen (2002a: 381-407).

the view that the quality of a person's life can be assessed to be good or bad to the extent that a person's preferences are satisfied (Scanlon 2000: 113; Parfit 1984: 493). Preferences are said to be 'revealed' either in actions people perform or in the choices they make (Sen 2002a: 121-157). Some of people's preferences might be 'personal' in the sense of what people want pertaining to their own life's goals and ambitions. Others, however, might be 'social' or 'political' in the sense of what people wish with regard to others, their community or environment at large (Dworkin 2000: 11ff.).

Sen's key objection to a preference-satisfaction view is the problem of adaptive preferences. Preferences are often formed by the circumstances in which people grow and are socialized; they are conditioned and shaped by the law and institutions under which people live. Sen directs his attention particularly to people who live in deprived conditions.

> The problem is particularly acute in the context of entrenched inequalities and deprivations. A thoroughly deprived person, leading a very reduced life, might not appear to be badly off in terms of the mental metric of desire and its fulfilment, if the hardship is accepted with non-grumbling resignation. In situations of long-standing deprivation, the victims do not go on grieving and lamenting all the time, and very often make great efforts to take pleasure in small mercies and to cut down personal desires to modest – 'realistic' – proportions ... The extent of a person's deprivation, then, may not at all show up in the metric of desire-fulfilment, even though he or she may be quite unable to be adequately nourished, decently clothed, minimally educated and properly sheltered. (Sen 1992: 55)

The types of people that Sen has in mind are battered housewives, bonded labourers, oppressed minorities, exploited immigrants, and so on (Sen 1999a: 62-63). Because these people have to endure situations of severe deprivation, and often do not see an immediate way out of their misery, they tend to adjust their preferences to what is seen as feasible. Elster (1982) has used the metaphor of 'sour grapes' to describe this phenomenon, precisely because people in such conditions spurn what is beyond their reach, similar to the fox which judged the unobtainable grapes to be sour. In severely harsh or coercive situations, people's perceptions and desires about their well-being are just too malleable to be reliable guides in assessing their quality of life. Even though their lives might 'objectively' lack some basic functionings such as adequate nutrition, literacy, good health and freedom of labour, their 'subjective' view might misjudge that perspective.[3] Marxists have called attention to this with the theory of 'false consciousness' – a condition in which workers' perceptions are deformed by capitalist economy and institutions so that they are unable to see their true interests in socialism. It is perhaps unwise and even illiberal and harmful to lump together all preferences which appear adaptive as a point of departure for social engineering. Out of commitment or for other autonomous reasons people might

---

3 Sen (1987c: 52-53), for instance, illustrates this with a survey conducted by the All India Institute of Hygiene and Public Health in an area near Calcutta (now Kolkata) in 1944 regarding the health situation of widows in the area. Among the people surveyed, surprisingly only 2.5% of the widows, in comparison with 48.5% of the widowers, ranked their health as being 'ill'. This was in striking contrast to their real situation, because widows in general tend to be more deprived in terms of health and nutrition.

choose to forgo certain options and narrow their feasible sets. Social policy and political deliberation must be alert and responsive only to those adaptive preferences that are formed without one's own awareness and control.

In general, Sen has been more alert to the problems of the underdogs of society. Yet by a similar line of reasoning, it can be pointed out that a preference-based view has problems with regard to 'expensive tastes' as well (Dworkin 2000: 48ff.). While in the case of adaptive preferences the person in question does not desire what can be rightfully claimed as components of his or her well-being, in the case of expensive tastes the person has costly preferences and expects society to subsidize them. Should society subsidize people's preferences for expensive banquets and exotic holidays? If one goes by a preference-satisfaction theory, then people's expensive tastes have to be satisfied, otherwise they would be miserable without them and in some sense, even worse off than those in similar circumstances with cheaper tastes. Yet most people think that social policy should not be responsive to such preferences, but instead make individuals pay for their expensive tastes.[4] Racist, sadistic and other antisocial preferences raise similar difficulties. Obviously, it is bad to satisfy them on the grounds that without their fulfilment people who have them would be worse off.

On an abstract level, it seems important to satisfy people's preferences since doing so upholds consumer sovereignty. Nevertheless, an unqualified preference-satisfaction theory without any additional conditions leads to ethically unsatisfactory implications. In the case of adaptive preferences, it suggests that we should take preferences as they are for their face value regardless of whether or not they have been malformed due to coercive and harsh circumstances. With regard to expensive and antisocial preferences, it recommends that these too should be counted for social policy considerations.

One promising and persuasive response to these troubling issues is to reject the preference-satisfaction view and endorse an objective theory of well-being. As Scanlon (1975) suggests, well-being can be assessed on the basis of certain 'objective criteria', such as 'urgency', which appeal not to preferences but to a reasoned 'consensus' of values about the content of well-being. For example, Scanlon points out how the idea of 'urgency' can play a crucial role in arriving at a consensus regarding our obligation to help. Generally we tend to agree that we have more obligations to feed a person than to satisfy his worship needs, to attend to someone's health requirements than to his amusement wishes, even if the person concerned prefers to use the help he receives for the latter. The notion of 'exploitation' – a

---

4   Here, I have in mind not only the positions of philosophers and academics, but also the commonsense or popular conceptions of social justice. When we look closely at empirical research on what the people themselves think about social justice, there is a clear consensus that people's expensive tastes should not be subsidized and that society should do something about people's debilitating adaptive preferences. Moreover, the commonsense view also endorses the idea that meeting demands of justice should involve a number of non-welfarist criteria. For illuminating discussions about popular conceptions of social justice, see Schokkaert, 'Mr. Fairmind is Post-welfarist: Opinions on Distributive Justice' (1998); Elster (1992); Miller, D. (2001: 61ff.). A theory of justice cannot be merely an aggregation of popular beliefs and opinions, but nevertheless conceptions of justice defended by philosophers cannot also be far remote from and insensitive to popular conceptions.

recurrent theme not only in Sen (e.g. 1978; 1992: 118ff.), but also in Roemer (1988), Anderson (1999), Van Parijs (1995) and Cohen (2000) – can be another such objective criterion to look at deprived conditions of well-being. We would be able to come to a reasonable agreement about whether a socio-economic relationship is exploitative, despite the fact that exploitation might be found in a wide variety of situations as different as feudalism, capitalism and child labour. The notions of urgency and exploitation, in other words, are indicative of certain objective contents of well-being, without having to entirely rely on individual preferences. But such an objectivist approach need not disregard preferences or be paternalistic about what people should prefer. In fact, on an objective view one can 'allow for' variations in individual preferences and give individual autonomy an important place. Yet we do not have to make subjective preferences the foundation of that theory. The following two chapters (Chapters 2 and 3) take up for discussion two such plausible objective theories – Rawls's theory based on 'primary goods' and Sen's theory based on 'functionings' and 'capabilities'.

A second, and perhaps a less convincing, type of response to the problems of the preference-satisfaction view is not to take the objective route to well-being, but rather to remain within the utilitarian framework and try to modify the preference-satisfaction view. Instead of maintaining that well-being is the satisfaction of actual preferences, the modified theory holds the view that well-being consists in the satisfaction of 'rational', 'true' or 'well-informed' preferences. Rational preferences are those preferences that a person *would* have in an ideal condition of information and rationality. Accordingly, social policy should be responsive only to people's 'laundered' preferences rather than to their 'dirty' or 'unrefined' preferences (Goodin 1995: 132ff.). Normally the laundering process takes place in the form of 'self-laundering' where individuals refine their preferences according to the institutional expectations and contexts they are placed in. However, this also takes place in the context of collective decision-making where public officials and policymakers acting on behalf of the people rule out or censor certain perverse preferences that might by-pass individual scrutiny. Harsanyi (1982), for instance, defends a modified view:

> All we have to do is to distinguish between a person's manifest preferences and his true preferences. His manifest preferences are his actual preferences as manifested by observed behaviour, including preferences based on erroneous factual beliefs, or on careless logical analysis, or on strong emotions that at the moment greatly hinder rational choice. In contrast, a person's true preferences are the preferences he *would* have if he had all the relevant factual information, always reasoned with the greatest possible care, and were in a state of mind most conducive to rational choice. (Harsanyi 1982: 55)

Besides holding the view that well-being should be assessed on the basis of rational preferences rather than actual preferences, Harsanyi points out that in matters of social policy certain antisocial preferences such as sadism, envy, resentment, and malice should not count (Harsanyi 1982: 58). The motivation behind discounting such preferences, for him, is 'a general goodwill and human sympathy' and the idea that utilitarian ethics makes all of us members of the same 'moral community'.

Perhaps it is easier to defend a modified rather than a straightforward and unqualified preference-satisfaction theory. The modified version remains vague insofar as it does not set out any criteria for discriminating between rational and actual preferences. Economists who might want to implement this theory would not only have a hard time figuring out what people prefer, but also face the problem of determining which of these preferences are 'rational', 'refined', 'well-informed', etc (Hausman and McPherson 1996: 79-81). Moreover, the modified version might hardly be an effective answer to Sen's concern with adaptive preferences, the battered housewife for example. The problem for people in severely deprived conditions is that an abstracted, ideal world with full information and rationally chosen preferences does not exist. Extreme conditions of manipulation and oppression can hardly be conducive to 'rational' choices. To ask therefore what one would rationally prefer in unspecified circumstances is to overlook the fact of the circumstantial and institutional contingencies of preferences.

One can in principle overcome the problem of vagueness by specifying certain criteria for rational preferences in order to make it a well-defined theory. However, to do that one needs an objective theory of value. As Harsanyi has done, one might have to identify and censor a number of antisocial preferences, even if they would positively contribute to and maximize social utility. In the instances of adaptive preferences, we might have to identify and put in place non-exploitative and non-coercive conditions that would make the rational choice process work for poor people. But when we begin to do that we would be indeed moving far from a standard utilitarian approach and moving in the direction of objective theories of well-being.

So, over the years, utilitarianism has spoken in different voices, depending on the type of content one imputes to utility or welfare. It has also evolved by refining and modifying certain elements in order to make it as relevant a moral theory as possible. Yet from the perspective of Sen's capability approach, the experiential as well as preference theories turn out to be inadequate to assess the quality of human well-being not only because these are subjective, but also because they exclude non-utility information such as functionings, capabilities, rights and obligations. Sen (1979: 478) advocates the view that a social ethics that wishes to incorporate such principles as 'equal pay for equal work', or 'elimination of exploitation', or 'priority for feeding the hungry', requires essential use of non-utility information. It is not that the socially conscientious utilitarians do not address these issues, but rather they defend these principles on some instrumental grounds, namely, in terms of their favourable influence on outcomes judged on the basis of some notion of utility. Therefore, in as much as utilitarians do not value realization of freedoms or the fulfilment of rights or duties on their own terms, there is a fundamental gap in their moral approach.

1.2 Utilitarianism and Consequentialism

Utilitarianism is a consequentialist doctrine – also traditionally called a teleological doctrine – in the sense that actions, rules, motivations and institutions are assessed on the basis of their consequences, and assessment of consequences in terms of utility or welfare. Accordingly, act utilitarianism, by far the simplest form, maintains that an action is right if it results in a state of affairs with at least as high a sum of total utilities as any other alternative act. Rule utilitarianism holds the view that actions are right if they conform to rules whose general observance can be expected to produce a state of affairs which is at least as good as the state of affairs that would have resulted from the adoption of alternative feasible rules (Smart 1973; Sen 1979). Utilitarianism as a consequential ethics also combines *two* more features. First, it involves 'sum-ranking' because the value of the consequent state of affairs is determined by aggregating or adding up individual utilities. Second, as implied by the utilitarian maxim 'the greatest happiness of the greatest number', utilitarianism's consequentialism requires 'maximizing' total or average utility for the reason that, if something is good, it seems irrational to choose to produce smaller amounts of it when one can produce larger. If human welfare is a valuable end, then the more fully one promotes it the better.

Consequentialist ethics in general and more particularly, the type of consequentialism involved in utilitarianism has been widely criticized by moral philosophers. As Williams (1973: 81) observes, 'some undesirable features of utilitarianism follow from its general consequentialist structure. Others follow more specifically from the nature of its concern with happiness.' Along with other leading economists and philosophers, Sen draws attention to the implications of utilitarianism's consequentialist morality and tries to search for alternatives.

a) The Logic of Sacrifice

Utilitarianism is often criticized on the grounds that maximization of welfare consequences leads to sacrificing individuals for the sake of the common good. This is a familiar criticism in social philosophy against hierarchical conceptions of society where the common good is defined in terms of a privileged few. In a monarchy or oligarchy, the interests of the king and royalty take precedence over those of the commoners; in a feudal society, the welfare of the landowning elites, the 'haves', is given more weight than that of the 'have-nots', and so on. In a more philosophized version such as Hegel's, individual sacrifices are legitimized as part of a dialectical process of history and society towards some higher form of existence. In contrast to these, utilitarianism emerges as an egalitarian theory because it advocates the view that everyone matters equally.[5] However, utilitarianism also suggests that the best way to realize that egalitarian concern is to maximize the good conceived in terms of a particular conception of welfare.

Rawls finds this to be a fundamental weakness of utilitarianism: 'Utilitarianism does not take seriously the distinction between persons' (Rawls 1971: 187). According to Rawls, utilitarianism ignores the distinctness of individuals on two grounds. First, it makes a false analogy between the individual and society. It is normal for a single individual to sacrifice a present satisfaction for a greater satisfaction later. In fact, such cost-benefit analysis of present sacrifices against future gains is considered

---

5   In fact, utilitarian intellectuals and political activists in England were recognized to be 'Philosophical Radicals', particularly for their hostile views on feudal elitism and for their progressive political views on the extension of democracy, legal reforms and welfare provisions. See Kymlicka (1990: 45ff.).

as part of prudence and an individual's practical rationality. However, to apply the same principle on the social plane is to be unmindful of the fact that the cost-benefit analysis in the individual's case takes place in different time-periods within the life of the same person, whereas on the societal level it takes place across different individuals. Second, the teleological version of utilitarianism places value on a stipulated conception of welfare and requires that to be maximized for its own sake. This implies that the proposed ideal is not to respect *people* as 'sources' of certain inviolable claims and rights, but rather to respect the *goal* (*teleos*) to which certain people might or might not be useful contributors. As Sen and Williams (1982: 4) put it, in the teleological version of utilitarianism persons do not count as individuals any more than individual petrol tanks do in the analysis of the national consumption of petroleum. Utilitarianism's teleological version might appear to be in tension with its egalitarian doctrine expressed in the maxim 'everybody is to count for one, no one for more than one'. Yet this is only an incomplete interpretation of equality (§1.2.a) because it treats not persons as such, but only their desires as valuable.[6]

The charge of ignoring the distinction between persons with their own rights and claims is a Rawlsian way of expressing the Kantian principle that human beings are ends in themselves and cannot be treated as means to some other social ends or goals. In *Metaphysics of Morals*, Kant writes that '[i]n the kingdom of ends everything has either a *price* or a *dignity*. What has a price can be replaced by something else as its *equivalent*; what on the other hand is raised above all price and therefore admits of no equivalent has a dignity' (Kant 1997: 42). Accordingly, Kant suggests that since persons have 'dignity' and not just a 'price' they should be respected and never be subjected as a means to some other ends. Rawls is well aware of the fact that social living involves not only sharing of benefits, but also burdens that result from social cooperation. And there will be winners as well as losers in the way a society chooses to organize its social, economic and political institutions. As Berlin (1969: 167ff.) observes, there is no social world without loss; elements of conflict and tragedy cannot altogether be eliminated from human life, personal or social. We are often confronted with making choices between such equally fundamental values as liberty, or equality, or justice, or security, or happiness, and between different appropriate institutions that will best promote them. Making these hard choices and balancing them against one another is not an easy task. They inevitably involve a certain amount of loss and sacrifice for people. Even so what utilitarianism lacks are *fair* terms and principles of justice based on which burdens of social cooperation can be proportionately shared. It turns out that a utilitarian society might perhaps be a 'happy' society, but it is highly doubtful whether it would turn out to be a just society. For instance, Rawls's principles of priority of basic liberties and the difference principle (§2.1) are meant to act against the logic of sacrifice of individuals for the sake of

---

6   Kymlicka (1990: 30-35) rightly points out that Rawls's criticism of utilitarianism does not make a clear distinction between the teleological and egalitarian grounds on which utilitarianism might be defended as a moral and political theory. Rawls seems to conflate both presuming that they are one and the same. In fact, as Dworkin (2000: 62-64) observes, it is the egalitarian claim, more than the teleological one, that makes different forms of utilitarianism still an attractive theory in public philosophy.

the common good. By assigning absolute priority to basic liberties, Rawls refuses to admit any trade off between basic liberties and other social goals. Additionally, by introducing the difference principle, Rawls suggests that at the heart of a theory of social justice, there should be the concern to improve the lot of the least advantaged members in society, rather than just the maximization of social welfare.

b) Personal Integrity

Utilitarian ethics is found to be problematic not only in public philosophy, but also in the sphere of personal ethics. Traditional utilitarianism requires moral agents to do whatever act that will produce the best available consequences overall, even if that means doing something quite horrible. If ten murders can be prevented by a single murder, then utilitarianism would recommend that you do just that. If you can get the perpetrator to confess the location of the bomb by torturing his small child so that you can save the whole city, utilitarianism seems to imply not only that you may but that you must torture the child. An unqualified utilitarian theory does not say that murder and torture are wrong on their own and are not permitted even if they would bring about more favourable consequences. In some sense, utilitarianism is also an exceedingly demanding moral theory because it requires that individuals should not attach any importance to special relationships and commitments when they, even by a small measure, can increase the good overall. If the world were to benefit more if I turned out to be a vagabond artist by deserting my wife and children, from a utilitarian point of view, this seems to be the right thing to do. The duties that I have towards my family are no more different from my obligation to each person in the world.

As Williams has argued, the demands of utilitarianism on moral agents can be so extreme that they undermines personal integrity: utilitarianism 'makes integrity as a value more or less unintelligible' and suggests that 'we should forget about integrity, in favour of such things as a concern for the general good' (Williams 1973: 99). Williams finds this to be odd because morality is not just a decision-procedure or calculating exercise where only states of affairs are considered to be valuable and the rightness of actions is judged on the basis of comparison of different states of affairs. Morality, by contrast, should offer scope for a number of things including standing rules of conduct, uncalculating relationships and 'agent-relative' duties. Even though from an abstract point of view, it might be the case that one state of affairs is better than another, we do not seem to think that a given agent should regard it as her duty to bring it about – although it might be an option for her to do so. It might be the case from an 'agent-neutral' point of view, that committing a single murder in the place of ten, torturing the child rather than allowing the city to perish might be the best thing to do. But it does make a lot of difference from a moral point of view, what *I* as an agent would do or have done in that situation. The standard of utilitarian maximization fails to account and give shape to the complexity involved in morality.

Furthermore, a moral agent acting on utilitarian calculations is expected to presume that each person in the world stands in the same relationship to him, and he in turn is under obligation to fulfil the claims that each person in the world might have. Moral decisions of a utilitarian agent are, as Williams observes, 'a function of all the satisfactions which he can affect from where he is: and this means that the projects of others, to an indeterminately great extent, determine his decision' (Williams 1973: 115). The imposition of indeterminate responsibility on the part of the moral agent, which Williams calls the 'negative responsibility', does not seem to offer a coherent account of ordinary intuitions about how we ought to conduct our interpersonal life. We do think that an ethical theory should allow for special relationships and honouring context-specific commitments to family, friends, community, country, etc without of course ruling out the possibility for agents to take up more encompassing duties.

c) Consequentialism versus Deontology

The type of consequentialism involved in utilitarianism seems to lead to counter-intuitive conclusions both in the public and personal ethics. In the sphere of public morality, utility maximization leads to sacrificing individual rights for the sake of the common good. At the level of personal ethics, utilitarianism leads to unrealistic conclusions about the duties of moral agents. Because it is assumed that an individual is required to act so as to bring about the best of consequences, it does not assign any special significance to special relationships and context-specific obligations which nevertheless are important aspects of moral reasoning.

A common reaction to the problems of utilitarianism and its consequentialist structure is to propose a deontological ethics as an alternative perspective. From a deontological perspective, people act, not because their actions will maximize consequences, but from a sense of duty. This is a sort of Ten-Commandment view where morality is essentially a list of 'dos' and 'don'ts' – a list of things that are right or wrong in and of themselves, quite irrespective of any consequences that might issue from doing them. For example, in moral philosophy, one traditional alternative to utilitarian consequentialism is Kantianism. Kant sought to make morality based on norms and duties. The rightness or wrongness of an action purely depends on the principle of action that lay behind it, and in particular, whether the agent could regard the principle as one that everyone ought to follow in all possible situations.

However, pure deontology is as little defensible as utilitarian consequentialism. Often, both in personal life as well as in public affairs, people have to make 'hard choices' between conflicting values. There is no single established hierarchy of norms which could be applied to all conflicting situations. Also, in the real world not everybody complies with the highest norms of morality. As discussed in Chapter 4, Sen is attracted to consequentialism, but seeks to overcome the traditional opposition between consequentialism and deontology by suggesting a 'broad consequentialist' approach to social ethics. Broad consequentialism implies that states of affairs are evaluated not only on the basis of welfare, but also on the basis of respect for rules, norms and values as well as the fulfilment of basic human capabilities. Actions themselves are treated as intrinsically valuable and become an integral part of the evaluation process of the state of affairs.

1.3 Are Human Beings Rational Fools?

One standard economic explanation of individual behaviour starts from the model of *homo economicus* – a view that human beings under all circumstances strive for their self-interest, and choose alternatives which would maximize their self-interest to the greatest possible extent. The idea behind this is that the pursuit of individual self-interest leads to the greatest happiness of the greatest number. This egoistic view of human beings was not only considered to be the basis of economic behaviour such as production, exchange and consumption, but it was also presumed to be the motivation behind social interactions and moral behaviour.[7] Often self-interested behaviour is also allied with rationality in the sense that rational choices are determined by the consistent pursuit of one's own preferences rather than by anyone else's.

a) Commitment and Plurality of Motivations

Quite rightly, many economists as well as philosophers have found this standard economic model to be a rather reductionist and impoverished understanding of human behaviour. The idea that people look out for their self-interest and welfare is only partially true. Often, people also genuinely care about their children, family, community, and so on – and they do this, not out of their egoistic interests, but in the interests of those they care about. In this connection, Sen (1977; 1982a; 2005) makes a distinction between *sympathy* and *commitment* as possible foundations for altruistic behaviour.

> Sympathy – including antipathy when it is negative – refers to one person's welfare being affected by the position of others (e.g., feeling depressed at the sight of misery). Commitment, on the other hand, is concerned with breaking the tight link between individual welfare (with or without sympathy) and the choice of action (e.g., acting to help remove some misery even though one personally does not suffer from it). Sympathy alone does not require any departure from individual-welfare maximization: but commitment does involve rejection of that assumption. (Sen 1982a: 7-8)

More than sympathy, it is commitment that undermines the assumptions of the standard economic model. If people are moved only by sympathy, then most other-regarding gestures can be explained in terms of self-interest: people care about others because others' situation affects their own welfare in some way. But people are also altruistic when there is no direct connection to their own welfare, and even when it minimizes or goes against their own welfare. In other words, sympathy consists in giving weight to other people's interests, whereas commitment involves letting moral concerns override one's preferences.

Political action seems to be one such instance where people demonstrate committed behaviour. In large elections, the prospect of an individual's vote determining the

---

7   One can associate such a view with social Darwinism propagated by Herbert Spencer and his followers. Social Darwinists hold the view that society, as it were, progresses, not by goodwill and collaboration among human beings, but by sheer individual competition and confrontation. See Sen, 'On the Darwinian View of Progress' (2002a: 484-500).

outcome is uncertain or extremely small. Yet people participate in elections, even in circumstances which involve considerable effort and risk, not so much because this will maximize the expected utility, but simply because they wish to 'symbolically' register their judgements on policies, politicians, and government. In cases of anti-war, anti-globalization, pro-environment or other forms of public protests, people turn out in large numbers not only because such public demonstrations will have substantial effect, but also because they view these as matters of social justice and are willing to stand by them. It is commitment rather than just selfishness, judgement rather than pure self-driven preferences that brings people together for collective action. The same may be said about people's willingness to contribute and collaborate in the provision of public goods such as public transport, a clean environment and social security. Public goods are such that they are non-rival and non-excludable in the sense that these are 'consumed' collectively, and once they are in place, individuals cannot prevent others benefiting from them. If people were concerned solely about their own consumption, there would be neither economic incentives nor political justification for providing for different public goods.[8]

Can we then conclude that because people are capable of, and do commit themselves to persons, values and institutions that they always act selflessly? To do so would be to portray human beings as unrealistically as the standard economic self-interest model. We cannot deny the fact that the economic mind does have a 'virtual presence' in the generation of human actions in market as well as non-market situations (Pettit 1995). In other words, self-interest does play an important part in many choices including economic transactions. Also, selfish or selfless behaviour depends a great deal on the circumstances, and on the social, economic and legal institutions people find themselves in. During civil war or times of scarcity people tend to be selfish and less trustworthy, whereas in times of peace people tend to be sociable and caring (Vandevelde 2005). People who grow up in extended families and traditional village communities tend to be more accommodating and cooperative than those in cities and nuclear families. Again, these are not once-and-for-all established norms. People are full of surprises, and individuals do defy expected prognoses. What is however hard to sustain as an overarching explanation about human motivation and rationality is the view that people actually behave in an exclusively self-interested way.

Furthermore, the mainline economic theory works under the assumption that individuals have a single preference-ordering and that rationality consists in choosing according to these preference-orderings. Sen (1977) finds this to be an odd description of human rationality. People do not just have one set of preference-orderings which they then apply to different situations – their role as parents, lovers, colleagues, well-wishers, citizens and so on. Rather, people have more than one set of preference-orderings and often discriminate and deliberate among preference-orderings influenced by a variety of motives. Human beings are not, as Sen observes,

---

8   Economic and philosophical literature connected with the Prisoners' Dilemma also points to the complexity of human behaviour and action in social cooperation, free-riding and public goods provisions. Among others, see Sen, 'Goals, Commitment, and Identity' (2002a: 206-224); Hausman and McPherson (1996: 180ff.).

'rational fools' to be driven to action exclusively by selfish preferences. It might therefore be more appropriate to claim that human action is influenced by a plurality of motivations – commitment, moral norms, institutions, etc – of which pursuit of personal well-being is one. Indications of the plurality of motivations in human action and rationality can be seen in our common experience, or so at least we can argue (Sen 1977; Pettit 1995). We entertain a wide variety of considerations in our interaction with others: merit, beauty, attraction, admiration, friendship, fairness, justice, cooperation and compassion. Not only are we apparently moved by a variety of motives, we also trust each other and respond to claims that transcend and sometimes confound the demands of self-interest. This is the reason why we feel free to ask each other for favours and to ground our projects in the hope that others will honour their promises and commitments.

Committed behaviour in the form of 'group loyalty' to family, class, religion, language, or occupational groups, for example, is a complex phenomenon which would be difficult to fit in with the narrow self-interest perspective. Actions based on group loyalties are a mixture of selflessness and selfishness (Sen 1987a: 19-22). While in some respects, they require self-sacrifice, in some other respects, they enhance the fulfilment of personal interests. The relative balance between self-sacrifice and self-interest, between what one gives and what one gains also very much varies and is even asymmetrical in collaborative efforts. In a trade union agitating for a particular demand the emphasis might be not only on what one contributes to the group, but also whether all members would in some way benefit from this collaboration. But in the context of family relationships or socially motivated groups, the proportion of what one forgoes can be large, and people hardly keep a count of what they receive in return.

It is often said that capitalism has prevailed over socialism and that the success of the former can be attributed largely to individual greedy behaviour. But such a lopsided view only conceals the fact that market mechanisms – considered to be the engine of capitalist economy – do and would work effectively only when there are firm foundations of non-market institutions (Sen 2002a: 501-530). Political and legal structures that protect and promote rights issuing from contracts are imperative for smooth operations of the market. A general conducive climate of mutual trust and business ethics is indispensable for market success (Alexander and Vandevelde 2006). A comprehensive analysis of the functioning and the alleged success of a purely capitalist economy would have to take note of not only individual greed, but also of the role of moral values in personal behaviour and institutional arrangements.

b) Adam Smith, Sen and Beyond Homo Economicus

In the wake of the enormous influence of utilitarian theory, it was not uncommon among economists to invoke the eighteenth-century economist-philosopher Adam Smith in order to provide justification for the view that human beings are primarily moved by self-driven preferences. Among other things, the often cited passage in support of this view is the following: 'It is not from the benevolence of the butcher, the brewer, or the baker, that we expect our dinner, but from their regard to their own interest. We address ourselves, not to their humanity but to their self-love, and never talk to them of our own necessities but of their advantages' (Smith 1976: 26-27). Sen (1986; 1987a) contests whether this or any other passage can just be taken out in isolation in order to attribute to Smith a view that would be quite at odds with his broader concerns in economics and politics. Sen points out that a reading of even this passage in question indicates that what Smith – in *The Wealth of Nations* where this quoted passage occurs – is concerned with is the complexity with which 'division of labour' and routine 'market transactions' function, rather than just establishing self-love as an overall motivation for human behaviour. Smith certainly holds the view that through an 'Invisible Hand' individuals' pursuit of self-interest can lead to mutually beneficial results for everyone and contribute to the common good. Yet he also thinks that an unbridled pursuit of self-interest would lead to a waste of social resources. For example, he recommends legal restrictions on usury in the sense that governments should fix the maximum rate of interest that can be charged.

> In countries where the interest rate is permitted, the law, in order to prevent the extortion of usury, generally fixes the highest interest rate which can be taken without incurring a penalty ... The legal rate, it is to be observed, though it ought to be somewhat above, ought not to be much above the lowest market rate. If the legal rate of interest in Great Britain, for example, was fixed so high as eight or ten per cent., the greater part of the money which was to be lent, would be lent to prodigals and projectors, who alone would be willing to give this high interest. Sober people, who will give for the use of money no more than a part of what they are likely to make by the use of it, would not venture into the competition. A great part of the capital of the country would thus be kept out of the hands which were most likely to make a profitable and advantageous use of it, and thrown into those which were most likely to waste and destroy it. (Smith 1976: 356-357)

Smith was generally opposed to any interventionist policies where a market could work well. In this case, he was certainly opposed to any type of general prohibition on charging interest on loans. However, he advocates legal restrictions and intervention on the part of the state because an unregulated pursuit of self-interest of certain individuals – Smith calls them 'prodigals and projectors' – would distort the proper functioning of the market and would ultimately lead to social loss. In other words, Smith who in the butcher-brewer-baker example emphasized the mutual benefits that can issue from self-interest, was also, as the prodigals-projectors example demonstrates, deeply concerned about undesirable consequences that can arise due to purely myopic behaviour.

Sen suggests that on a less biased reading of Smith, and when Smith's thought is taken as a whole, Smith does emerge as an advocate of a 'pluralist' and rich understanding of human action. In Sen's widely quoted article 'Rational Fools' (1977), Adam Smith appears only once in a citation from Kenneth Arrow and Frank Hahn:

> There is by now a long and fairly imposing line of economists from Adam Smith to the present who have sought to show that a decentralized economy motivated by self-interest and guided by price signals would be compatible with a coherent disposition of economic resources that could be regarded, in a well-defined sense, as superior to a large class of possible alternative dispositions ... It is important to understand how surprising this claim must be to anyone not exposed to the tradition. The immediate common sense answer to the question 'What will an economy motivated by individual greed and controlled by a

very large number of different agents look like?' is probably: There will be chaos. That quite a different answer has long been claimed true and has indeed permeated the economic thinking of a large number of people who are in no way economists is itself sufficient ground for investigating it seriously. (Arrow & Hahn 1971: vi, in Sen 1977: 321)

My intention in citing this passage is to show that Sen's critique of the standard economic model is in fact a revival of an economic and philosophical tradition that takes into account the complexity of human motivations and behaviour. Moreover, in a number of Sen's subsequent writings (1981; 1986; 1987a; 1999a) that followed the above mentioned article, Smith becomes a chief representative of that 'forgotten' tradition and inspiration for the capability approach. At least three aspects of Smith's ideas become relevant for Sen's critique of utilitarianism and for the theoretical basis of the capability approach.

i) In Smith's understanding, self-interest should not be confused with prudence (Sen 1986). According to him, prudence is the union of two qualities of 'reason and understanding' on the one hand and 'self-command' on the other. The notion of self-command, which Smith seems to have taken from the Stoics, goes beyond self-interest insofar as it checks and restrains pursuit of self-interest. The Stoic roots of Smith's moral psychology also make it clear why Smith attached importance to self-discipline and sympathy as part of human behaviour. Moreover, alongside prudence – which, in Smith's understanding, is only helpful to the individual – Smith also emphasized qualities such as 'humanity, justice, generosity, and public spirit' which might be considered favourable toward others. Therefore, in contrast to monistic approaches such as Benthamite hedonism (§1.1), Smith's moral philosophy can be rightfully claimed as a pluralist approach. In the past, it was not unusual for commentators of Smith to discuss what is called the 'Adam Smith Problem': how to fit together Smith's sentimentalist ethics with his seemingly egoistic economics and politics? Along the lines suggested by Sen, scholars (e.g. Griswold 1999; Muller 1995) do find Smith to be a philosopher concerned with pluralism of values and richness of human motivation rather than just with self-interest.[9]

ii) The birthplace of Sen's capability approach is the study of the cause of famines and starvation (§3.1). Sen's analysis of the causes of famines revealed that millions of people died during famines not particularly because of the decline of food supply, but rather due to 'entitlement' failure, namely, their lack of purchasing power or ability to buy food due to unemployment, malfunctioning of the food market, etc. In this regard, contrary to many 'biased' readings of Smith, Sen is keen to point out that conceptual resources for such entitlement-capabilities-based analysis of famine can be found in Smith. Smith (1976: 526ff.) is generally against blaming market-mechanism as the sole cause of famines, and suppression of trade as a way out of famines. However, Smith's analysis of famines also acknowledged the possibility of famines arising from an economic process involving market mechanisms such

---

9   For example, Griswold (1999) presents Smith as an advocate as well as a critique of enlightenment. On the one hand, Smith is a champion of economic and political liberties, dignity of the individual and religious toleration. On the other hand, Smith also views human beings as profoundly social, and advances an ethics on the basis of values of sympathy and community.

as low real wages and unemployment, without being caused by 'a real scarcity' caused by a decline in food supply. This implies that Smith's ethical approach to public policy in general, and famines in particular, is in favour of interventionist strategies (e.g. income creation through work programmes) in order to supplement the operations of the market in support of the entitlements of the poor.

iii) In *The Wealth of Nations*, Smith discusses the idea of how 'necessaries' (goods and commodities) create not only consumption possibilities, but also play a crucial role in achieving the capability of 'appearing in public without shame'.

> By necessaries I understand, not only the commodities which are indispensably necessary for the support of life, but whatever the custom of the country renders it indecent for creditable people, even of the lowest order, to be without. A linen shirt, for example, strictly speaking, is not a necessary of life. The Greeks and Romans lived, I suppose, very comfortably, though they had no linen. But in the present times, through the greater part of Europe, a creditable day-labourer would be ashamed to appear in publick without a linen shirt, the want of which would be supposed to denote that disgraceful degree of poverty, which it is presumed, no body can well fall into without extreme bad contact. Custom, in the same manner, has rendered leather shoes a necessary of life in England. The poorest creditable person of either sex would be ashamed to appear in publick without them ... In France, they are necessaries neither to men nor to women; the lowest rank of both sexes appearing there publickly, without any discredit, sometimes in wooden shoes, and sometimes bare-footed. (Smith 1976: 869-870)

Smith's insights that 'necessaries' are valuable in achieving the capability of social respect and that the achievement of this capability would vary from society to society have clear linkages to Sen's capability-based analysis of poverty and inequality. Central to the capability approach is the idea that goods or commodities are only instrumentally valuable in achieving different functionings and capabilities. The real assessment of people's well-being should focus on what they are able to do and be rather than what they possess by way of income and commodities. Furthermore, Sen observes that poverty is 'relative' in the realm of commodities, but 'absolute' in the realm of capabilities. This implies that being relatively poor in a rich country can be a great capability handicap, even when one's absolute income is high in world standards. In a generally opulent country, more income is needed to buy enough commodities to achieve the same social functioning.

The above conceptual linkages between Smith's economic and philosophical views on the one hand and Sen's capability approach on the other are indicative of the fact that we need to go beyond the self-interest, *homo economicus* model of human beings. They also point to the fact that an acknowledgement of a more complex view of human motivations and inclusion of many more things that are valuable need not go against the spirit of economic concerns. In fact, they pave the way for the revival of a tradition that views economics and moral philosophy, efficiency considerations and ethical values, not as rivals, but as mutually beneficial approaches.

1.4 The Search for Alternative Paradigms

Williams (1973:150) predicted of utilitarianism that 'the day cannot be too far off in which we hear no more of it'. It is fair to say that the message of utilitarianism's demise is yet to reach the ears of some philosophers and many more economists. This is partly because utilitarianism has rejuvenated and adapted itself to modern criticisms and challenges, and partly because the emerging alternative theories have yet to establish themselves as ones which can be operationalized for social policy considerations. Some economists find the alternative theories to be too messy and less helpful for social engineering despite their conceptual persuasiveness.

We have taken utilitarianism mainly as an ethical theory with political consequences. As an ethical theory, it tells us that the most appropriate way to evaluate well-being is on the basis of a stipulated conception of welfare, namely, pleasure, happiness or preference-satisfaction. It is also a political doctrine in the sense that it purports to give guidelines as to what is right and wrong, good and bad, for us to do jointly, in the conduct of our lives as a political community. Both as an economist and a philosopher, Sen has been a leading critic of utilitarianism as an ethical theory and of its implications, if we were to follow its principles in the political sphere. This chapter has particularly focused on three major aspects of Sen's critique by confronting utilitarianism with some of the fundamental claims of the capability approach.

First, the different forms of utilitarianism turn out to be subjective approaches to well-being, leaving out elements that seem valuable, even if they are not treated as something prominent in a subjective evaluation. Utilitarianism seems to deal with something eminently important in human life – diminution of pain and suffering, promotion of happiness and satisfaction of preferences. Nevertheless, it is doubtful whether it deals with everything that might be regarded as reasonably valuable. Second, the type of consequentialism implied in utilitarianism requires the maximization of the common good. This leads to some unattractive conclusions for social justice. In the place of a theory that requires us to sacrifice individuals for the sake of the common good, we would be more inclined towards a theory that delineates and protects certain individual rights and capabilities as something vital and non-violable. Third, a theory of justice should strive to represent a rich and, at the same time, a realistic picture of human beings and motivations for human action. Unfortunately, the standard economic understanding has resorted to a partial and simplified anthropological vision (*homo economicus*) founded on self-interest. It is heartening to know that this has not been the case with all utilitarians. Utilitarian liberals such as Mill precisely embody the tension of having to incorporate a richer conception of human being within a purely utilitarian paradigm.

The dissatisfaction with utilitarianism has stimulated a search for non-subjective, non-utilitarian criteria of well-being. Related notions such as 'urgency', 'exploitation', 'functionings', 'capabilities' and 'human rights' allude to the prospect of objective theories of well-being. One such theory, as discussed in Chapter 2, is that of Rawls based on the idea of 'primary goods'. These theories are objective not in the sense that they are opposed to what individuals themselves would prefer and choose for themselves, but in the sense of what are most likely to emerge in a public and reasoned consensus as claims of justice.

Chapter 2

Rethinking Rawlsian Justice

I will give you a talisman. Whenever you are in doubt, or when the self becomes too much with you, apply the following test. Recall the face of the poorest and the weakest man you may have seen, and ask yourself if the step you contemplate is going to be of any use to him. Will he gain anything by it? Will it restore him to a control over his own life and destiny? In other words, will it lead to *swaraj* (self-rule) for the hungry and spiritually starving millions? Then you will find your doubts and yourself melting away.

Mahatma Gandhi, August 1947

To refuse to give, to fail to invite, just as to refuse to accept, is tantamount to declaring war; it is to reject the bond of alliance and commonality.

Marcel Mauss, *The Gift*

John Rawls is generally regarded as the most significant and influential political philosopher of the twentieth century in the English-speaking world. He is commended for subverting the pervasive influence of utilitarianism, the dominant mode of theorizing in the nineteenth and the first half of the twentieth century. More constructively, Rawls is acknowledged for revising the traditional social contract doctrine in political philosophy and innovatively reviving it to advocate and to justify an alternative systematic account of justice that would successfully counteract utilitarianism. In the monumental classic *A Theory of Justice* [*TJ*] (1971),[1] Rawls first outlined the basic tenets of his 'justice as fairness' theory. Here he is chiefly concerned with principles by which the major social institutions distribute fundamental rights and duties, and determine fair divisions of advantages issuing from social cooperation. This implies that Rawls's justice as fairness theory is primarily intended to apply to what he calls the 'basic structure' of society, the way that major institutions such as the political systems, legal structures, competitive markets and the family interact with each other in order to determine people's life prospects. Later, in another seminal work *Political Liberalism* [*PL*] (1993), Rawls, without making major alterations to the original theory, refines it as a 'political conception' of a liberal constitutional democracy regulated by reasonable pluralism and public reason. In *TJ*, Rawls advances justice as fairness in refutation of utilitarianism, perfectionism or other general conceptions; he portrays it as a universal moral ideal to be aimed at by all societies. In *PL,* he is no longer anxious to defeat utilitarians

---

1 Henceforth, Rawls's *Theory of Justice* (1971) and *Political Liberalism* (1993) will be referred to as *TJ* and *PL* respectively. The revised edition of *A Theory of Justice* (1999) will be referred to as *TJ revised*.

or any other moral theorists; he is directly concerned about the culture of a liberal constitutional democracy.

Until now, two sorts of criticisms – the first one by Sen and Eva F. Kittay (§2.2), and the second by Nussbaum (§2.3) – have been advanced by the capability theorists against Rawls's theory. Sen points out that a theory of justice should not assess people's well-being and their standing in society on the basis of *primary goods*, but rather in terms of *basic capabilities*. Rawls's primary goods account, Sen argues, does not pay sufficient attention to the interpersonal capability differences in the conversion of primary goods into valuable functionings. Kittay criticizes Rawls's theory for failing to incorporate the capability shortfalls and requirements of the dependent and of those who provide care for them. Nussbaum, on the other hand, focuses on the social contractarian nature of Rawls's theory, tracing some of the problems in his theory to the elements of social contract. Rawls has taken note of and responded to some capabilities-based objections to his theory.[2] He has defended his theory against the capability approach by pointing out that the endorsement of capabilities would entail a comprehensive conception of the good and hence, would be inappropriate to represent the capability approach as a liberal political conception.

The merit of the arguments for and against Rawlsian justice from the standpoint of the capability approach largely depends on addressing at least some of the following issues. To what extent can a capabilities-based critique of Rawls's theory be justified? If Rawls's theory, as some capability theorists claim, is found to be inadequate in respect to certain aspects of justice, does the capability approach have the potential to provide a better alternative to handling these issues? Do Rawls's theory and the capability approach compete with each other as rival approaches? The ongoing conversation between these two major approaches suggests that at least on certain fronts both approaches converge and complement each other in addressing contemporary challenges of justice. Yet it should also be emphasized that both approaches have different points of departure and offer distinctive elements to an understanding of social justice which cannot be so easily merged as one (§2.4). The capability approach starts from an inquiry about the components of the good life and remains a good-based approach to justice. In Rawls's political liberalism there is neither an attempt to define the good nor is there an endeavour to pursue it. While for Rawls and a Rawlsian the requirements of social justice are conceived as disconnected from, and accompanied by a degree of scepticism about the good, for a capability theorist they are related to an inquiry into the plural components of the human good and well-being that reasonable persons can acknowledge as a public conception of justice. In addition, the difference between Rawls's theory and the capability approach also consists in the way they envisage social cooperation and the underlying political conception of the person.

---

2   In *TJ*, Rawls has generously footnoted many references to Sen's contributions to social choice theory and his critique of utilitarianism. In *PL* and other later writings, Rawls has, however, specifically responded to Sen's capabilities-based criticism of his own theory. See Rawls (*PL*, 178-190; 2001: 176ff.).

2.1 The Core Claims of Rawlsian Justice

To be able to fully appreciate the import of Rawls's theory and to assess its strength and weakness against the capability approach, it is important to note that Rawls has tried to work out a 'realistic ideal'[3] of justice. It is 'ideal' in the sense that it is designed for the ideal conditions of a 'well-ordered society', where reasonable persons who are free and equal all accept the same conception of justice. It is 'realistic' because Rawls proposes an account of justice that is meant to apply neither to perfect altruists nor downright egoists, neither to moral saints nor devils, but instead to what human beings at their best are capable of, given the right type of social, economic and political institutions. Moreover, both in its realistic and idealistic dimensions, *reasonableness* as distinguished from mere *rationality* is crucial to Rawls's theory (*TJ*, 17-20; *PL*, 81-82; Rawls 1999a: 316-317). Rawls presumes that in a well-ordered society citizens are not merely rational in the sense of being concerned about pursuing what is advantageous from their own standpoint; but that they are also reasonable, since they are willing to propose and honour fair terms of cooperation with others and to take into consideration the consequences of their actions on others' well-being. Reasonableness implies that people are willing to live with others according to principles and institutions which other reasonable persons acknowledge and endorse; they would also want to justify with reasons and arguments the political principles and policies they support that other reasonable persons can recognize and accept.

Rawls proposes 'primary social goods' (or simply 'primary goods') as the most appropriate measure to evaluate individual benefits in social cooperation. In *TJ*, primary goods are defined as 'all-purpose means' that a rational person would want in order to be able to pursue his or her conception of the good (*TJ*, 92). In subsequent writings (e.g. *PL*, 178-179), primary goods are defined not as 'all-purpose means', but as goods that a rational person with two moral powers – the capacity for a sense of justice and the capacity to adopt and pursue a conception of the good – would want. The list of primary goods includes the following five items:

- basic rights and liberties
- freedom of movement and choice of occupation
- powers and prerogatives of offices and positions of responsibility
- income and wealth, and
- social bases of self-respect.

Rawls also proposes two principles of justice based on which the above list of primary goods can be fairly distributed among citizens. Rawls claims that these principles could be accepted by free and equal persons as fair terms of social cooperation. The principles are as follows:

---

3   Rawls has used the phrase 'realistic utopia' in *Law of Peoples* (1999b: 7) to describe the extension of his theory in the sphere of international relations and justice. Although this work was written after *TJ* and *PL*, in hindsight we can use this term to characterize Rawls's project as a whole. See Freeman (2003: 2-3).

1. Each person has an equal claim to a fully adequate scheme of equal basic rights and liberties, which is compatible with the same scheme for all; and in this scheme the equal political liberties, and only those liberties, are to be guaranteed their fair value.
2. Social and economic inequalities are to satisfy two conditions: [2a] first, they are to be attached to positions and offices open to all under conditions of fair equality of opportunity; and [2b] second, they are to be to the greatest benefit of the least advantaged members of society. (*PL*, 5-6)

The first principle is referred to as the *equal liberties principle*. Rawls provides a list of the most important basic liberties protected by this principle: political liberty (the right to vote and to hold public office) and freedom of speech and assembly; liberty of conscience and freedom of thought; freedom of the person, which includes freedom from psychological oppression and physical assault and dismemberment (integrity of the person); the right to hold personal property; and freedom from arbitrary arrest and seizure as defined by the concept of the rule of law (*TJ*, 61). The second principle is generally further separated into its first part, the *fair equality of opportunity principle* and its second part, the *difference principle*.

In addition, Rawls accords a strict lexical priority among the principles: 1 over 2, and 2a over 2b. This implies that one is not allowed to trade off basic liberties for gains in the other two justice principles. One should not settle for lesser civil and political liberties when such acceptance would bring about greater fulfilment of the fair equality of opportunity principle or bring about greater improvement for the least advantaged members of society. Also, the fair equality of opportunity principle has lexical priority over the difference principle. As pointed out in §1.2, Rawls's stipulation of lexical priority among justice principles is a critique of utilitarianism. In utilitarianism, it is possible to legitimize unequal distribution of basic liberties and opportunities, when such an arrangement would contribute to 'the greatest happiness for the greatest number'. But Rawls refuses to make such trade offs.

Central to Rawls's presentation of the justice as fairness theory is the issue of political legitimacy: why should one accept the primary goods measure and the principles of justice? Rawls presents two lines of argument explaining why reasonable people would accept his principles of justice rather than any other on offer, for example utilitarianism, intuitionism or perfectionism. First, Rawls suggests that the principles of justice he proposes match our 'considered convictions' about matters of justice. We are inclined to support the idea that every individual should be guaranteed at least a limited number of basic rights and liberties which should not be arbitrarily violated by another individual or the state. Furthermore, traditionally, people were inclined to condone economic and social inequalities if there was 'formal equality of opportunity' in the sense of equal competition for political offices, social positions and entrepreneurial prospects, and no one is discriminated against on the basis of race, religion, sex, etc. Such a norm for instance, could be satisfied in a society where only relatively rich and well-placed children are able to gain the required skills and abilities, and thus have an edge over others in occupying competitive positions.

Rawls suggests that this would go against some of our deepest intuitions about what justice requires. Instead of a mere formal equality of opportunity, we are likely to accept 'fair equality of opportunity'. The latter requires that society's institutions are arranged such that any individual with the same native talent and ambition should have the same prospects for competitive success. Moreover, people who occupy higher positions and offices are not automatically entitled to a greater or unlimited share of society's resources. An ideal social cooperation requires that we pay attention to the lot of the worst off group in society and find some ways of combining meritocracy that says society's offices and positions should be filled on a competitive basis *with* the redistribution of wealth and income ensuing from these offices and positions. Rawls claims that his principles would come close to some of these considered convictions regarding justice.

The second line of argument – Rawls's more innovative argument – consists in the original position, a procedure or an 'expository device' (*TJ*, 21) that Rawls uses to derive principles of justice. He envisions the original position to be an analogue to the state of nature in traditional social contract theory. It is a hypothetical position from which representatives of citizens in a well-ordered society choose principles of justice that would regulate the basic structures of their society. Rawls constructs the original position in such a way that people choose principles of justice that would shape the basic institutions of their society while behind a 'veil of ignorance'. The veil of ignorance is indeed thick in the sense that the participants do not know any particular facts about themselves, namely, their social position, abilities and talents, race, gender and class. Nor are they aware of their aims and values, and more generally of their life plans and conceptions of the good. All that they know are such general facts as social sciences provide: general knowledge about human psychology, social interactions, and basic economic and political principles.

The idea behind such a veil of ignorance is that when people abstract themselves from their social positions, circumstances or life plans, it enables them to be impartial and arrive at principles of justice that will be fair for everyone. The original position is also, so to speak, a situation of uncertainty where people do not know what they are going to be in real life and whether their own interests are any better than those of others. This forces them to distance themselves from their own particular standpoints so that they can propose principles that would be ideally fair to all. Rawls maintains that in the hypothetical original position so constructed participants would choose the primary goods standard and his two principles of justice.

The details of Rawls's theory and its development are important, but for the purpose of comparison with the capability approach, it is worthwhile recapitulating its main traits that make it an influential theory in contemporary political philosophy.

i) Rawls's theory views persons as sources of inviolable claims
The simple and profound intuitive idea which motivates and informs Rawls's theory is the following: 'Each person possesses an *inviolability* founded on justice that even the welfare of society as a whole cannot override. For this reason justice denies that the loss of freedom for some is made right by a greater good shared by others' (*TJ*, 3-4, my emphasis). Inviolability of each person is preserved in Rawls's theory from the fact that certain basic liberties are made absolutely important and non-

negotiable. Rawls reiterates this by describing citizens in the well-ordered society as 'self-originating sources of valid claims' (Rawls 1980: 543) and 'self-authenticating sources of valid claims' (*PL*, 32).[4] As pointed out in §1.2, this is Rawls's own way of expressing the Kantian maxim about the invaluable worth and dignity of each person. At the same time, by viewing citizens as sources of certain rights and claims, Rawls also clearly rejects the principle of utility. In utilitarianism, persons are viewed not as sources of valid claims, but as sources of welfare for the common good.[5]

ii) Rawls's theory promotes individual responsibility

Rawls's theory is not an outcome theory. It aims only at a fair distribution of the primary goods of basic liberties and opportunities and not their outcomes in the sense of what people do or achieve with their primary goods. This reserves a space for individual responsibility and enables individuals to act as responsible agents. Once primary goods have been fairly equalized, if one makes a judicious use of them, while another squanders them, the latter would not be compensated in the name of justice. As Rawls puts it:

> Justice as fairness … *does not look behind* the use which persons make of the rights and opportunities available to them in order to measure, much less to maximize, the satisfaction they achieve. Nor does it try to evaluate the relative merits of different conceptions of the good. Instead, it is assumed that the members of society are rational persons able to adjust their conceptions of the good to their situation. (*TJ*, 94, my emphasis)

This implies that people as agents must take responsibility and adjust their conception of the good, and in particular their tastes and ambitions in accordance with the amount of primary goods they can expect to get in a fair term of social cooperation. Thus, people with expensive tastes and ambitions should normally be made to pay for them rather than expect society to subsidize them.

Some philosophers have expressed doubts as to whether Rawls's theory enjoins an *effective* sense of responsibility (Dworkin 2000: 330-331; Arneson 1990; Kymlicka 1990: 73ff.). The difference principle in Rawls's theory requires improving the situation of the worse off without taking into account the impact it will have on people who do not belong to this group. People's hard-earned income and wealth would be transferred by way of taxes to support welfare programmes in favour of the worse off, even when the beneficiaries choose not to work or do not make effective uses of their basic liberties and opportunities. The difference principle

---

4   The change of terminology from 'self-originating' to 'self-authenticating' is perhaps to clarify a possible communitarian criticism that Rawls's theory is individualistic. While the former gives the impression that only individuals and their self-interested claims matter, the latter gives the scope to think that individuals can also take into consideration and endorse or authenticate others' claims and interests as well.

5   Rawls (*PL*, 33) notes how in the case of slavery this is taken to an extreme point. Slaves are not counted as sources of claims and as capable of having duties and obligations. Laws which prohibit the maltreatment of slaves, for example, are *not* based on the claims of the slaves, but on the claims originating from slaveholders or from the general welfare of society.

works under the assumption that sacrifice at the top is better than sacrifice at the bottom, despite Rawls's pronounced aspiration to prevent the sacrifice of individual claims for the sake of social goals. It can also cause incentive problems, since those with better native talents and who slog it out are likely to get much less in the regime of difference principle than in a free market.

Rawls does foresee that the hard-working and the naturally gifted will complain, and hence will have some negative effect on efficiency. Nevertheless, he sees this as a more *reasonable* arrangement than the one where there would be no redistribution at all. As he puts it, 'we can ask the willing cooperation of everyone only if the terms of the scheme are reasonable. The difference principle, then, seems to be a fair basis on which those better endowed, or more fortunate in their social circumstances, could expect others to collaborate with them when some workable arrangement is a necessary condition of the good of all' (*TJ*, 103). Also, for Rawls, toleration of inequalities subject to the condition of the difference principle is important from the view of 'social responsibility' of maintaining a 'decent' level of social-base for self-respect: no citizen should be so poor that he or she cannot *decently* take part in normal social life (*TJ*, 535).[6]

iii) Rawls's theory involves ethical individualism rather than ontological individualism

As with most liberal theories, the primary focus of Rawls's theory is the *individual*. Society's different economic and political institutions are evaluated in terms of what they can contribute to the enhancement of individual rights and opportunities. Rawls does not mean to deny the social nature of human beings and the communal values that individuals might find important. Nevertheless, Rawls thinks that the fundamental basis of a theory of justice should be individual freedom and rights. In a crucial passage in *TJ*, he makes his position clear:

Justice as fairness has a central place for the value of community ... The essential idea is that we want to account for the social values, of the intrinsic good of institutional, community, and associative activities, by a conception of justice that in its theoretical basis is *individualistic*. For reasons of clarity among others, we do not want to rely on an undefined concept of community, or to suppose that a society is an organic whole with a life of its own distinct from and superior to that of all its members in their relations with one another ... From this conception, however individualistic it might seem, we must eventually explain the value of community. Otherwise the theory of justice cannot succeed. (*TJ*, 264-65, my emphasis)

Most communitarians[7] find that Rawls's focus on the individual and the accordance of priority of individuals over the value of community would lead to serious errors. The most common fault that communitarians attribute to Rawls's

---

6 Chapter 5 discusses in detail the principle of individual responsibility in relation to a theory of social justice. From the vantage point of the capability approach, the chapter develops the idea that Rawls, Dworkin and other liberal theories need to envisage a broader scope for the interdependence between social and individual responsibility.

7 Communitarianism comprises a rich variety of authors such as Sandel, McIntyre, Taylor and Walzer whose intellectual trajectories vary vastly. I will therefore consider only

theory is with regard to its conception of the person, according to which individuals are essentially distinct from and even prior to their ends, or values or conceptions of the good.[8] The reason for this is often traced to Rawls's use of the device of the original position: a just agreement about the distribution of primary goods can be reached only if the participants to that agreement step behind a veil of ignorance that strips them of their particularity and communal embeddedness, namely, their natural endowments, social positions and their particular conceptions of the good. The communitarians point out that such a radical detachment from one's nature and ends as Rawls suggests is not only psychologically impossible, but is also not helpful in reasoning about social justice. In contrast, communitarians advocate the view that the complex network of language, meaning systems, moral norms and socialization processes form an 'authoritative horizon' from which individuals necessarily derive their self-understanding and conception of the good. Moreover, even if we grant that Rawls's theory takes into account the value of community, communitarians find it to be biased in favour of a particular understanding of the individuals' relation to their community. Society is viewed as nothing more than an association for the pursuit of one's own advantage. Conceptions of the good that are communal in content and that value relations with others as valuable in themselves are set aside.

A Rawlsian response to the communitarian concerns can take the following directions. Because Rawls's theory focuses on individual freedom and rights, it might be considered to involve *ethical individualism* rather than ontological individualism. The latter implies that people can and do exist as atomistic individuals and that their dependence on society is more or less contingent and not indispensable. Individuals might require other individuals or a collection of individuals such as the family or other larger forms of associations for fulfilling some of their needs, but this dependence is not anything intrinsically important to the existence of the individual. Ethical individualism, by contrast, treats individuals and their interests as the basic unit of moral analysis. The normative value of social, economic and political institutions depends on their effects on individuals, but this is done not in view of negating or denying individuals' relations to society and their embeddedness in communal values and tradition.

In fact, Rawls is well aware of the significance of social embeddedness and authoritative horizons for individuals: 'social life is a condition for our developing the ability to think and speak … No doubt even the concepts that we use to describe our plans and situations often presuppose a social setting as well as a system of belief and thought that is the outcome of the collective efforts of a long tradition' (*TJ*, 522). This is one of the reasons why Rawls envisions his theory to be an 'institutional' approach to social justice and focuses on the 'basic structure' of society as the subject

---

some crucial arguments that might be applied to Rawls's theory and how Rawls or a Rawlsian would respond to communitarian criticisms. See Mulhall and Swift (2003); Sandel (1982).

8   Rawls gives such an impression when he, in *A Theory of Justice*, explicitly states the following: 'Self is prior to any of its ends' (*TJ*, 560). Kymlicka has demonstrated that this statement of Rawls ought to be understood as emphasizing the individual's capacity to critically distance oneself and evaluate one's communal values and projects rather than as a denial of communal affiliations and embeddedness. See Kymlicka (1990: 207ff.).

of justice: society's basic economic and political institutions shape the 'wants and aspirations that its citizens come to have' and determine 'in part the sort of persons they want to be as well as the sort of persons they are' (*TJ*, 259).

However, what Rawls refuses to accept is the idea that we should accept our communal values as 'given' without subjecting them to critical evaluation and scrutiny. More importantly, Rawls does not so much fail to acknowledge the importance of communal values. In fact, he is happy to see them flourish in the context of family life, churches, universities, scientific societies and other private associations. But what he denies is their appropriateness and legitimacy in the political sphere. Some communitarians such as Taylor (1985b; 1995b; 1995c) might find this unconvincing because even in the political sphere without the affirmation of shared communal values and (civic) virtues it might be difficult to envisage a more intimate relationship between individual liberty and the state. Shared understandings and values are the proper starting points of political argument. People no doubt would like to be free in the sense of doing what they want, but they also want their choices to be communally recognized and valued. Communitarians doubt that Rawlsian liberalism would be able to achieve that.

iv) Rawls's theory is a freestanding political conception of justice
As pointed out earlier, one crucial shift that Rawls makes from *A Theory of Justice* to *Political Liberalism* is that in the latter, Rawls's conception of justice is presented specifically as a 'political' conception. Rawls himself acknowledges this:

> The distinction between a comprehensive doctrine and a political conception is unfortunately absent from *Theory* and while I believe nearly all the structure and substantive content of justice as fairness ... goes over unchanged into that conception as a political one, the understanding of the view as a whole is significantly shifted. (*PL*, 177, n.3)

For Rawls, deep and irresolvable differences among citizens on matters of fundamental significance are a 'permanent condition of human life'. People are different in their religious, moral and philosophical beliefs and it might be possible to justify the principles and institutions of justice as fairness on the basis of any of these comprehensive conceptions. In *PL*, however, Rawls makes it clear that justice as fairness should be viewed as 'freestanding' or independent of religious, moral, and any general philosophical conceptions. A freestanding theory aims to avoid such philosophical questions as the original source of moral principles, how we come to know them, and so on. These should be avoided in order to maintain the full freedom of conscience of citizens and provide them with a 'neutral' conception that all can reasonably accept. Therefore, what distinguishes a political conception of justice from others is that it strives to affirm ideas and principles of justice that people in their capacity as citizens in a constitutional democracy can share publicly, whatever their conceptions of the good may be. Only such a freestanding political conception of justice can serve as reasonable basis for an overlapping consensus among citizens.

Some have wrongly interpreted Rawls's argument for a political conception of justice as being 'tolerant' to all types of conceptions of the good. Because justice as fairness distances itself from passing judgements on religious, moral or metaphysical inquiries, it would be neutral to all comprehensive conceptions. This would be a misinterpretation of Rawls's theory. Rawls's political conception is not based on 'open' pluralism or 'pluralism as such', but rather on 'reasonable' pluralism. It is not a theory that is unconditionally open to all conceptions of the good, regardless of the content that goes to make up these conceptions. Rather, it is open only to reasonable conceptions that are compatible with principles and institutions of justice as fairness. A comprehensive doctrine that condones or actively promotes, for example, slavery, untouchability, or violation of freedom of conscience does not stand a chance of being accepted.

2.2 Who are the Least Advantaged?

a) Sen's Critique

Sen (1980: 213ff.) criticizes Rawls's idea that primary goods are the appropriate measures to evaluate people's benefits and standing in society. He points out that people's variations in physical traits, talents and circumstances play a crucial role in converting primary goods into different functionings. In applying the case-implication critique (Chapter 1), the most obvious case that Sen thinks of is a person in a wheelchair. Equalizing the amount of primary goods between an able-bodied and a handicapped person overlooks the fact that the latter would require more material and social resources to be mobile and to achieve other functionings including overcoming social discrimination against disability. What about Rawls's difference principle that stipulates to improve the situation of the least advantaged? Would it not be favourable to the lot of the person in the wheelchair? As Sen points out, 'the Difference Principle will give him neither more nor less on grounds of his being a cripple' (Sen 1980: 215). Sen's observation seems right because in Rawls's theory someone is counted as the least advantaged not on account of his or her natural handicaps, but rather according to the holding of primary goods, particularly income and wealth. The least advantaged, for Rawls, are those who are the least favoured by each of the following three kinds of factors:

> Thus this [the least advantaged] group includes persons [i] whose family and class origins are more disadvantaged than others, [ii] whose natural endowments (as realized) permit them to fare less well, and [iii] whose fortune and luck in the course of life turn out to be less happy, all within the normal range and with the relevant measures based on social primary goods. (*TJ, revised*: 83)

By qualifying the above three factors with 'all within the normal range', Rawls presupposes that everyone has physical and psychological capacities within the normal range. The special requirements and needs of people who fall below the normal range do not arise. Rawls's reason for this assumption is not so much that these issues necessarily fall outside the scope of social justice, but that these kinds of 'hard cases' should be dealt with at the 'legislative stage' when the prevalence and the extent of these kinds of disadvantages are known and the costs of treating them can be balanced against the total government expenditure. Sen questions the adequacy of postponing these issues instead of integrating them into the theoretical structure of justice.[9] If principles of justice are intended to shape the basic structure of society, then it becomes pertinent to include concerns of capability variations right from the beginning. Moreover, Sen calls attention to the fact that the variations between people, and the advantages or disadvantages arising thereof in converting primary goods into functionings go beyond the case of physical disabilities. The 'pervasive fact of interpersonal heterogeneity' at different levels indicates that primary goods are an inadequate measure to evaluate people's benefits.

> The primary goods approach seems to take little note of the diversity of human beings … If people were basically very similar, then an index of primary goods might be a good way of judging advantage. But, in fact, people seem to have very different needs varying with health, longevity, climatic conditions, location, work conditions, temperament, and even body size (affecting food and clothing requirements). So what is involved is not merely ignoring a few hard cases [e.g. handicaps], but overlooking very widespread and real differences. Judging advantage purely in terms of primary goods leads to a partially blind morality. (Sen 1980: 215-216)

Chapter 3 discusses in detail how different elements of human variations such as personal heterogeneity, social circumstances and distribution within the family can either enhance or hamper individual freedom to varying degrees and whether a capabilities-based understanding of justice can be more sensitive to human diversity than Rawls's. However, the upshot of Sen's objection to using primary goods as the measure is that primary goods are only a *means* to a life of freedom (Sen 1980: 216). People's life of freedom, Sen points out, is determined not only by the primary goods that are at their disposal, but also by a variety of capability factors that influence to what extent they can transform these primary goods into relevant doings and beings. So, instead of focusing just on the means we should focus directly on people's capabilities to different doings and beings. Focusing on the means, namely, primary goods rather than on the ends to which primary goods are only instrumental, for Sen, entails a sort of fetishism.

b) The Dependency Critique

Reflective of Sen's capabilities-based critique, Kittay (2003) advances a 'dependency critique' against Rawls's theory, focusing on the 'human condition' of dependency and on the problems of people who provide care to the dependents.

---

9   Rawls does admit the fact that a certain amount of arbitrariness cannot be avoided in identifying members who would belong to this group: 'It seems impossible to avoid a certain arbitrariness in actually identifying the least advantaged group' (*TJ revised*: 84). Nevertheless, he gives two indications as to how one may proceed in identifying the least advantaged. First, giving the example of an 'unskilled worker', Rawls says that we may define the least advantaged as all those with approximately the income and wealth of the unskilled worker or similar categories. Second, Rawls also suggests that we can define the least advantaged as all those with less than half of the median income and wealth. These two suggestions further confirm Sen's point that Rawls omits the cases of people with physical disabilities.

It is my view that liberal political theory and Rawls's theory, in particular, are flawed in that they do not take the issue of dependency to be central. All of us are dependent in childhood; most of us are dependent for long periods of time (sometimes throughout a life) because of ill health. Dependency is thus a matter for us all in our lives as social beings. Most women – by virtue of their traditional roles and the ineluctable demands of dependency – and some men, primarily those from marginalized classes, find themselves with the responsibility to care for dependents. In assuming these duties, they have too often found themselves stigmatized as dependents. As such, they have been unable to function as equals in a society of equals. (Kittay 2003: 169)

Kittay's critique of Rawls reiterates, and at the same time, extends Sen's capabilities-based objection. It draws attention to the fact that 'dependency is a feature of our human condition' and that people who are dependent to varying degrees require care and caring persons to meet their needs. A theory of social justice cannot ignore the capability shortfalls of dependents and any special needs and requirements they might have. However, Kittay by extension also calls attention to the problems of justice with regard to 'dependency workers' – people who attend to dependency needs of others, whether full or part time and through paid or unpaid work. These, by virtue of their attention to dependents, become vulnerable to a condition of 'derived' dependence particularly when society does not duly recognize or reward their work economically or otherwise. Consequently, they also cannot offer an effective and fulfilling service. Also, the issue of dependency and dependency workers is closely linked to gender justice because most care for the dependents is provided by women, most of which might not be recognized by the market as work.

Kittay points out five presuppositions in Rawls's theory that makes it inadequate to address the issues of dependency.

i) In Rawls's theory, the issue of justice arises only under 'circumstances of justice', an idea that Rawls takes over from Hume.[10] Rawls particularly mentions two kinds of circumstances which make us aspire to principles of justice: objective and subjective. Among objective circumstances, he refers to 'a definite geographical territory' and 'moderate scarcity', a condition in which natural resources are neither so abundant that social cooperation becomes superfluous nor so scarce that cooperative arrangements cannot be obtained. Regarding subjective circumstances, Rawls alludes to the fact of persons and associations having different and contrary conceptions of the good as well as of how to realize them. Kittay points out that Rawls does not consider human dependency to be part of the circumstance of justice. Yet in Kittay's view, human dependency continues to be an important and unavoidable 'circumstance' of justice. People do have the need and the desire to be cared for and to care for someone, and these can be very much part of their conception of the good.

ii) Rawls's list of primary goods does not include *care* as a primary good and hence, does not adequately address the needs of dependents and of those who care for them. This is partly because Rawls envisages primary goods as serving

---

10 On circumstances of justice that Hume appeals to see Hume, *A Treatise of Human Nature* (2000), Book 3, Part 2; *An Enquiry Concerning the Principle of Morals* (1998: 83-98).

the requirements of citizens with the attributes of two moral powers, namely, the
capacity for a sense of justice and the capacity to form and revise a conception of
the good. Kittay suggests that if we consider individuals in dependency relations and
those who care for them as citizens, then we need to expand the list of citizens' moral
powers. The moral powers of the citizens would not just include (a) a sense of justice
and (b) capacity to pursue a conception of the good, as Rawls suggests, but also (c)
a capacity to respond to vulnerability with care. Such expansion of moral powers
would also lead to a revision of the list in order to include care as a primary good.

iii) As pointed out in §2.1, one important merit of Rawls's theory is that it
views persons as 'self-originating' sources of valid claims. This, in Rawls's view,
asserts the freedom as well as the inviolability of each person. Kittay argues that
such portrayal of individuals is an inadequate characterization of freedom for the
dependency workers and fails to take account of the claims they might have on
behalf of those related to their charge. A mother's claim for her child or professional
caretakers' claim for their charge cannot be totally identified as self-originating
claims. They are distinct claims, even though those who 'voice' them may or may
not endorse or authenticate those claims as their own. A theory of justice should
represent persons not only as sources of 'self-originating' claims, but also involved
in a complex network of interdependent relationships.

iv) In Rawls's theory, social cooperation is not just a coordinated social activity
efficiently organized by publicly recognized rules to achieve some overall end.
Instead reciprocity and fair terms of cooperation become central to the notion of
social cooperation. The relationships between dependents and dependency workers
and to larger society do not fit within this framework. Moreover, such a conception
of social cooperation excludes permanently dependent and severely disabled people
from social cooperation and hence, citizenship. Kittay suggests that an adequate
conception of social cooperation should also include dependency concerns. A
society that does not care for its dependents, and that cares for them only by unfairly
exploiting the goodwill and labour of those who actually care for them cannot be
considered a just society.

v) Rawls's theory is based on the idealization that all citizens are fully cooperating
members of society. Kittay points out that such idealization is counterfactual and
misleading. A strong interpretation of Rawls's idealization – particularly with
reference to Rawls's phrase that 'citizens are to be fully cooperating throughout
their lives' – would be quite far from reality because not a single citizen approaches
the ideal of full functionings *throughout* a lifetime. A weaker interpretation of this
idealization – especially when we emphasize Rawls's term 'over the course of a
complete life' – can be understood such that people are fully cooperating members
of society just at certain periods of their lives when it would be reasonable to expect
an individual to be fully functioning. Even a weaker interpretation would not take
into account those in conditions of extreme dependency and the requirements of
those who care for them.

c) Rawls's Response

Is it an oversight on the part of Rawls to omit the problems of capability shortfalls and variations highlighted in different ways by Sen and Kittay? In Rawls's writings, we can find two lines of response to capabilities-based objections. As an initial type of response, Rawls points out that Sen's capability approach entails a comprehensive conception of the good. Any capabilities-based theory that is concerned with identifying people's basic capabilities would have to appeal to a particular conception of the good life and value judgements, and as a consequence, cannot respect the diverse comprehensive conception of the citizens in a plural society. Rawls in contrast insists that a theory of justice should be a freestanding 'political' conception that not only avoids inquiries into the nature of the human good, but works towards an overlapping consensus based on principles of justice that citizens with different conceptions of the good can endorse.

The second type of Rawls's response is more promising, acknowledging the significance of human diversities and in particular the different levels of people's capability deprivations as important components of a theory of justice. In *PL*, Rawls writes: 'I agree with Sen that basic capabilities are of first importance and that the use of primary goods is always to be assessed in the light of assumptions about those capabilities' (*PL*, 183). In *Justice as Fairness: A Restatement* (2001) his acknowledgement is even more yielding and sympathetic:

> The more extreme cases I have not considered, but this is not to deny their importance. I take it as obvious, and accepted by common sense, that we have a duty towards all human beings, however severely handicapped. The question concerns the weight of these duties when they conflict with other basic claims. At some point, then, we must see whether justice as fairness can be extended to provide guideline for these cases; and if not, whether it must be rejected rather than supplemented by some other conception … If Sen can work out a plausible view for these, it would be an important question whether, with certain adjustments, it could be included in justice as fairness when suitably extended, or else adopted to it as an essential complementary part. (Rawls 2001: 176, n. 59)

While these statements may suggest an amendment or extension of Rawls's theory in the direction of the capability approach, the difficult question however is whether such an extension can be realized without violating the core intuitions of Rawls's theory. The greatest concern for Rawls or a Rawlsian is whether a transition to a capabilities-oriented understanding of justice would still be able to maintain the 'political' character of justice as fairness and avoid the risk of reverting back to some form of comprehensive conception.[11]

---

11 Norman Daniels (1990; 2003) and Yvonne Denier (2005) have made compelling arguments to illustrate how it is possible to relax certain assumptions of Rawls's theory so as to address capabilities-related concerns particularly in the area of health care.

2.3 Social Contract and Motivations for Social Cooperation

Sen and Kittay criticize Rawls's theory for its failure to adequately address the needs and requirements of people with physical disabilities and extreme dependency. Among other things, both identify primary goods to be problematic as a measure of a person's well-being and standing in society. A key suggestion that emerges from their critique is that we ought to add the need for care for the disabled and dependents to the Rawlsian list of primary goods and view primary goods as means to people's basic capabilities.

a) Nussbaum's Critique

Nussbaum (2006: 146ff.) endorses Sen-Kittay's critique of Rawls's theory. She, however, identifies the limitations of Rawls's theory to be structurally linked to its contractarianism and the corollary idea of justice as mutual advantage. Rawls no doubt revises the traditional social contract theories, selecting only those elements that would best suit his theory. Nonetheless, since Rawls on the whole envisages his project to be part of that tradition, he retains the key elements associated with it. As in the case of most social contract theories, in Rawls's theory the idea of mutual advantage plays a central role in designing principles of justice. People agree to cooperate with one another primarily because it is beneficial to their own well-being. In *TJ,* Rawls defines society as a 'cooperative venture for mutual advantage' (*TJ*, 4). He further elaborates upon this idea by claiming that 'social cooperation makes possible a better life for all than any would have if each were to live solely by his own efforts' (*TJ*, 4). In *PL,* Rawls no longer uses the term 'a cooperative venture for mutual advantage'. Instead, he speaks of society as 'a fair system of cooperation over time' (*PL*, 14). In fact, he denies that mutual advantage is the right way of thinking about his theory. He prefers to replace the earlier term 'mutual advantage' with the idea of reciprocity: 'the idea of reciprocity lies between the idea of impartiality, which is altruistic (being moved by the general good), and the idea of mutual advantage understood as everyone's being advantaged with respect to each person's present or expected future situation as things are'; '[f]inally, it is clear … that the idea of reciprocity is not the idea of mutual advantage' (*PL*, 16-17). Despite this change of terminology, Nussbaum (2006: 54ff.) finds that the idea of mutual advantage remains a strong motivation in Rawls's idea of social cooperation.

On a deeper level, Nussbaum (2006: 127-145, 159-160) finds the Kantian conception of the person that Rawls deploys to be narrow and insufficiently rich to address the needs of people with a low level of capabilities, despite the fact that Rawls sees justice as fairness giving expression to the Kantian principle of treating every person as an end, and does not allow the subordination of any individual to the cause of the common good. Kant makes a division between the realm of nature on the one hand and the realm of reason on the other. He associates all non-human animals as well as the natural and non-rational part of human life with the former. In contrast, he elevates the human capacity for rationality as different from and superior to the realm of nature. In fact, morality and moral freedom for Kant consists in acting in accordance with the pure good will untainted by elements of nature. In *Metaphysics*

of Morals (1997: 393-405), Kant refers to the good will as that which 'shines like a jewel' and is superior to any of the other human characteristics such as needs, desires, talents and temperaments. Only when the good will excludes and harnesses all desires, inclinations and needs, and external influences, would it be able to freely determine itself and act autonomously. Rawls does not accept the metaphysical baggage of Kantian personhood, but he nevertheless retains the Kantian concept of the person insofar as rationality and reciprocity become the fundamental basis for deriving political principles.

Nussbaum realizes that the Kant-Rawlsian conception of the person can be misleading and consequential for issues of justice. By making a division between what is rational and natural and privileging the former over the latter, it gives the impression that our rationality is something independent of our human vulnerability and dependency. We are moral and rational, but we cannot ignore the fact that our rationality and morality are deeply intertwined with human needs, dependency, disease, and so on. Furthermore, the Kant-Rawlsian idea of the person seems to suggest that only those who possess a certain threshold level of rationality and moral agency are eligible for social cooperation and claims of justice. Those who are seen not to be reaching the threshold – people with learning or physical disabilities, for example – might have claims of charity or benevolence, but not justice.

b) *Mutual Advantage or Impartiality?*

Nussbaum is right to remark that Rawls proposes justice as fairness as belonging to the social contract tradition and that some of the problems of his theory might be identified as coming from its allegiance to that tradition. However, her critique of this aspect of Rawls's theory seems only partially applicable particularly because Rawls inherits, and at the same time reworks and improves upon the idea of social contract. Until the seventeenth century, philosophers were mostly inclined to appeal to a naturalistic vision of society, and attempted to derive political principles based on such a vision. We can find this in Aristotle, Plato and other ancient philosophers. Later, this continues to find a prominent expression in theistic or deistic theories in the Middle Ages. In the seventeenth and eighteenth centuries, however, the hegemony of the naturalistic vision was seriously challenged and replaced by the notion of social contract. Most political philosophers of this period – with the important exception of Hume – tried to justify political principles and institutions based not on natural laws, but on the fact that people could make a contract with one another to live in a political society. Therefore, the crucial question for the social contract philosophers was the following: how can we legitimize the existence and organization of the state, its coercive laws and institutions, the rights and duties of individuals without resorting to any naturalistic or religious explanations? Even though philosophers of the social contract tradition come up with somewhat different answers to this question, at least two common features can be identified.

The first is related to the state of nature and the idea of contract. Society in general and particularly a political entity such as the state comes about not through some natural process – as for example, Aristotle tried to explain it (§6.1) Instead, it is an *artefact*, distinctively created by human beings through contract. In order to

Nature
origin

explain this, social contract thinkers invoke the idea of the 'state of nature' – a kind of fictitious pre-political situation where there was no sovereign, government, laws, courts, property rights, etc. Hobbes describes it as a state of 'war of all against all'. Locke and Rousseau do not describe it as a state of war; for them even in the state of nature human beings have some moral values. Nevertheless, in the absence of a proper political society there is really nothing to prevent the state of nature from turning into a state of war. People could continue to live in the state of nature, but it would be besieged by insecurity, distrust, violence and chaos. So, people leave such volatile states by making a contract with one another. The state of nature that these thinkers imagine is therefore not a historical moment or reality. Rather, it is a counterfactual, hypothetical situation contrived in order to legitimize contemporary state and society: the reason why rational persons would agree to live together and socially cooperate and why they would surrender themselves to a legitimate authority such as the state, its laws and institutions.

And the second feature concerns the motivations for contract. Why would free, equal and independent individuals agree to enter into a social contract? The parties are envisaged as entering into a contract mainly in order to secure a mutual benefit which otherwise would not be available, if they lived alone and without social cooperation. However, there are variations from one social contract thinker to another regarding the motivations for contract. For Hobbes, it is chiefly self-interest and mutual advantage: people would forego some advantages in the state of nature only in exchange for some other advantage for their own well-being. Locke however, does not paint such a pessimistic picture. People are motivated to enter into a contract to protect themselves and their property, but they also have concerns for others.

Rawls works out a contemporary version of the contractarian theory. He remains a contractarian philosopher in as much as he shares some aspects of the above two elements. Rawls himself acknowledges and sees his project as part of the social contract tradition: 'My aim is to present a conception of justice which generalizes and carries to a higher level of abstraction the familiar theory of the social contract as found, say, in Locke, Rousseau and Kant' (*TJ*, 11). Furthermore, he compares the original position in his theory to the state of nature in the traditional social contract: 'In justice as fairness the original position of equality corresponds to the state of nature in the traditional theory of social contract' (*TJ*, 12). However, Rawls turns out to be a rather different contractarian because he diverges from the traditional theories in some important ways, sifting ideas and authors of this tradition. He shows distaste for the Hobbesian version of contract and keeps his distance form it: 'For all its greatness, Hobbes's *Leviathan* raises special problems' (*TJ*, 11, n.4). He is more attracted to the Kantian version, particularly its 'constructive' approach to moral values and justice, and its emphasis on the inviolability of each person. While early uses of the contract arguments were predominantly intended to explain and legitimize the authority of the state and its institutions, Rawls uses them mainly to justify a conception of justice. Legitimization of the state and its authority over the citizens plays only an ancillary role in Rawls's theory. More pertinently, Rawls's 'political psychology' – the reasons and motivations why people socially cooperate – differs from that of his contractarian predecessors. Rawls achieves this by introducing a completely new idea into the notion of contract, namely, the veil of ignorance. Through this he emphasizes that the contracting parties, in drawing up the principles of justice, are not only motivated by *mutual advantage*, but also by *impartiality* (Barry 1989: 145ff.). In other words, there is a calculation of self-interest behind the veil of ignorance embodied in impartiality. In traditional social contract theories, particularly those of Hobbes and Locke, we have neither the Rawlsian veil of ignorance nor anything indicative of the motive of impartiality.

On account of the fact that Rawls's contractarian theory involves mutual advantage *and* impartiality, Nussbaum's critique cannot be attributed to the whole corpus of Rawlsian contractarianism. However, Nussbaum is right to insist and demand from Rawls a more complex political psychology of what motivates people to live together and socially cooperate. Sometimes people tend to cooperate because of what they in turn can get out of cooperation. At other times people also cooperate of other motives such as a sense of justice, justice for justice's sake, compassion and benevolence, without keeping an account of what they get out of cooperation. Sen makes a similar point in his critique of the traditional economic model of rationality, *homo economicus* (§1.3). He criticizes utilitarianism for assuming that people behave solely on the basis of self-interest. He points out that human beings are not 'rational fools' acting only on self-interest. Human beings are moved to act not only because of self-interest, but also because of other-regarding interests such as sympathy and commitment. Rawls has certainly come quite far from the utilitarian model and the traditional social contract model which appeal only to self-interest or mutual advantage. As emphasized at the beginning of this chapter, *reasonableness* as differentiated from rationality is central to Rawls's political psychology. Human beings are not only rational in the sense of looking for what is advantageous from their viewpoint. They are also reasonable insofar as they are willing to honour fair terms of cooperation and justify their support for principles and policies with arguments and reasons that other reasonable persons can acknowledge and endorse. Furthermore, Rawls also considers that citizens possess the capacity for a sense of justice, along with the capacity to form a conception of the good, to be essential for justice as fairness theory. Nonetheless, Rawls does not go to the extent of considering moral sentiments such as sympathy, commitment and benevolence as part of motivations for social cooperation. As pointed out in Chapter 6, Nussbaum by contrast suggests that social cooperation should be envisaged as originating from a plurality of motivations which includes not only reciprocity and impartiality but also benevolence, compassion and commitment.

2.4 The Liberal Scepticism of the Good

In 'Social Unity and Primary Goods' (1982), Rawls makes a distinction between liberal and non-liberal political theories. In a liberal theory, the purpose of the state is to allow each citizen to pursue his or her own conception of the good. In a non-liberal theory, by contrast, some conception of the good is taken as established, and the aim of the state is to realize that conception. Rawls's favoured example of a non-liberal theory is classical utilitarianism. As he points out, utilitarianism is a non-liberal theory, since it takes the goodness of the maximization of preference-satisfaction

END ALIENATION

as both philosophically established and capable of justifying a political conception. An Aristotelian theory that takes the purpose of the state to educate the citizens for a virtuous life, or a Marxist theory which aims at rendering us truly human, or even a type of Kantianism that strives to make its citizens into autonomous individuals would also be non-liberal. In contrast, Rawls defines a liberal theory as one that allows for 'a plurality of different and opposing, and even incommensurable, conceptions of the good' (Rawls 1982: 160).

The most frequently stated reason for this is the stability of a political society – namely if we begin to focus on the components of the good we would not succeed in obtaining an overlapping consensus among citizens with different and conflicting conceptions of the good. As Korsgaard (1993) points out, there is also another accompanying reason – perhaps not so explicitly acknowledged. This is what might be called the scepticism of the good.[12] According to this view, there is no best life, or at least we cannot prove that there is, so we have no solid ground for forcing people to lead or choose to lead one kind of life rather than another. Moreover, it is also important to realize that often the 'unknowability' of the good comes mixed up with a sort of epistemological individualism (Korsgaard 1993; Nussbaum 1990b; Arneson 1990; Raz 1990). As a result, the goodness of a life essentially depends on its being chosen by the person who lives it; as a matter of fact, it is the individual, and individual alone, who is best placed to find out for himself or herself what the best life is. It is with these theoretical presuppositions that Rawls associates liberal theories with ones that, on the one hand hold the view that we do not know enough about the final goods to use them in political justification, and on the other hand advocate that the goodness of life by nature is best left in the hands of individuals.

Rawls is rather open to the idea that there can be different versions of liberal political theories. However, a central aspiration of his work on justice is to *free* the idea of what is right and just from the idea of what is good or advantageous for a person, exemplified in his well-known statement 'the priority of the right over the good'. Rawls therefore suggests that what makes his own theory of justice as fairness attractive, and a paradigm for all liberal theories, is that it gives priority to the right over the good. That is, it has an account of people's rightful claims that is not derived for any particular idea or conception of the good. Principles of right – equal basic liberties, fair equality of opportunity and the difference principle – are prior to, and constrain the pursuit of the good. In contrast, what makes utilitarianism or Aristotelian or Marxist theories unattractive and disqualifies them as liberal theories is that they give priority to the good over the right. That is to say, they

---

12 Raz (1990) makes a parallel criticism by noting that Rawls's theory embraces epistemic abstinence in order to defend pluralism as part of a theory of justice. He writes: 'Rawls's epistemic abstinence lies in the fact he refrains from claiming that his doctrine of justice is true. The reason is that its truth, if it is true, must derive from deep and possibly nonautonomous, foundations, from some sound comprehensive moral doctrine. Asserting the truth of the doctrine of justice, or rather claiming that its truth is the reason for accepting it would negate the very spirit of Rawls's enterprise. It would present the doctrine of justice as one of many competing comprehensive moralities current in our society, and this would disqualify it from fulfilling its role of transcending the disagreement among these many incompatible moralities' (Raz 1990: 9).

have an independent account of the good (happiness, virtues, or classless society, for example) and the right is defined as maximization of that good. People's rightful claims (basic rights and opportunities, for example) are entirely dependent on what best promotes the good. Having distinguished liberal and non-liberal theories this way, Rawls confronts us with a dilemma: either we accept his liberal theory of justice (with its scepticism of the good and epistemological individualism) or else we fall back into some form of non-liberal theory founded on a single, monistic conception of the good. This way of setting up the either/or dilemma also makes it convenient for Rawls to look *as if* there are no alternatives to his liberal theory other than those that endorse the maximization of the good, chiefly utilitarianism; it also makes it appear that the choice between a liberal and non-liberal political theory is actually a choice between a conception of justice in which individual rights are intrinsically valuable and a conception of justice where individual rights are not at all or at the most only derivatively important in maximizing the common good.

This was probably at the back of Rawls's mind, when he initially expressed reluctance to accept Sen's capabilities-based criticism of his theory, and he in turn criticized the capability approach as involving one, unique or comprehensive conception of human well-being or the good (§2.2). A capability theorist might find Rawls's reluctance and charge against the capability approach to be unnecessarily fretful. Central to the capability approach is the distinction between functionings and capabilities. While the former refers to people's *achieved* doings and beings, the latter refers to the extent of *freedom* that people have in order to achieve certain basic valuable functionings. Pluralism is therefore preserved insofar as the capability approach as a political objective aims at equalizing citizens' life prospects for basic capabilities (opportunities) rather than what they do with these opportunities, namely functionings. Also, pluralism is protected from the fact that one could sign on to a list of basic capabilities such as nutrition, health, education, social recognition and political participation, without having to justify it from any one particular conception of the good. Nonetheless, the capability approach remains a good-based approach to justice. Hence, what distinguishes the capability approach from Rawls's theory is that while for Rawls the requirements of justice are conceived as disconnected from, and accompanied by a degree of scepticism about the human good and well-being, for Sen (as well as for Nussbaum and Anderson) they are related to an inquiry into the human good and well-being.[13] To the extent that we have an adequate and public

---

13 A closer examination of Rawls's theory brings to light that it is not always easy or possible to maintain an attitude of scepticism towards the good. One paradigmatic place where Rawls does implicitly invoke the idea of the good is in maintaining the priority of basic liberties and balancing it against other human interests which cannot strictly be enlisted as basic liberties – although Rawls would call this a 'thin' conception of the good (Barry 1973; Sen 1999a: 63-65). Rawls accords a strict lexical priority to basic liberties that cannot be overridden by other interests. Yet he acknowledges that there could be situations such as famines, war, public order, security, health and safety when we have to digress from this priority rule (*TJ*, 97ff.). He refers to this as the need to balance liberties with the 'principle of common interest'. One can point to the fact that determining the form and content of things that must come under the principle of common interest invariably involves an inquiry into and validation of the human good.

conception of the human good and well-being which delineates what is truly worth caring about and what makes a life really go better for the person who is living it, it makes sense to hold that what people in a society fundamentally owe to each other is a fair distribution of the human good. An adequate and public conception of the good need not turn out to be single or monistic like the utilitarianism that Rawls is seriously concerned about. Most surely, it would be pluralistic, taking cognizance of the fact that there are many distinct components of well-being and valuable ways of life. Further, it would not strive for more than a partial consensus among the citizens. Just as Rawls believes that reasonable people can come to agreement about principles of justice, so too they can come to an agreement about certain basic capabilities that would inform and support what we owe to each other in the name of justice. On some matters and some capabilities there would not be many controversies, but on others disagreements are bound to arise, as would be the case with any public conception of justice. What is however difficult to sustain is Rawls's suggestion that appealing to substantial claims about the content of human good or well-being necessarily leads back to utilitarianism or any of its allies. In fact, a good-based theory of justice – as it is the case with the capability approach – can affirm that we should choose actions and institutions that go against utilitarianism or any monistic conception of the good.

2.5 Similar and Yet So Different

Rawls's theory of justice and the capability approach are best thought of as 'first cousins', sharing a number of similar features in understanding what we owe to each other in the name of social justice (Roemer 1996: 164). The most striking element is the fact that both are non-utilitarian approaches, evaluating people's benefits and standing in society on the basis of objective criteria. While it is primary goods in Rawls's theory, it is people's basic capabilities to valuable functionings in the case of Sen's capability approach. In both theories, the equalisandum is not *utility*, but rather *primary goods* or *basic capabilities*. In addition, it turns out that both are not outcome theories. Neither advocates a fair distribution of final outcomes, but rather opportunities that each individual can deploy in order to achieve his or her life plans. Primary goods or basic capabilities are inputs into what individuals can achieve in exercising their agency and responsibility.

Despite these commonalities, Rawls's theory and the capability approach differ from each other. This chapter has particularly studied three problem areas in Rawlsian justice from the viewpoint of people's basic capabilities. First, from the standpoint of the capability approach Rawls's primary goods measure proves to be inadequate in addressing some crucial capability variations and shortfalls of individuals. A fair distribution of primary goods to all would still leave some people disadvantaged – the person in the wheelchair, people with physical and mental disabilities, and people who provide formal or informal care for dependents, for example. Sen and Kittay seem to be right to insist on broadening the scope of the difference principle in order to accommodate needs for care and capability shortfalls of people.

Second, Rawls's allegiance to the social contract doctrine in political philosophy leads him to envisage social cooperation in terms of reciprocity. As Nussbaum suggests, motivations for social cooperation need not be confined to reciprocity alone. People tend to cooperate with each other also on the basis of plurality of motivations including moral sentiments of sympathy, commitment and compassion. Envisioning social cooperation in this way would be more sensitive to the problems of justice that Rawls's theory overlooks. However, this would ask for deviation and a break from some of the crucial elements of the social contract doctrine.

Third, Rawls is a product of his own times. He was working largely under the shadow of and in response to utilitarianism and other forms of monistic theories of the good. This motivated him to assume that the requirements of justice are best known and formulated on the basis of scepticism of the good or at most a 'thin' conception of the good. We have shown that the alternative to utilitarianism or any other monistic conception of the good need not necessarily lead to scepticism about the nature of the human good and well-being. Rather, the requirements of justice are better understood on the basis of an inquiry into the plural components of the human good and making certain basic capabilities part of the public conception of justice. A capabilities-based approach to social justice advocated by Sen, Nussbaum and Anderson aspires to achieve such a vision of social justice.

Chapter 3

Towards a Capability Theory of Justice

It will be seen how in place of the wealth and poverty of political economy come the rich human being and rich human need. The rich human being is simultaneously the human being in need of totality of human life-activities – the man in whom his own realization exists as an inner necessity as need.

Karl Marx, *Economic and Philosophical Manuscripts of 1844*

Development is the strategy of evasion. When you can't give people land reform, give them hybrid cows. When you don't send the children to school, try non-formal education. When you can't provide basic health to people, talk of health insurance. Can't give them jobs? Not to worry. Just redefine the words 'employment opportunities'. Don't want to do away with using children as a form of slave labour? Never mind. Talk of 'improving the conditions of child labour'. It sounds good. You can even make money out of it.

P. Sainath, *Everybody Loves a Good Drought*

The preceding chapters have reviewed two prominent approaches in political philosophy. Among other things, the main objection to utilitarianism was that it is *subjective*, and does not intrinsically value the importance of individual freedom and rights. Equalizing people's welfare – pleasure, happiness or preference-satisfaction – would turn out to be equalizing too much. Welfare differences such as expensive tastes and antisocial preferences ought to be treated as matters of individual responsibility and do not have a claim on justice. In the case of adaptive preferences, since a person's subjective perceptions of well-being are malleable to circumstances, alluding to objective notions such as 'functionings', 'urgency', 'exploitation' and so on is helpful in discerning the essential components of well-being. In contrast to utilitarianism, Rawls's theory is *objective*, since it aims at a fair distribution of primary good, with basic liberties and opportunities. A person's benefits and standing in society, in Rawls's theory, are judged not on the basis of utility, but rather in terms of the holding of primary goods. Nonetheless, from the perspective of people's capability variations, even Rawls's theory turns out to be inadequate in certain respects. Giving the same stock of primary goods to people with significant capability shortfalls as to anybody else would leave them rather disadvantaged. Capability deprivations can range from physical and learning disabilities to uneven distribution within the family to the lack of institutional arrangements for the dependent and for those who care for them. Equalizing the holding of primary goods in such instances might amount to equalizing too little. Capability variations which are not the responsibility of individuals, but nevertheless impede people from living valuable human lives should fall under the purview of justice.

Can a capabilities-based approach to social justice respond to the limitations of other influential theories on offer? So far, three versions of the capability approach – as developed by Sen (§3.1), Nussbaum (§3.2) and Anderson (§3.3) – have emerged contributing in their own way to the theoretical foundations of a capability theory of justice. Initially, Sen advocated an 'entitlement' approach, particularly in the context of famine and poverty analysis. Later, he broadened the scope of the idea of entitlements and reinvented it in the form of the capability approach that aims at evaluating people's well-being and their standing in society in terms of certain basic capabilities to achieve valuable functionings. Although Sen has defined the relevant concepts and has even shown the possibility of operationalizing the approach for social policy considerations, he does not endorse any specific list of basic capabilities. As highlighted in Chapter 7, Sen advocates the idea that the selection of relevant capabilities should be linked to, and justified by public reasoning and democracy. Nussbaum in contrast has developed the approach on the basis of a list of (ten) basic capabilities. She has particularly enriched the philosophical foundations of the approach in two directions: first, by showing its connections to Aristotle's ethics and political philosophy and second, by developing the approach as a promising form of political conception. Anderson's version of the capability approach can be viewed as a mid-way point between Sen and Nussbaum. While Sen seems shy of endorsing a predetermined list of basic capabilities and Nussbaum advocates a rather extensive list, Anderson insists only on a relatively few important capabilities considered essential for a regime of democratic equality against oppression and exploitation. It is also important to note that the differences between these leading capability theorists concern not only the endorsement of a list, but also the justification they seek for the capability approach.

In recent philosophical literature, a number of objections have been raised regarding the nature and justification of the different versions of the capability approach (§3.4). One major objection against the capability approach is that it collapses into either a resource-based view or a variety of welfare theories, since the theory is basically concerned either with resources or with welfare derived from the utilization of resources. This objection raises doubts as to the distinctiveness of the capability approach. Often enough the lack of distinctiveness can be traced to the ambivalence in the capability approach as to whether the focus should be on functionings or capabilities. Another important objection is that since the primary intent of the capability theorists is to realize certain basic capabilities for all they are basically concerned with developing a sufficientarian approach and, in the process, are hardly concerned about the inequalities above a stipulated threshold level of well-being. This casts doubts on the scope of the capability approach to function as a fully-fledged theory of justice. The prospect of developing the capability approach as a persuasive theory of justice would very much depend on satisfactorily responding to these objections.

3.1 Sen: The Capability Approach Defined

a) Entitlements and the Political Economy of Hunger

The idea of 'entitlements' that Sen advocated in his earlier study of famines and poverty is a conceptual forerunner to the idea of capabilities, and sheds much light on the motivations of the capability approach to justice. In *Poverty and Famines* (1981: vii), he writes: 'Much about poverty is obvious enough. One does not need elaborate criteria, cunning measurement or probing analysis to recognize raw poverty and to understand its antecedents.' Paradoxically, Sen's theoretical analysis of famines and poverty not only reveals surprising, and not-so-obvious results, but also contains a number of invaluable public policy implications for overcoming world hunger. Traditionally, it was believed that famines occur because of declining of food production and supply in the region. Sen's economic analysis of famines, however, challenged this conventional wisdom. Sen showed that famines occur not mainly because there is any significant fall in the supply of food, but because people lose their 'entitlements' and the 'purchasing power' to acquire and have access to food. This happens to be the stark reality with most of the major famines that have occurred or continue to occur in the world. In 1943, Bengal experienced a devastating famine in which around three million people died. During this year, there was no significant fall in the production of food, but the relative prices of food shot up with the implication that only people in the cities and those with higher wages could afford to buy food. Rural populations with meagre or unstable incomes and who lived on daily wages and a life of hand-to-mouth existence were badly hit. In 2005, Niger was on the brink of a serious crisis of famine and hunger. Although insufficient rain reduced the country's total output of cereals, it was not so disastrous: in fact, it was 22% greater than the harvest of 2001, a year that went without starvation. Yet a sizeable section of the population, particularly the pastoralists, was hungry, sick and malnourished because while the prices of what they can sell (their livestock) plummeted, the prices of what they must buy (food) soared. This made them suffer a lack of power to purchase food, despite the fact that there was no lack of food to purchase.[1] So, Sen emphasizes that hunger and deprivation relate not only to food *production* and availability of food, but also to the *distribution* of food and to the economic, social and political arrangements which can directly or indirectly influence people's capacities or abilities to acquire food and to achieve health and nourishment.

What then are the best ways to prevent famines and overcome deprivations? Since famines and deprivations occur largely because of 'entitlement failures' of one or more occupational groups in particular regions, one pertinent way to prevent them is to focus on 'social safety nets' for entitlement protection (Sen 1981; 1988a). In relatively developed countries, such protection is provided by unemployment insurance and antipoverty programmes. Most developing countries do not have any

---

1   For illustrations of famines in China, Ireland, Bangladesh and Ethiopia see Sen (1981). For details about the recent hunger and poverty crisis in Niger, see *The Economist*, 'Destitution Not Dearth' (20 August 2005), 53.

general system of unemployment insurance, but some of them do provide emergency measures such as 'public employment' (construction of public roads, deepening of public wells and agricultural lakes, etc) by which people could earn a sufficient wage to overcome starvation. Sen also insists on viewing the interconnections between people's basic *economic* freedoms such as living a life without hunger, disease and deprivations on the one hand and *political* freedoms such as freedom of the press, democracy and political participation on the other. Sen's thesis is that 'no famine has ever taken place in the history of the world in a functioning democracy' (Sen 1999a: 16).[2] A country with periodic elections, opposition parties, critical media and press, and a culture of public debate has better prospects of averting famines and other extreme disasters. Political freedoms and rights enable people to criticize government and politicians, and demand attention on urgent issues. Sadly enough, democracy and public debate have been more sensitive to extreme disasters such as famines. Other societal failures such as endemic hunger, malnutrition, infant mortality, severe health crises for the poor and systematic social exclusion of women and minorities continue to co-exist with democracy and public debate. Progress on these issues requires strengthening and improvement rather than the rejection or bypassing of democracy and public discussion.

b) Functionings and Capabilities, Achievements and Freedom to Achieve

Sen (1992; 1993) refines and transforms the concept of entitlements into capabilities. While the term 'entitlements' was mostly used to designate a lack of capacities or abilities to meet basic necessities for bare survival, the term 'capabilities' is used to refer to a wide range of capacities and opportunities required for human well-being as a whole.[3] Accordingly, Sen advocates that people's well-being and standing in society should be evaluated on the basis of their 'capability to achieve valuable functionings' (Sen 1993: 31). This consists of two related but distinct notions: *functionings* and *capabilities*. Sen defines functionings as a number of 'doings' and 'beings' that a person manages to achieve at a time or accumulates over time. Thus goes one of Sen's clear formulations of what functioning means:

> A functioning is an achievement of a person: what he or she manages to do or to be. It reflects, as it were, a part of the 'state' of that person. It has to be distinguished from the commodities which are used to achieve those functionings ... It has to be distinguished also from the happiness generated by the functioning ... A functioning is thus different both from (1) having goods (and the corresponding characteristics), to which it is posterior, and (2) having utility (in the form of happiness resulting from that functioning), to which it is, in an important way, prior. (Sen 1987c: 7)

---

2   It should be noted that democracy, for Sen, is more than just a majority rule. In Chapter 7, I shall discuss the interconnections between capabilities, democracy and public reasoning.

3   As far as I am aware, neither Sen nor any other capability theorist justifies the switch over of terminology from 'entitlements' to 'capabilities'. The most plausible reason could be that the term 'capabilities' seems to indicate more clearly the agency and active participation of the person than 'entitlements'. When we say that someone is 'entitled to' something, it can give the impression that the person himself or herself does not have to do anything.

By way of example, Sen mentions not only basic functionings like nutrition, life expectancy, health and education, but also complex functionings like self-respect, social recognition and political participation which are relevant to the assessment of well-being. In order to achieve these simple and complex functionings, we would certainly require resources such as money, private goods and public goods. We would also derive certain psychological sensations (happiness, fulfilment, etc) from achievement of these functionings. Sen, nonetheless, insists that functionings should be the basis of assessment of a person's well-being.

Sen defines capabilities as the various combinations (or vectors) of functionings that a person *can* achieve or could have achieved. 'The capability of a person reflects the alternative combinations of functionings the person can achieve, and from which he or she can choose one collection' (Sen 1993: 31). Capabilities therefore stand for the extent of freedom that a person has in order to achieve different functionings. There has been a considerable debate and discussion among philosophers and capability theorists (e.g. Williams, Cohen, and Crocker) as to where exactly Sen places emphasis when he uses the term capabilities. David Crocker (1995: 163) states that in Sen's writings the notion of capabilities does not directly refer to people's capacities, or 'internal powers'. Cohen (1993: 20-25), by contrast, notes that the notion of 'capability to do' carries with it an overactive 'athletic' character and hardly has any reference to opportunities and conditions that are required to develop capabilities. Sen (1993) has, however, clarified this as follows:

> The freedom to lead different types of life is reflected in the person's capability set. The capability of the person depends on a variety of factors, including personal characteristics and social arrangements. A full accounting of individual freedom must, of course, go beyond the capabilities of personal living and pay attention to the person's other objectives (e.g. social goals not directly related to one's own life), but human capabilities constitute an important part of individual freedom (1993: 32).

In Sen's understanding therefore, the term 'capabilities' refers to two interrelated elements. First of all, it refers to *capacities* or *powers* of people as human beings; these can range from the most basic ones required to fulfil nutritional and health needs to more complex ones such as the exercise of practical reason and living with self-respect in a community. Secondly, it refers to the *opportunities* that people have to nurture and to exercise their capacities; indeed, people's capacities can be enhanced or hampered depending on the opportunities they face in their familial, social and political circumstances.[4] Sen is well aware that there is a certain unavoidable 'ambiguity' in the term 'capability' in comparison with 'functionings', since the latter stands for a person's 'achievements', whereas the former stands for the person's 'freedom to achieve'. Yet he points out that this should not deter us from focusing on a person's choice and freedom: 'In so far as there are genuine

---

4   Bernard Williams has also suggested an understanding of the term 'capability' along these lines: 'you have to think about sets of co-realizable capabilities *and* about social states in which people acquire various ranges of capability' (Williams 1987: 100, my emphasis). I have basically followed Williams' interpretation and suggestion. See Alexander (2003a; 2005a). Nussbaum's idea of 'combined capabilities' (§6.1) supports this line of interpretation.

ambiguities in the concept of freedom, that should be reflected in corresponding ambiguities in the characterization of capability' (Sen 1993: 33).

c) Well-being and Agency, Control and Effective Freedom

Not only does Sen envisage capabilities to be a reflection of people's freedom to achieve certain valuable functionings and lead the type of life they have reason to value, he also elaborates on the different aspects of freedom that could be important in assessing people's benefits and standing in society. As William Cowper puts it: 'Freedom has many charms to show, that slaves, howe'er contented, never know.'[5] Sen points out that in assessing the extent of freedom that a person enjoys, it is important to pay attention to both 'well-being' and 'agency' aspects. Well-being refers to individuals' own advantage, where advantage can be assessed in terms of valuable states of being such as being well-nourished, healthy, decently educated and so on. Agency on the other hand, refers to the different ways the persons themselves act, and exercise their choice to achieve valuable states of being including goals, commitments and obligations, the outcomes of which need not be advantageous to the agents themselves.

These are two different perspectives in the sense that while in the agency aspect the person is primarily seen as an 'agent' who pursues various goals and accomplishes different things and takes responsibility for his actions, in the well-being aspect the person is seen as a 'patient' or 'beneficiary'. However, it is also important to notice the substantial interconnections between the two, and most often the proven way to enhance people's well-being is to follow the 'agency' and 'participation' route (Sen 1999a: 189ff.). For example, it has been shown that women's well-being in developing countries is tremendously improved by such things as women's ability to earn an independent income, to find employment outside the home, to be literate, to be informed participants in decision-making within and outside the family, and to have ownership rights. These things make a positive contribution to women's voices and agency and hence, enhance the social standing of women in the household and family. Even infant mortality and overpopulation are more effectively tackled by the agency and participatory approaches of educating and empowering women than through some coercive health policies.

Furthermore, Sen also contrasts *control* freedom with *effective* freedom. Control freedom refers to opportunities that are the outcome of a person's own exercise of choice. The role of other agents might in such cases be minimal. Effective freedom, by contrast, refers to opportunities that are the outcome of other agents such as the family, community or the state. The person is either a mere beneficiary or his exercise of control is very minimal.

> The contrast between effective power [effective freedom] and procedural control [control freedom] is important in practice. It is often not possible to organize society in such a way that people can directly exercise the levers that control all the important aspects of their personal lives. To try to see freedom exclusively in terms of control is to miss the

---

5   As quoted in Sen (1999a: 298).

demands of freedom when control cannot feasibly be exercised by the persons themselves (Sen 1985a: 210).

Sen's motivation for retaining the distinction between control and effective freedom is to recognize the importance of economic, social and political structures that can either facilitate or hamper individual capabilities. Persons acquire, exercise and enhance their capabilities depending on their social conditions. Instead of advocating the view that freedom is an exclusive result of the individual's privilege and achievement, Sen reminds us of its other important dimension: 'Freedom is one of the most powerful social ideas' (Sen 1992: 69). Freedoms and opportunities generated by public goods are results of effective freedom brought about by interventions of responsible communities and governments. It would be unreasonable to expect individuals to exercise direct control in these situations.

d) Sen and Social Policy

Sen's capability approach has served as an inspiration for social policy priorities on different fronts. As Sen (1987c) himself has shown, one important application of the capability approach relates to the concept of poverty. Poverty can be relative in the space of income, but absolute in the dimension of capabilities (§1.3.b). This has led to viewing poverty as a capability deprivation rather than merely as low income. Among the most well-known uses of the theoretical insights of the capability approach is the annual Human Development Report (HDR) published since 1990 by the United Nations Development Programme (UNDP). Sen's idea that development is not merely economic growth, but is also an expansion of people's capabilities to be and to do certain valuable things is the starting point of the Human Development paradigm. Accordingly, the main aim of the HDR is to shift focus from traditional 'income-centred' accounting to 'people-centred' policies (Fukuda-Parr 2003). One important part of the HDR is the Human Development Index (HDI) that ranks countries in the world based on the three basic capabilities of *life expectancy* (ability to live long and avoid premature death), *literacy* (ability to read, write and communicate better) and *economic standard of living* (ability to buy goods and services that one wants measured by GDP per capita). This index does show that the traditional income-based GDP per capita measure is an imperfect indicator of human development and that capabilities-based indicators show different results than the former. Despite certain 'valuational' and measurement difficulties and shortcomings, the HDI exerts significant policy impact on national and international agenda. For example, when it becomes rather clear that some countries and regions such as Costa Rica, Sri Lanka or the state of Kerala in India manage to achieve higher levels of 'human development' in comparison to countries or regions with similar or greater income levels, it sets governments and policymakers thinking about the right kinds of policies.

Even at the micro levels, a capabilities-based analysis seems to show important consequences for policy attention. Schokkaert and Van Ootegem (1990) were among the first to operationalize the capability approach using micro-data on the unemployed in Belgium. They conclude their inquiry with a modest but promising note: 'the concept of (refined?) functionings certainly has given us an attractive line of approach. At least it helped us formulate the questions to ask when going beyond the traditional income or utility framework. More empirical work along these lines therefore seems to be eminently useful' (Schokkaert and Van Ootegem 1990: 445). Their research favours the conclusion that the well-being of the unemployed should not be viewed only in monetary terms, that is to say the loss of income, but also in terms of non-monetary factors such as the loss of self-esteem, psychological health and social exclusion. Hence along with the monetary support, non-monetary policy programmes targeted towards the unemployed would prove beneficial. Alkire (2002) illustrates the incongruence between the traditional cost-benefit analysis and a capabilities-based analysis of three Oxfam projects in Pakistan: goat rearing, rose garland production and female literacy classes. In a pure cost-benefit analysis of these projects, the first two are likely to be favoured over the third because of the immediate and tangible returns which can be quantified in economic terms. In a capabilities-motivated evaluation, by contrast, the female literacy class project would be justified as much as the others because of the 'transformative' and 'empowering' effect on the beneficiaries.[6]

Valuable though the various attempts and possibilities to operationalize the capability approach for appropriate social policies are, these cannot however overwrite certain theoretical difficulties with the capability approach. Given the fact that different people and societies vary with regard to which functionings (doings and beings) should count as important and which trivial, it is difficult to identify, discriminate and select the most important functionings as a measure for evaluating people's quality of life and their equal standing in society. The valuational exercise becomes much more complex when attention is shifted from achieved functionings to substantive freedoms represented by the capability set (a combination of functionings that can be achieved). Sen insists that a full assessment of a person's well-being and advantage should take account of '*counterfactual choice* – what one would have chosen if one had the choice' (1992: 67). The difficulties involved in the valuation of capabilities complicate the task of constructing a proper index of capabilities. For example, the Human Development approach which tries to evaluate well-being and quality of life across countries, continents and cultures faces the formidable challenge of deciding which capabilities are most important: why only capabilities related to life expectancy, education and decent living standard, and not others? (Fukuda-Parr 2003). The range of basic capabilities is indeed extensive and the value that individuals assign to each can vary from person to person. Although some capabilities might be deemed vital, deserving social policy attention, their relative importance can and does vary with social and cultural contexts. Sen has not so far proposed a complete ordering of capabilities that would help to discern that one person's capability set is richer or better than another's. He has advocated the idea that value selection and discrimination are an 'intrinsic part' of the capability

---

6   There are many notable empirical applications of the capability approaches. Among others see Chiappero-Martinetti (2000), Robeyns (2003), Bojer (2003), Kuklys (2005), Deneulin (2006), and Subramanian (2006).

approach and that any definite list of capabilities should be avoided. Nussbaum and Anderson disagree with Sen precisely on this point.

Furthermore, Sen has pointed out that the ability to convert resources such as income and wealth into relevant functionings is affected by a 'multiplicity' of individual and social differences. This implies that some people would need more resources than others for the same range of capabilities. 'Differences in age, gender, special talents, disability, proneness to illness, and so on can make two different persons have quite divergent opportunities of quality of life *even when* they share exactly the same commodity bundle' (Sen 1999a: 69). For example, distributive patterns and social norms followed within the family can make a major difference to the capability prospects of individual members. In a gender-biased society, boys and men would normally have priority for many opportunities. In such instances, the fact of being a man or a woman does make a difference. Sen has (1992: xi) referred to these elements of human diversities as 'empirical facts', and sees the inevitability of counting some diversity and discounting others. 'There are diversities of many different kinds. It is not unreasonable to think that if we try to take note of all the diversities, we might end up in a total mess of empirical confusion. The demands of practice indicate discretion and suggest that we disregard some diversities while concentrating on the more important ones' (Sen 1992: 117). However, as Pogge (2002b: 179-190) has highlighted, the question remains how these diversities could be quantitatively measured and what procedure we should follow in choosing certain diversities and rejecting others in order to propose concrete political and distributional arrangements

3.2 Nussbaum: The Capability Approach Philosophized

a) Nussbaum, Aristotle and the Capability Approach

Nussbaum strengthens and enriches the theoretical foundations of the capability approach by showing its connections to Aristotle's ethics and political philosophy. Even though Sen from time to time alludes to the Aristotelian, along with the Marxist, idea of a 'truly human functioning', he has not gone in a major way towards providing a philosophical justification of the approach based on Aristotle. Sen acknowledges this to be Nussbaum's significant contribution: 'Though at the time of proposing the approach, I did not seize its Aristotelian connections ... [t]he Aristotelian perspective and its connections with the recent attempts at constructing a capability-focused approach have been illuminatingly discussed by Martha Nussbaum' (Sen 1993: 30, n. 2). Aristotle's ethics and political philosophy are based on a reflection on the good life. Unlike a hedonist – or his contemporary analogue a utilitarian – who seems to reduce the constituents of the good life to a *single* good of pleasure or preference-satisfaction, Aristotle argues that the components of the good life are *many* and irreducibly plural.

On the basis of her life-time engagement with the textual interpretation of Aristotle's views and a number of path-breaking contributions to Aristotelian scholarship,[7] Nussbaum connects the capability approach to Aristotle's philosophical method of an ongoing normative reflection on the 'valuable human functionings' that ought to constitute the good life. The concept of a 'flourishing human life', for Nussbaum, would play an important role in discerning the different capabilities that should draw the attention of ethical and political reflections. Thus, Nussbaum places the capability approach within the tradition of political philosophy that justifies political principles and the legitimacy of the state on the the basis of the 'political' nature of human beings to come together in the polis. This implies that, in the footsteps of Aristotle, Nussbaum does not appeal to the notion of social contract doctrine and all the elements connected with it (§2.3) for justifying a public conception of basic capabilities.[8] Nussbaum however, is a vigilant reader of Aristotle. Although she envisages the capability approach to be largely an Aristotelian project, she makes important corrections to Aristotle. No reader of Aristotle can ever miss the most striking normative deficit in his work: the absence of any reference to universal human dignity. His understanding of human beings was rather hierarchical: masters, men, women and slaves. He just did not think of natural slaves and women as equal human beings, who deserved to be included in the polis. He also excludes from citizenship people like craftsmen (*banausoi*), who do not have enough leisure to get the education that Aristotle thinks citizenship requires. Nussbaum infuses the idea of equality and human dignity into Aristotelian thinking. She finds that an appropriation of Aristotle for contemporary political purposes would have to necessarily extend Aristotelian thought in the direction of egalitarianism insofar as Aristotle himself was deeply interested in identifying 'truly human functionings' and advocated that the polis should provide the necessary and appropriate conditions for the exercise of these human functionings. Besides the obvious rejection of all forms of slavery and its related institutions, Nussbaum (1988a) holds the idea that we need to work politically with the assumption that 'all children of two human parents' are capable of the major functions of human life and hence, deserve attention and respect. In the case of severely disabled and dependent children and adults, she points out that we need to provide material resources, education and social recognition, so that they too like others would be socially accepted and integrated.

Also, Aristotle seems to exhibit perfectionist and paternalistic attitudes in the realm of politics. He advocates the idea that the state should not only discern what the good life is, but also actively promote different virtues and ways of life among citizens. Any contemporary reader of Aristotle's *Ethics*, and in particular, his *Politics* is likely to find that a robust distance between the state and citizens is missing, when especially citizens are commanded in such personal matters as what to study and how much exercise to take everyday, without realizing that this is a morally

---

7   Among other works, see Nussbaum, *The Fragility of Goodness* (1986), *Love's Knowledge: Essays on Philosophy and Literature* (1990a), *The Therapy of Desire* (1994), *Upheavals of Thought* (2001a) and *Hiding From Humanity: Disgust, Shame, and the Law* (2004).

8   In Chapter 6, the points of convergence and divergence between Nussbaum's hybrid theory of capabilities and Aristotle's 'naturalistic' moral and political philosophy are taken up for review.

controversial role for the state. Nussbaum insists that Aristotle's lack of a conception of political liberty calls for a major departure: 'In this area the *Aristotelian* must depart from *Aristotle*' (Nussbaum 1990b: 239, my emphasis). She alludes to, for example, the Athenian tradition of free speech that might prove helpful in correcting and reorienting Aristotle, since some Athenian laws required 'the protection, around each citizen, of a sphere of privacy and non-interference within which what goes on will not be the business of political planning at all, though politics will protect its boundaries' (Nussbaum 1990b: 239).[9] Nonetheless, as argued in Chapter 7, neither Nussbaum nor Sen would settle for a conception of liberty only as non-interference. Nussbaum points out that in some respects the liberal conception of freedom as non-interference can be effectively critiqued by the Aristotelian and capability theorist, advocating that certain types of apparent 'interferences' as in the case of economic redistribution, income tax, land reforms, etc might actually be required in order to enable citizens to be capable of choice and derive the full benefit of freedom. Insofar as the types of interferences envisaged are capabilities-promoting, non-dominating and under the purview of the law, they could be justified and need not be debilitating to citizens' freedom.

It is important to note that over the years Nussbaum's thinking, particularly with regard to the capability approach, has gone through refinement and changes. In *The Fragility of Goodness* (1986) the concept of capabilities and its moral and political implications remain only in the background. In a number of subsequent articles (e.g. 1988a; 1988b; 1990b; 1995c) she explores the possibility of developing a distinctive approach to social justice drawing inspiration from Aristotle on the one hand and Sen's capability approach on the other. However, in *Women and Human Development* (2000a) and *Frontiers of Justice* (2006) she tries to develop a hybrid view of capabilities that critically aligns elements of Aristotelian social democracy with certain liberal doctrines.[10]

b) The List of Capabilities

While Sen is contented in advocating a capabilities-based understanding of justice as an open approach, without endorsing a definite list of capabilities, Nussbaum (2000a) develops it as a substantive conception of justice based on a list of (ten) capabilities. She argues: 'It seems to me, then, that Sen needs to be more radical than he has been so far ... by introducing an objective normative account of human functioning

---

9   Aristotle, however, is not as illiberal and paternalistic as he sometimes is portrayed to be. As demonstrated in Chapter 5, for Aristotle the idea of 'choice' played an important role in the context of individual responsibility. Furthermore, as Nussbaum (1990b: 235-236) notes, Aristotle did not advocate any particular guidelines concerning the religious identity of the polis. This seems to be an obvious omission and departure, given the fact that during and prior to the period of Aristotle, city state contained not only a conflicting plurality of Olympian deities, but also a host of foreign cults. In particular, this turns out to be a significant departure from Plato's *Republic,* where all speech about the gods is carefully regulated. We do not seem to find such regulation in Aristotle.

10   The conceptual connections as well as the differences between Aristotle and the capability approach are discussed in detail in Chapter 6.

and by describing a procedure of objective evaluation by which functionings can be assessed for their contribution to the good human life' (1988a: 176). Thus, the list of capabilities is one of the important differences between Nussbaum and Sen's version of the capability approach. Nussbaum, no doubt, agrees with Sen that capabilities are the most appropriate criterion or space to evaluate people's quality of life. She also agrees that the capability approach as a theory of justice should focus on people's capabilities rather than on functionings so that people are not compelled to act in particular ways but are given ample opportunities to choose the types of functionings they consider valuable. Yet, Nussbaum will traverse a more radical path. As she puts it: 'Sen has focused on the role of capabilities in demarcating the space within which quality of life assessments are made; I use the idea in a more exigent way, as a foundation for basic political principles that should underwrite constitutional guarantees' (2000a: 70-71). Sen of course speaks of the need for paying attention to 'a relatively small number of centrally important' (Sen 1992: 77) capabilities such as nutrition, health, mobility, political and civil liberties, free choice of labour, social respect and so on. However, he does not commit himself to a definite list of capabilities in the way Nussbaum does.

Drawing inspiration from Aristotle-Marx's conception of 'truly human functioning' and focusing on the idea of 'human dignity', Nussbaum proposes a systematic list of central capabilities that might serve as benchmarks for governments, policymakers and international institutions. The list of capabilities is as follows (Nussbaum 2006: 76-78):

1. *Life*. Being able to live to the end of a human life of normal length; not dying prematurely, or before one's life is so reduced as to be not worth living.
2. *Bodily Health*. Being able to have good health, including reproductive health; to be adequately nourished; to have adequate shelter.
3. *Bodily Integrity*. Being able to move freely from place to place; to be secure against violent assault, including sexual assault and domestic violence; having opportunities for sexual satisfaction and for choice in matters of reproduction.
4. *Senses, Imagination, and Thought*. Being able to use the senses, to imagine, think, and reason – and to do these things in a 'truly human' way, a way informed and cultivated by an adequate education, including, but by no means limited to, literacy and basic mathematical and scientific training. Being able to use imagination and thought in connection with experiencing and producing works and events of one's own choice, religious, literary, musical, and so forth. Being able to use one's mind in ways protected by guarantees of freedom of expression with respect to both political and artistic speech, and freedom of religious exercise. Being able to have pleasurable experiences and to avoid non-beneficial pain.
5. *Emotions*. Being able to have attachments to things and people outside ourselves; to love those who love and care for us, to grieve at their absence; in general, to love, to grieve, to experience longing, gratitude, and justified anger. Not having one's emotional development blighted by fear and anxiety.

(Supporting this capability means supporting forms of human association that can be shown to be crucial in their development.)

6. *Practical Reason*. Being able to form a conception of the good and to engage in critical reflection about the planning of one's life. (This entails protection for the liberty of conscience and religious observance.)

7. *Affiliation*

   A. Being able to live with and toward others, to recognize and show concerns for other human beings, to engage in various forms of social interaction; to be able to imagine the situation of another. (Protecting this capability means protecting institutions that constitute and nourish such forms of affiliation, and also protecting the freedom of assembly and political speech.)

   B. Having the social bases of self-respect and non-humiliation; being able to be treated as a dignified being whose worth is equal to that of others. This entails provisions of non-discrimination on the basis of race, sex, sexual orientation, ethnicity, caste, religion, national origin.

8. *Other Species*. Being able to live with concern for and in relation to animals, plants, and the world of nature.

9. *Play*. Being able to laugh, to play, to enjoy recreational activities.

10. Control over one's environment.

    A. Political. Being able to participate effectively in political choices that govern one's life; having the right of political participation, protections of free speech and association.

    B. Material. Being able to hold property (both land and movable goods), and having property rights on an equal basis with others; having the right to seek employment on an equal basis with others; having the freedom from unwarranted search and seizure. In work, being able to work as a human being, exercising practical reason and entering into meaningful relationships of mutual recognition with other workers.

i) *Character and justification of the list*

Nussbaum's list of capabilities contains a number of attractive features, arguably both complementary and corrective in respect of Rawls's list of primary goods and the current list of human rights in thinking about the obligations of social justice.[11] The list, first and foremost, is rather 'generous' and elaborate enough to include a wide range of capabilities for a flourishing human life: from the most fundamental ones like long life, health and bodily integrity to some complex ones such as practical reason, affiliation and control over one's material and political environment. Second, although the list is intended to be specific with regard to the focus on crucial areas

---

11 For discussion about the complementary and corrective role between Nussbaum's list of capabilities on the one hand and human rights and Rawls's primary goods on the other, see Nussbaum, 'Capabilities and Human Rights' (1997a); *Women and Human Development* (2000a: 96-100) and Alexander (2004). Besides the inclusion of many more items on the list, one crucial difference between Rawls and Nussbaum's list is that while Rawls includes income and wealth, Nussbaum omits them.

of capabilities, the items on the list are somewhat general and abstract so as to allow room for further specifications and implementation by consequent constitutional, legislative and judicial procedures. Third, the list does entail a 'thick' conception of human being in comparison to philosophical positions such as Rawls's (§2.4) that claim to be independent of endorsing any particular conception of human being, and yet it remains a 'thin' moral conception that could be compatible with different moral, religious and philosophical doctrines.[12] Finally, the list of capabilities affirms the idea that human life ought to be irreducibly heterogeneous: each component, as different as health, education, political liberties and self-respect, is qualitatively distinct and important in its own right; indeed, the distinctness of each of them puts moral limits on the practice of comparing them or weighing them on a single scale for trade offs and cost-benefit analysis.

Some critics of Nussbaum have disputed the inclusion or the absence of certain items on the list. Some others find the very procedure of drawing up a universal list to be paternalistic and culturally insensitive (Ackerly 2000; Hurka 2002; Menon, 2002; Kekes 2003: Ch. 7). However, we need not always be misled or dismayed by the implications that the term 'list' may suggest. Perhaps, philosophically, it may be more rewarding to switch attention away from the detail of Nussbaum's list of capabilities and turn to the complex structure and theoretical underpinnings that the list involves. The critique of existing political theories and the search for a more appropriate alternative can, following Nussbaum, begin with a blueprint, a working hypothesis: a list of what is good and correspondingly what is bad for a human life; that long life, health, pleasure, friendship, solidarity, humour and so on are good and that premature death, hunger, pain, sickness and loneliness are in themselves bad. At the same time, our aptitude to list things that are good and bad for a human life may not necessarily be accompanied by a deeper understanding of the nature and implications of the items on the list.

Consider for instance bodily integrity, fundamental among capabilities found on Nussbaum's list (see number three on the list). Spontaneously we seem to think that everyone should enjoy this human good; certainly, we would consider it a misfortune when someone is deprived of it. But when asked why this should be considered as something valuable in terms of a human life, we might then have to explicitly state that a person's life interrupted by physical torture, sexual assault, or domestic violence cannot be considered a proper human life. Consequently, societies and governments which do nothing or very little to guarantee everyone the opportunities for a life without physical intimidation and harm, we would think, are deficient in matters of social justice. The list, therefore, has to be constantly accompanied and supported by critical reflection, public discussion and democratic deliberation.

---

12 Nussbaum has referred to it as a 'thick vague' conception of the good. She writes: 'The Aristotelian uses a conception that is not "thin", like Rawls's "thin theory" – that is, confined to the enumeration of all-purpose means to good living, but "thick" – dealing, that is, with human ends across all areas of human life. The conception is, however, vague and this in a good sense. It admits, that is, of many concrete specifications; and yet it draws, as Aristotle put it, an "outline sketch" of the good life' (1990b: 217).

ii) Universalism versus particularism

Nussbaum's universal framework consisting of a list of capabilities has generated an ongoing philosophical debate on the urgency and relevance of universal values for assessing people's quality of life. Apparently one might, like Nussbaum, argue that there are certain universal values such as the dignity of the person, the integrity of the body, basic political rights and liberties, basic economic opportunities and so on which people from different nations and cultures can recognize and have reasons to see as valuable. Certain universal norms of human capabilities ought to be considered central for political purposes in thinking about constitutional guarantees in all nations. One might, at the same time, also be seriously concerned about the appropriateness and legitimacy of universal values and paradigms. These tend to advocate and support paternalist states and international institutions: 'we' know what is good for you; 'you' had better listen to us! It's for your own well-being that we do this! Any claim to a set of cross-cultural values and norms as benchmarks for culturally different countries and societies across the world might run the risk of disrespecting people as autonomous agents and as democratic citizens to determine for themselves what is good for them. A 'colonial universalism', for example, works with the assumption that the ways of the colonial powers and 'developed' societies are progressive and enlightened and the ways of the colonized and 'developing' societies primitive and reactionary. A 'globalization universalism' works with a single-minded purpose of maximizing profit, overlooking human values.

On a more fundamental level, one might express concerns about a universalist project for cultural reasons. Any attempt to pick out some elements of human life as more important and fundamental than others is bound to be insensitive to actual historical and cultural differences. People understand human life and in particular family, social and religious life in widely different ways, and any attempt to produce a set of most important values is bound to reflect and promote certain cultural or religious conceptions, while disadvantaging others.

Nussbaum does not deny the potential dangers of a universalist project. Nonetheless, she is of the opinion that respect for cultural pluralism and people's autonomy are themselves universal values which are not respected everywhere. Protecting and promoting them therefore requires a commitment to some cross-cultural principles as fundamental entitlements. Moreover, when the list of universal human capabilities is informed and animated by public dialogue, it can maintain a rich flexibility to cultural contexts and sensitivity to the individuality of the agents and social situations involved. Culture is a space of contestation and debate. One might identify certain social norms, values and practices as representative of a particular culture, but one needs to also be aware of traditions of 'internal criticism' and 'dissidence' present in the culture. For Nussbaum, a universal aspiration to human capabilities would have to draw resources from the dynamics of cultural dialogue and debate rather than mindlessly using them as a platform for meddlesome interference.

3.3 Anderson: The Capability Approach Democratized

a) Capabilities and Democratic Equality

Anderson's (1999) version of the capability approach draws inspiration from three characteristics of what she calls a regime of 'democratic equality'. First, like social and political movements that have historically struggled and pressed for certain egalitarian claims against *oppression* and social hierarchies, democratic equality seeks to abolish all forms of socially created oppression, particularly those forms of social relationships by which some people dominate, exploit, marginalize, demean, and inflict violence upon others. It asserts the social and political equality of everyone on the basis of the equal moral worth of persons. This implies that although people do not have equal talents or capacities, no one shall be discriminated against on the basis of birth, race, ethnicity, gender and so on. Second, democratic equality views social justice in a *relational* perspective. Most contemporary theories of justice are concerned with attaining a fair distribution of some distributable goods such as income, resources and opportunities for welfare. Social relationships that affirm equal worth of persons are often seen to be instrumental to achieving such patterns of distribution. In contrast, democratic equality considers social relationships of equality as fundamental. Certain patterns of distribution of goods might enhance such relationships, but distribution of goods is only a means to the end of equal, meaningful and rewarding social relationships. Third, democratic equality accommodates demands of equal *recognition*, particularly by ensuring that resources are distributed according to principles and procedures that express respect and dignity. Specifically, this would mean avoiding a condescending attitude in coming to the aid of people. In the name of promoting individual responsibility and agency, some stringent theories of distribution – Anderson calls them 'luck egalitarian' theories – tend to abandon citizens to fend for themselves.[13] Theories that do stipulate some forms of compensation and redistribution of resources to unfortunate citizens do so in such a manner that it degrades the dignity of the beneficiaries. Against such schemes of compensation or redistribution, democratic equality insists that people should not be required to demean themselves before others as a condition of laying claim to their share of goods.

Anderson appreciates the fact that the conception of democratic equality circumscribed by the above three characteristics would be best fulfilled by adopting the theoretical insights of the capability approach: 'Amartya Sen has proposed a better way to understand freedom … We can understand the egalitarian aim to secure for everyone the social conditions of their freedom in terms of capabilities. Following Sen, I say that egalitarians should seek equality for all in the space of capabilities' (Anderson 1999: 316). She is drawn towards the capability approach mainly because it focuses directly on what people are able to do and be rather than on goods or

---

13 Under luck egalitarian theories, Anderson includes the works of R. Dworkin, G.A. Cohen, R. Arneson, J. Roemer, E. Rakowaski, P. Van Parijs and others. For details about her critique of each of these theories, see Anderson (1999). Chapter 5 discusses her specific objections against Dworkin's equality of resources.

resources which are only means to people's doings and beings. Such a direct focus, Anderson points out, would empower people with necessary entitlements to avoid or overcome entanglement in oppressive social relationships. More positively, it would also enable people to participate in and to function as equal citizens in a democratic society.

However, Anderson, like Nussbaum, is troubled by the open and unspecified character of Sen's version of the capability approach.

> Sen's capability egalitarianism leaves open a large question, however. Which capabilities does society have an obligation to equalize? Some people care about playing cards well, others about enjoying a luxury vacation in Tahiti. Must egalitarians, in the name of equal freedom, offer free card-playing lessons and state subsidized vacations to exotic lands? Surely there are limits to which capabilities citizens are obligated to provide one another. (Anderson 1999: 316)

Instead of leaving it open and unspecified, Anderson holds the view that it is possible to identify certain core areas of capabilities that would be deemed essential for avoiding or overcoming oppression and for social and political participation on the basis of equality and dignity. She advocates three relevant spheres of capabilities, namely capabilities required to function: (1) as a human being, (2) as a participant in a system of co-operative production, and (3) as a citizen of a democratic state. They are as follows:

1. To be capable of functioning as a *human being* requires effective access to the means of sustaining one's biological existence – food, shelter, clothing, medical care – and access to the basic conditions of human agency – knowledge of one's circumstances and options, the ability to deliberate about means and ends, the psychological conditions of autonomy, including the self-confidence to think and judge for one's self, freedom of thought and movement.
2. To be capable of functioning as an *equal participant in a system of cooperative production* requires effective access to the means of production, access to the education needed to develop one's talents, freedom of occupational choice, the right to make contracts and enter into cooperative agreements with others, the right to receive fair value for one's labour, and recognition by others of one's productive contributions.
3. To be capable of *functioning as a citizen* requires rights to political participation, such as freedom of speech and franchise, and also effective access to the goods and relationships of civil society. This entails freedom of association, access to public spaces such as roads, parks, and public accommodations including public transportation, the postal service and telecommunications. This also entails the social condition of being accepted by others, such as the ability

,to appear in public without shame, and not being ascribed outcast status. (Anderson 1999: 317-318, my emphases)

b) *Anderson between Sen and Nussbaum*

Anderson's version of the capability approach might be best understood and interpreted as a mid-way point between those of Sen and Nussbaum. Although Sen has referred to certain basic capabilities like nutrition, health, education, self-respect and political participation which no society can afford to ignore, he has in principle refused to endorse any definite list of capabilities. Such a position might, on the one hand, make the capability approach sensitive to cultural contexts: each society can through a process of public discussion determine the basic capabilities that citizens in the name of justice are obligated to provide one another. But, on the other hand, a refusal to delineate and specify some focus areas of attention or basic capabilities can leave the approach vulnerable to different interpretations and outcomes. Nussbaum, by contrast, has specified a list of basic capabilities, thus giving a substantive content to the approach. This to a large extent overcomes the problem of imprecision and the risk of uncertain outcomes found in Sen's position. However, since the list is extensive and tries to cover many areas of capabilities, it can give the impression of being utopian. One might dismiss it under the pretext of being insensitive to the human condition of scarcity and the necessity of having to make difficult choices between conflicting values.

By restricting the number of capabilities and grouping them together under three main areas, Anderson aims at a more realistic version of the capability approach. More importantly, as pointed out at the beginning of this chapter, the difference between Nussbaum and Anderson concerns not only the number of capabilities on the list, but also the justification that supports them. What motivates Nussbaum's approach is a sort of universalism informed by the concept of a 'flourishing human life', a concept from which it might require demanding efforts to derive a political consensus. Anderson in contrast, focuses on capabilities required to overcome 'oppression' and 'exploitation'. One should, no doubt, like Nussbaum aspire for a full-blown conception of the good life, but often it turns out that we make progress on moral and political fronts on the basis of what is 'unjust', 'urgent', 'exploitative' and 'oppressive'.

The difference in the justification of the list is further reflected in the fact that Anderson singles out the sphere of economic production and emphasizes the capabilities required to effectively and meaningfully participate as an equal in a system of cooperative production. Under the capabilities required to have 'Control Over One's Environment' (number 10 on the list of capabilities), Nussbaum does mention the need to engage in meaningful and rewarding relationships in the work place: 'In work, being able to work as a human being, exercising practical reason and entering into meaningful relationships of mutual recognition with other workers' (Nussbaum 2006: 78). However, unlike Anderson, Nussbaum does not separate it out as a productive sphere in order to give it a special attention.

From the viewpoint of democratic equality, this seems significant particularly because modern forms of oppression and capability deprivation take place in the context of productive relationships rather than in the traditional sense of slavery – humans owning other humans. In democratic equality, it is true that citizens' entitlement to basic goods does not originate from an obligation to produce them. Yet it promotes and encourages work-ethics. So much so that people's capacities to participate in non-exploitative productive processes and to engage in a reciprocal economic relationship are themselves valued as crucial capabilities. This means that most people who are fit and capable of doing some work will gain access to the resources they require by earning a wage or some equivalent compensation on the basis of their role in the division of labour. Nevertheless, in a democratic society, economy is not equated with market sector. It recognizes the fact that people's access to jobs, resources and social positions are more like the gifts one receives in a network of relationships with varying degrees of reciprocity than market transactions where one receives only what one pays for. Such a view is particularly important for recognition of the 'invisible' and 'non-quantifiable' contributions of non-wage-earning dependent caretakers to the economy.

3.4 Objections

a) A Distinctive Non-welfarist Approach?

A central claim which is prominent in all three versions of the capability approach – Sen, Nussbaum and Anderson's – is that people's benefits and standing in society ought to be assessed neither in terms of resources they own nor welfare they derive from the utilization of these resources, but rather on the basis of certain basic capabilities to achieve valuable functionings. Positively, this would imply that the capability theorists envision the capability approach to be a distinctive non-welfarist approach, since it aims at 'equality of certain basic capabilities' rather than equality of resources or equality of welfare. Dworkin (2000: 285ff.) has argued that the capability approach does not really provide a genuine alternative to welfare equality. In fact, according to Dworkin, Sen's capability approach turns out to be equality of welfare, since it suggests that people should be made as nearly equal as possible in their capacity to realize the 'complex' achievements of happiness, self-respect, and a significant role in the community (Dworkin 2000: 301). Consequently, Dworkin's contention is that people cannot be made equal in their capabilities for 'happiness', 'self-respect' and 'community participation'. These capacities are subjective and vary from person to person and from community to community, and hence Sen's suggestion that government should take steps to bring about equality in these capacities is unacceptable. Roemer (1996) raises the problem of 'residual welfarism' in the capability approach. Here is how he voices his objection:

> [I]ncluding happiness as one of the functionings weakens the extent to which an index of functionings will be independent of self-conceived notions of welfare ... The pleasure that I receive from satisfying my offensive and expensive tastes will also generate happiness, and this weakens the detour around these kinds of taste that focusing on functioning was supposed to facilitate. (Roemer 1996: 191-192)

Dworkin and Roemer are right to notice that the capability approach involves not only simple 'capabilities to achieve valuable functionings' but also complex ones and that this brings in certain 'arbitrariness' and 'subjective' elements to the approach. For a capability theorist however, the alleged arbitrariness need not lead to the conclusion that the capability approach collapses into a sort of welfarism (Williams, A. 2002). For example, Sen seems to anticipate a possible misunderstanding in this regard.

> There are different problems with different interpretations of utility, but they share the programme of getting the evaluation done *indirectly* through using some psychological metric like happiness or desire. This is precisely where the main difficulty lies. *While being happy may count as an important functioning, it cannot really be all there is to leading a life (i.e. it can scarcely be the only valuable functioning).* If the utility-based functioning is done in terms of pleasure or happiness, then in effect the other functionings would get disenfranchised, and would be valued only indirectly and only to the extent that they contribute to pleasure or happiness. (Sen 1992: 54, my emphases)

Happiness, self-respect and participation in community life are no doubt complex matters to objectify and quantify. These are not like simple well-being indicators such as life expectancy, nutrition, literacy and educational levels, infant mortality and absence of severe illness. Nevertheless, the understanding and role of happiness in the capability approach can be differentiated from welfarism. In welfarism, happiness is associated with subjective *psychological states* and becomes the sole criterion through which a person's well-being is viewed. In contrast, in the capability approach, happiness is associated with *actions* – as in the case of Aristotle's eudaimonism. So goes the argument of Aristotle in *Ethics*.

> Let us now turn back again to the good which is the object of our search, and ask what it can possibly be; because it appears to vary with the *action or art* ... In medicine this is health; in strategy, victory; in architecture, a building – different things in different arts, but in *every action and pursuit* it is the end. (*Ethics* I, 7: 73, my emphases)

This implies that even though there might be some apparent affinities between *eudaimonism* and *welfarism*, both can be differentiated: while the former is concerned with what a person is 'able to do', the latter is associated with what the person 'feels'; while in eudaimonism happiness is only a by-product or side-effect of what one is able to achieve by different worthwhile activities, in welfarism happiness is considered as a goal in itself. Moreover, in the capability approach, the overall quality of life of the person is evaluated looking at the *capability set* as a whole, not just happiness. The residual welfarism that could arise because of a subjective interpretation of happiness, self-respect and community participation is counter-checked and counter-balanced by other functionings in the capability set. For instance, a battered housewife and a bonded labourer (§1.1) might have psychologically 'educated' themselves to be happy. However, looking 'objectively' at their condition of lack of freedom and opportunities, their vulnerability to abuse and violence, it is not difficult to determine the deprived state of their lives. Finally, the capability approach does recognize the value of certain complex capabilities to achieve valuable functionings even when these are complex, and often prove to be challenging to measure objectively.

b) Functionings or Capabilities?

One of the central claims of the capability approach is that as far as adult citizens are concerned what we owe to each other as claims of justice are a set of basic capabilities and not functionings. As Nussbaum formulates it: '*capability, not functionings, is the appropriate political goal*' (2000a: 87); 'The government aims at capabilities and leaves the rest to citizens' (1990b: 214). This means that despite having access to food, a person may prefer to fast, whether as a political protest or as part of religious beliefs or for some other reason; having adequate opportunities to get educated, a person might decide on what and how long to study; having the required facilities for play and recreation, a person may decide to be a workaholic, taking no advantage of relaxation opportunities; having the necessary opportunities to actively participate in politics, a person might decide not to play a public role; and so on. In all of these instances, the basic idea of a capability theorist is that social justice would be violated if people are in want of the capability to be adequately nourished, to be educated, to enjoy leisure and to participate in politics. In contrast it would be no social injustice if functionings or the actual achievement of nourishment, education, play and political participation are not achieved. In fact, forcing or pressurizing people to convert their capabilities into achieved functionings would amount to unwarranted paternalism and injustice.

The idea that justice is fulfilled when individuals have relevant basic capabilities, whether or not they are actualized into corresponding functionings is attractive and resonates with a number of liberal values. It gives much more information on the options and choices available to the person, which may not be available when we focus only on the achieved functionings. Not only do we know that a person is adequately nourished, educated and the like, but we also have relevant information on whether or not the person has had the opportunity to exercise his or her agency to realize these functionings. Moreover, forcing people to achieve a particular level of functionings would mean that we push people into particular ways of doing and being. This would be a paternalistic interference on the part of the state, society or any interested third party in the lives of individuals. A benevolent dictator might just as well achieve a good distribution of functionings while suppressing agency and freedom of choice. Finally, equalizing people's capability sets rather than their functionings allows space for individual responsibility. People who waste or do not make an effective use of the opportunities provided to them, do not have claims of justice for their capability shortfalls.

Some social philosophers [e.g. Arneson (2006); Phillips (2004); Fleurbaey (2002)] point out that it is unnecessary, and even dangerous to shift the ethical perspective from a theory of achievements (functionings) to a theory of opportunities (capabilities). The point of social justice is, these philosophers argue, not just about some abstract opportunities which may or may not materialize, but rather about effectively having them. A socially conscientious philosopher should always be asking why in the social competition some succeed and others do not. The losers do not always lose because they are lazy, irresponsible or less talented. It often depends on how the social game is played. So, probably in the case of essential goods such as food, education, health, and jobs, focusing on capabilities or sets of opportunities is not enough. Moreover, the capability theorists who have tried to operationalize the approach point out that for the formulation and evaluation of social policies, it is relatively easier and more useful to look at people's achieved functionings. Sen, however, does not want to reduce the scope of the capability approach to the evaluation of achieved functionings, although in some contexts we might have to be content focusing on functionings: 'Ideally the capability approach should take note of the full extent of freedom to choose between different functioning bundles, but limits of practicality may often force the analysis to be confined to examining the *achieved* functioning bundle only' (Sen 1992: 53).

Sen is rather hopeful and optimistic that the gap between the concept of capabilities and its measurement can be narrowed down by the deployment of 'pragmatic reason' and by adopting different strategies for using the capability approach in further research. On the one hand, it can be used as a *direct approach* that directly analyses and compares vectors of functionings or capabilities: 'In many ways this is the most immediate and full-blooded way of going about incorporating capability considerations in evaluation' (1999a: 81-82). The direct approach could take the form of 'total comparison' (complete ranking of all vectors), or 'partial ranking' (ranking of some vectors *vis-à-vis* others without demanding completeness) or 'distinguished capability comparison' (comparison of some particular capabilities such as employment, nutrition, literacy and so on). On the other hand, the capability approach can be also used as a supplementary and indirect approach. The *supplementary approach* would consist of supplementing the more traditional income comparisons with capability considerations. This approach can lead to a more comprehensive picture and broadening of the informational base. The *indirect approach* would take the form of using the traditional income comparisons but calculating incomes 'adjusted' by capabilities. For example, the family income levels could be adjusted downwards or upwards depending on literacy levels in order to make them equivalent in terms of capability achievement.

c) A Sufficientarian Approach?

 Arneson (2000; 2006) notes that the capability approach adopts a sufficientarian approach to social justice, since it aims to guarantee to all citizens basic capabilities to realize 'good enough' levels of all essential functionings. As he puts it:

> The Nussbaum and Sen approach can usefully be interpreted as sufficientarian. On this view, justice above all requires that each and every person be sustained at a threshold adequate level of capability to function in all of the ways that are important to human well-being ... The nub of the difficulty with sufficiency is that it overstates the moral importance of sustaining each and every person at the 'good enough' level, come what may (Arneson 2006: 17).

Arneson finds sufficientarian theories such as the capability approach to be objectionable because taken literally these would lead to unrealistic conclusions.

Some individuals are extremely unable, but nevertheless can be brought to the level of threshold by means of enormous amounts of resources siphoned off in their favour. Some others are so severely disabled that they cannot be brought to a threshold of basic capabilities whatever the amount of assistance rendered to them, unless one sets the threshold level very low. Severely disabled people with low level of capabilities, then, become 'basins' of attraction, or 'bottomless pits', demanding enormous levels of social resources even though their capability levels would improve only to insignificant levels. This might pressure the society so much that no above threshold level of capabilities can be sustained for anybody at all.

Furthermore, sufficientarian views are indifferent to inequalities above the threshold (Frankfurt 1987; Arneson 2000; Parfit 1995; Pogge 2002b: 176). Since from a moral point of view each and every person must be provided basic capabilities which are stipulated to be necessary for a satisfactory level of functionings, egalitarian demands, on a sufficientarian view, are strict but also limited. Inequalities among persons above the stipulated threshold turn out to be irrelevant or at most play an ancillary role. Finally, there is also the difficulty of how one might non-arbitrarily set the appropriate level of threshold. Why at this level, and not higher or lower? People's lives are more of a 'mixture' and 'continuum' of different capabilities rather than a compartmentalization of different capabilities and of each capability according to distinguishable threshold levels.

The observation that the capability approach adopts the principle of sufficiency, and hence fails to meet the fuller demands of justice might be attributed more to some versions of the capability approach than to others. Sen is not vulnerable to this criticism. He holds the view that social justice demands equality of basic capabilities, but allows that equality must be balanced and traded off against other worthy social goals such as efficiency, respect for human rights and so on. He stresses the importance of efficiency as follows:

> I have tried to emphasize that this capability perspective can be used not just for evaluating equality, but also for assessing efficiency. Efficiency in the capability space, if defined analogously to the usual definitions of 'economic efficiency' (characterized in terms of utility space), would require that no one's capability can be further enhanced while maintaining the capability of everyone else at least at the same level. (Sen 1992: 143-144)

Sen's explicit admission of efficiency considerations indicates that Sen does not advocate an unqualified sufficientarian view which would be indifferent to the consequences it will have for society's other goals. As elaborated in the following chapter, Sen advocates a broad consequentialist approach so that a society can achieve a maximum of basic capabilities for all, paying particular attention to those with low levels of basic capabilities. Moreover, Sen does not advocate 'shortfall' or 'levelling down' equality in the space of capability. For example, when there are disparities in life expectancy and levels of education between sections of population in a country or region, Sen recommends that the gap should be narrowed not by dragging down the capability levels of those who are better-off in terms of capabilities, but through social policies of nutrition, access to health care, and public education that improve the situation of those who are worse off in terms of basic capabilities.

In some sense, Anderson and Nussbaum's versions are susceptible to the limitations associated with sufficientarian theories insofar as both work with the notion of a threshold level of capabilities. Anderson advocates the idea that democratic equality requires all citizens be guaranteed of basic capabilities that would enable them to overcome oppression and exploitation. This implies that the set of basic capabilities she proposes cannot be traded off or balanced against other social goals. Nussbaum (2000a: 75) however, holds a subtler position. She envisages the list of capabilities to be an expression of a 'decent social minimum' that ought to be ensured for all citizens, and thus it has to be viewed only as a statement of a 'partial' conception of justice, although a demanding one. And yet she does not foreclose the possibility of addressing inequalities above the threshold.

3.5 Three Visions, One Theory

At the beginning of the 1980s, Sen raised a crucial question that was to frame much of the literature on social justice through the following decades: 'Equality of What?' (Sen 1980: 197). While this generated a wide variety of answers ranging from 'welfare' (utilitarianism), 'primary goods' (Rawls), and 'resources' (Dworkin) to 'equality of opportunity for welfare' (Arneson) and 'equality of access to advantage' (G.A. Cohen), Sen's own favoured candidate is 'capability to achieve valuable human functionings'. But over the years, even Sen's answer has been developed somewhat differently thus making the capability approach an assortment which offers manifold ways of critiquing the inadequacies of existing moral and political theories and building up an understanding of social justice on the basis of human capabilities. At one end of the spectrum is Nussbaum's philosophized version that situates the capability approach in the Aristotelian tradition of moral and political philosophy which derives and justifies principles of justice on the basis of an ongoing reflection on the components of the good life. The components of the good life are not only irreducibly plural, but they can also be public in the sense of what reasonable people can acknowledge and endorse for political purposes. Nussbaum, however, distinguishes herself from other capability theorists by her willingness to take a stand on a list of basic capabilities that would inform a public conception of capabilities. She distinguishes herself also from Aristotle by infusing egalitarian sensibilities and a robust sense of political liberty into the capability approach.

Anderson's version of the capability approach is reminiscent of the historical origins of social justice movements that have struggled to overcome exploitation: Marxist movements against class oppression, anti-apartheid movements against racism and segregation, women's movements against gender discrimination and Dalit movements against caste segregation, for example. We can and should aspire towards a fuller expression of what social justice demands and this, even at the risk of being utopian. Nevertheless, there are good reasons why we should focus on the few 'urgent' and 'crucial' areas of capabilities that we owe to each other as claims of justice. Probably, consensus and endorsements are more easily obtained across persons and societies on things that are 'unjust' rather than 'just', although making progress on one front means advancement on the other.

Sen is perhaps much imbued with realism and is concerned about what may be realistically achievable and what can make a real difference to people's well-being and living standards, particularly the underdogs of society, without of course foreclosing the possibility of aiming at the ideal. The strength of Sen's vision consists in its openness. Insofar as Sen is able to draw elements from different theories and traditions and envisages the capability approach to be intimately linked to a process of public reasoning and democracy, he emerges as an ecumenical philosopher.

Despite the diversity of emphases by these leading capability theorists, there are a number of common moral and political principles that underpin the theoretical foundation of the capability approach. The following chapters identify and engage with these principles with a view to illustrate and to examine the plausibility of a capabilities-focused theory of justice.

PART II
Capabilities, Morality and Politics

Chapter 4

The Theory of Broad Consequentialism

An ethical theory is a theoretical account of what ethical thought and practice are, which account either implies a general test for the correctness of basic ethical beliefs and principles or else implies that there cannot be such a test.

Bernard Williams, *Ethics and the Limits of Philosophy*

We ought not to plan for a final reconciliation of conflicting moralities in a perfect social order; we ought not even to expect that conflicts between moralities, which prescribe different priorities, will gradually disappear, as rational methods in the sciences and law are diffused. We know virtually nothing about the factors determining the ebb and flow of moral beliefs, conventions and commitments; and we know very little about the conditions under which an intense and exclusive attachment to a particular way of life develops, as opposed to a more selective and critical attitude to the moral conventions that prevail in the environment.

Stuart Hampshire, *Morality and Conflict*

Rights have come to occupy a central place in normative reflections on social justice. The idea that individuals have rights and that these rights set important limits on what might be done to them by the state or in the name of any social goal, has developed to the stature of an entrenched conviction in political philosophy. The idea is widely upheld in political practice as well. Most countries have a list of rights written into their constitutions, affirming, for example, that the state will not interfere with citizens' freedom of speech, religious liberty, freedom of movement and choice of work, sexual privacy, and their equal access to law. The international community has agreed to respect the Universal Declaration of Human Rights, motivated by the fact that there are liberties and interests so basic that all nations should strive to secure them despite their varying history, cultural tradition and position on the economic ladder. The rhetoric of rights has been and continues to be passionately invoked by social movements pressing for certain claims.

Sen envisages rights to be fundamental among moral principles. He has upheld the importance of rights and human rights in particular against different critiques.[1]

---

1 There are at least two rather distinct concerns that critics advance concerning the theoretical foundation of human rights. The first one can be called the *legitimacy* critique. Since human rights are presumed to be pre-legal entitlements of every human being in virtue of being 'human', the critics point out that they lack a clear legal status and legitimacy. The second type of criticism can be called the *coherence* critique. Rights, on this view, are entitlements that require correlated duties. If person A has a right to x, then there has to be some agency, say B, which has the duty to provide A with x. If no such duty is recognized,

He has also been in the forefront of the debate between the universality of human rights and the particularity of 'Asian values' and has denounced the idea that the so-called Asian values can overrule human rights. However, Sen has been less attracted towards a side-constraint view of rights as represented for instance in the libertarian social ethics and political philosophy (§4.1). Even though a constraints-based approach helps to affirm the 'absoluteness' and 'sacredness' of rights, it fails to confront certain 'difficult choices' that are part and parcel of social living and political morality. Normally we uphold property rights and find them valuable for individual freedom. We would therefore support economic, legal and political institutions that protect and promote private ownership. However, if it turns out that unqualified property rights directly or indirectly cause famines and starvation, and are responsible for environmental problems and aggressive depletion of natural resources, should we not put a restriction on them? Just because we find certain rights to be intrinsically valuable, it does not foreclose the fact that they can come into conflict with other values. In the case of famines and starvation, the right to property should be balanced against another equally valuable human right not to die of hunger. In such cases, it might be irresponsible to adhere mindlessly to antecedent rights and moral precepts literally, no matter whatever the consequences.

Sen however, does not suggest that an alternative to the constraints-based view is a consequentialist ethics where consequences would be viewed in terms of a single measure – as in utilitarianism, for example. He, by contrast, advocates a pluralistic consequentialism in which different incommensurable values and actions are taken into consideration. Hence Sen is more keen on advocating rights within a broad consequentialist perspective where people's fundamental rights as well as their capability interests are to be considered as morally demanding principles in social ethics (§4.2). Rights are not equivalent to capabilities, but nevertheless without the possession of some basic capabilities it would not be possible to make an effective  use of the existing rights recognized in a political community. Similarly, some capabilities are so basic and vital to a decent human life that it is vital to formulate them in the language of rights. The rights to free speech and political participation would make no meaning and will remain purely nominal when citizens are illiterate or inadequately educated. At the same time, citizens' educational capabilities can be enhanced when they can have recourse to appropriate environment and institutions and when they can freely and without fear criticize government policies and programmes.

Seeking to represent the interdependence between rights and capabilities, Sen evolves an ethical paradigm to evaluate the effectiveness of the basic structure of society in promoting the maximum possible condition for the realization of basic capabilities for all. Among the basic structures of society that greatly affect citizens' capability prospects is the market (§4.3). A justification of the market purely in terms

---

then the presumed right, on this view, cannot but be empty. Since human rights such as the right to food or to medicine, or generally to a decent standard of living do not or cannot stipulate agency-specific duties, these turn out to be mere rhetoric, lacking coherence. For Sen's response to these critiques, see Sen (1999a: 227ff.; 2004a). Also see Pogge (2002a), Nussbaum (1997a) and Alexander (2004).

of certain antecedent rights without really caring about their impact on the lives of people is likely to end in favour of a totally unregulated market and a sort of Nozickian 'minimal state'. Sen therefore is drawn to validate the need for a broad consequential reasoning by focusing on the strengths as well as the limits of the market in protecting and promoting citizens' capabilities. If the market causes good consequences, then it should be deemed as efficient. When it is found to be responsible for an undersupply of public goods and for causing huge social and economic inequalities, it should be regulated such that equity in terms of basic capabilities for all can be realized.

4.1 Rights as Side-constraints

In *Anarchy, State and Utopia* (1974), the libertarian philosopher Robert Nozick maintains that rights should be viewed as side-constraints constituting the foundations of morality. Accordingly, on this view, an individual's obligation is not to strive for a maximum of any social goal such as achieving equity or a minimum of rights violations. Instead, agents, whether individual or institutional, may do as they wish, within the constraints imposed by rights. Rights are simply not to be violated.

> A more appropriate view of individual rights is as follows. Individual rights are co-possible; each person may exercise his right as he chooses. The exercise of these rights fixes some features of the world. Within the *constraints* of these fixed features, a choice may be made by a social choice mechanism based upon a social ordering; if there are any choices still left to make! Rights do not determine the social ordering but instead set the *constraints* within which a social choice is to be made, by excluding certain alternatives, fixing others, and so on. (Nozick 1974: 166, my emphases)

The set of absolute individual rights which on Nozick's view express the 'inviolability' of the person and the fact of 'separate existence', includes such rights as the right of the individual not to be killed or assaulted, to be free from all forms of coercion, and the right to acquire property by inheritance or transfer and not to have one's property seized or the use of it limited. Individuals also have a right to punish and claim compensation for violations of their rights, to defend themselves and others against such violation. As long as these rights are not violated, it is not for morality – except perhaps in extreme cases of catastrophe – to be concerned about how social systems actually work or should work, what needs and capabilities of people they fail to meet, and what sort of miseries and inequalities they generate.

Nozick's side-constraints view of rights has implications for the type of state that he envisions. The state should be a 'minimal state', limited to the narrowest functions – or as he calls 'the night-watchman' functions – such as protection against violence, theft, and fraud, and the enforcement of contracts (Nozick 1974: 26ff.). In particular, the state should not impose burdens on the wealth or income of some citizens in order to redistribute it in the name of equity and to support various welfare programmes. At most, a state may tax its citizens only as much as necessary to provide for the police, the armed forces and the legal institutions. A state that extends its functions beyond this narrow range of functions would turn out to be a totalitarian and unjust state.

Given the fact that Nozick holds individual rights to be absolute and supreme, what is it that leads him to advocate a minimal state rather than simply endorse anarchism – a situation where there would be no state all? If he, like Hobbes, had defined the 'state of nature' as a situation of continuous 'war of all against all', then it would have been easier for him to justify the state as an alternative to anarchism. However, Nozick does not justify the state this way. Instead, he is more attracted to the Lockean version of the state of nature where even in the state of nature people are moral beings and moral rights and duties are respected. Nozick tries to show that a Lockean state of nature would spontaneously develop into a minimal state. He suggests that the transition from the state of nature to a minimal state takes place not through a single hypothetical contract – as in the case of Locke's social contract theory – but through a series of actual mutually advantageous economic free exchanges between individuals. As Nozick puts it: 'Out of anarchy, pressed by spontaneous groupings, mutual protection associations, division of labour, market pressures, economies of scale, and rational self-interest there arises something very much resembling a minimal state or a group of minimal states' (Nozick 1974: 16-17).

It is important to note that Nozick derives support for the side-constraint view of rights and the minimal state from his 'entitlement theory'.[2] This theory works under the assumption that 'things come into the world already attached to people having entitlements over them' (Nozick 1974: 160). Hence everyone is entitled to the goods and property they currently own, their 'holdings'. A just distribution is whatever results from people's free market exchanges of these holdings. Therefore, the principle of just distribution is as follows: 'From each as they choose, to each as they are chosen' (Nozick 1974: 160). This is just the reverse of what egalitarians from the left are likely to say: 'from each according to their capacity, to each according to their need'. Accordingly for Nozick, if I steal or buy from someone who stole, then I am not entitled to the goods I own. Instead, if I acquired them through gift or inheritance or through a fully voluntary transfer from a just situation then I am entitled to them. Justice consists in following a 'fair' procedure of acquisition and exchange: 'whatever arises from a just situation by just steps is itself just' (Nozick 1974: 151).

Nozick in fact, rejects the idea that justice consists in (re)distribution of resources according to some pre-established distributive patterns and principles. Liberty, according to him, upsets patterns. Furthermore, respect for individuals as self-owners also requires us to reject what he refers to as a 'pie-cutting' approach to justice. The latter approach, Nozick points out, assumes that society's resources are like the 'manna from heaven' in need of some distributive principles such as needs, desert, etc. Yet for Nozick justice consists in respecting the already existing just entitlements and the resulting holdings that issue from individual's free market transactions. In this regard, Nozick criticizes Rawls's theory and its redistributive aims. He says that Rawls's theory cannot be realized without continuous interference with people's lives (Nozick 1974: 183ff.). This is because the difference principle

---

2   Nozick's use of the term 'entitlements' is different from the way Sen uses it (§3.1). While Nozick refers to entitlements as ownership rights, Sen refers to them as people's abilities or capacities to establish command over commodities.

in Rawls's theory (§2.1) stipulates redistribution of resources in favour of the least advantaged in society. In contrast, Nozick claims that his theory avoids interference in people's lives, since it does not require that people's free exchanges conform to any predetermined distributive pattern, and thus does not require any intervention in those exchanges.

Nozick's libertarian defence of property rights and market freedoms is a powerful antidote to any complacent interventionists, who under the pretext of achieving some social goals interfere in the lives of individuals. Social ethics cannot be founded on a careless idea that individual liberties can just be abdicated and interfered with for the sake of social goals, however noble they might be. Social philosophers should learn this important lesson from Nozick. Nevertheless, there are a number of reasons to be dissatisfied with Nozick's libertarianism (or extreme liberalism). It turns out that for Nozick rights are the *only* source of moral principles for our social life. There are no other principles that could be important from a moral point of view. Hart (1979) voices his criticism:

> Even if social philosophy can draw its morality as Nozick assumes only from a single source; even if that source is individual rights ... why should rights be limited as they are by Nozick to what Bentham called negative services of others, that is abstention from such things as murder, assault, theft and breach of conduct? Why should there not be included a basic right to the positive services of the relief of great needs or suffering or provision of basic education and skills when the cost of these is small compared with both the need to be met and with the financial resources of those taxed to provide them? Why should property rights, to be morally legitimate, have an absolute, permanent, exclusive, inheritable and unmodifiable character which leaves no room for this? (Hart 1979: 835)

Hart's criticism that rights cannot cover the whole backdrop of what we owe to each other and that political morality cannot disregard 'positive' rights is an important corrective to Nozick's views and resonates a great deal with the intuitions of the capability approach. If we are to be serious in our defence of rights, it is important to recognize not only the traditional libertarian rights on which Nozick seems to so much concentrate, but also certain socio-economic or 'welfare' interests and claims such as the right to education, housing, health care, employment and an adequate standard of living (Waldron 1986; 1988; Shue 1980). People can hardly make use of a right that they are presumed to have, if they lack the essential capabilities for a decent and healthy life. Even if one were to consider that most rights are meant to support the exercise of freedom and agency, it cannot be denied that things like hunger, illiteracy and disease can smother or destroy human capacities for agency and freedom.

A more radical formulation of these capabilities-focused concerns would be to point out the intrinsic value of socio-economic interests which may or may not be formulated and legislated into precise rights. Instead of stating that economic well-being is necessary in function of other rights, it states directly that certain socio-economic rights are as valuable as any other interests and that an ethical theory that neglects them would turn out to be inadequate. The merit of this straightforward critique is that it does not privilege traditional libertarian rights over welfare rights: we no doubt need civil and political liberties, but we also need socio-economic rights.

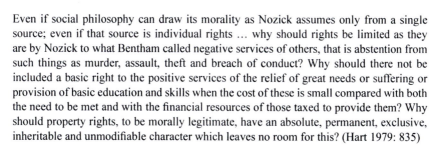

This position, one might point out, can lead to 'rights explosion' – to which we should certainly pay attention. However, it is far from evident that in order to avoid undue proliferation of rights, it is welfare rights that should be abridged. From Nozick's standpoint, however, recognition of socio-economic rights and redistribution of the material resources required to realize them would interfere with people's already existing entitlements and property rights. Individual entitlements and ownership, for Nozick, 'fill the space of rights, leaving no room for general rights to be in a certain material condition' (Nozick 1974: 238). However, a capability theorist can also reverse Nozick's order of priorities and insist that no system of entitlements would be justified if it leaves a large number of people poor and with capability deprivations (Waldron 1986; Sen 1982c). It is not that we first and foremost determine who owns what and then think about what to do about people's capability shortfalls. Instead, people's socio-economic rights should right from the start play a fundamental role in governing the initial allocation of entitlements.

A capability theorist might pitch this critique a little higher by pointing out how Nozick's theory is reflective of a general contemporary liberal tendency to view social living as a market. Individuals require the state only insofar as they can keep their consumer preferences and guard their interests in property and entitlements. One thing that seems to be conspicuously absent in Nozick's thought is a robust sense of democracy. For the libertarian camp of liberalism, society is more of a marketplace than a public forum. In the minimal state there is hardly any mention of political arguments and parliamentary debates about conflicting values and policy priorities which are unavoidable in contemporary societies. Economic freedom and consumer sovereignty play a greater and more decisive role than political freedom. The space of democracy, public discussion and political action is usurped by the market.

4.2 Rights and Capabilities in a Broad Consequentialist Perspective

Sen (1982b; 1985b; 2000a) points out that it is possible to permit rights to have an important role without accepting the extreme side-constraint and procedural view that libertarianism espouses. The libertarian proposal for a consequence-independent theory of rights is imbued with a considerable indifference to the enhancement – or the deprivation – of basic capabilities that are important to people's life of freedom. We have reasons to disagree with a social ethics that relies only on procedural rules no matter what the consequences it generates in the lives of people involved. Social justice cannot be just a matter of procedures without paying attention to the substantive inequalities and lack of freedoms that the procedures may generate. However, the alternative to libertarianism is not utilitarianism, where consequential reasoning takes on a very narrow and monistic character. In a utilitarian consequentialism (§1.2), the value of states of affairs is assessed solely in terms of utility. Individual freedoms and rights are either omitted or they are only instrumentally valued for the contribution they make to utility and the maximization of the good. Sen by contrast advocates a broad consequentialist approach where consequential reasoning can attach fundamental importance to the fulfilment or violation of individual rights without ignoring other non-rights considerations, including the actual impact of having certain rights on the basic capabilities that people actually come to have. Here is one of Sen's succinct definitions of broad consequentialism: '[It is] a moral system in which fulfilment and nonrealization of rights are included among the goals, incorporated in the evaluation of states of affairs, and then applied to the choice of actions through consequential links' (Sen 1982b: 15). Emerging from this definition are the following three traits that form the theoretical edifice of Sen's broad consequentialism.

a) Pluralistic Consequentialism

'Roughly speaking', says Pettit, 'consequentialism is the theory that the way to tell whether a particular choice is the right choice for an agent to have made is to look at the relevant consequences of the decision: to look at the relevant effects of the decision on the world' (Pettit 1993: xiii). On the basis of this definition, we might identify utilitarianism to be a consequentialist doctrine insofar as the assessment of actions in a utilitarian framework is done on the basis of neither some *a priori* deontological principles nor a set of inviolable rights, but rather in terms of the consequences they generate on the states of affairs, or on the world, as Pettit puts it. However, utilitarianism is a *monistic* consequentialism because in the assessment of the state of affairs nothing matters morally except utility, utility of course can be defined differently such as pleasure, happiness or preference satisfaction (Scheffler 1982; Scanlon 2001). One might, for example, make a connection between hedonism and consequentialism. If pleasure and absence of pain are the *only* morally relevant values of worth, then the value of the state of affairs is evaluated in terms of this single value (§1.1.a). Consequently, what morality requires is that we produce a state of affairs with the greatest amount of this value. In such a consequential reasoning, actions in general and rights violations in particular are excluded as not having intrinsic value in the evaluation of the state of affairs. Sen finds this to be a fundamental limitation:

> There is no general reason for an a priori exclusion of any part of the state of affairs in evaluating the state of affairs. Some ethical theories (like utilitarian ethics) insist, however, that nonutility features, such as actions, must not be considered to be of any value or disvalue on their own (rather, only for the utilities or disutilities they generate). But since there are good reasons to be concerned about some of these features such as actions, motives, and the like (for reasons which are close enough to those which move deontologists, among others, to take note of them, in their own special way), the utilitarian exclusion ends up being an arbitrary exclusion of a class of reasoned demands. (Sen 2000a: 487-488)

Sen departs from the monistic model of consequentialism by rejecting the assumption that *only* utility has to be taken into account in evaluating a state of affairs. He includes actions as parts of the states of affairs that are to be evaluated, and insists that part of this evaluation should consider whether or not they involve violation of people's rights. This implies that Sen is drawn not to a monistic consequentialism, but instead to a version of *pluralistic* consequentialism.

Pluralism becomes a distinguishing feature of Sen's consequentialist ethics at least in two important ways (Sen 1985a: 176-181). First, it is plural in terms of *principles*. Entrenched human rights such as civil and political liberties would be among the principles. Yet along with them certain basic capabilities which may or may not be formulated in the language of rights would be included. Often when a right is formulated and recognized by a society, it is presumed that people have the necessary capabilities to make use of the rights in question. However, this need not always be the case. Capability deprivations in terms of illiteracy and lack of education can be a barrier to making a full use of the right to freedom of speech and to actively participate in public discussion and criticism. Social norms and prejudices may in effect prevent women and minorities from access to careers, social space and political participation even though formal rights might assure them of these benefits. This implies that social ethics needs to recognize a multiplicity of fundamental principles. It is imperative to respect their distinctness and allow to them to be so. These multiple principles need not be combined into one general principle that would count as the ultimate standard. Second, Sen's consequential approach requires a plural informational base. Utilitarianism includes only information concerning personal utilities understood in term of happiness, satisfaction, or desire-fulfilment. Information concerning freedom, rights, and distributive justice is excluded. Libertarianism suffers from the limitation of focusing only on certain rights, neglecting information on people's capability interests. In Sen's approach, by contrast, a broad informational base plays a crucial role.

 Perhaps this is a prudent middle way between two extreme kinds of moralists that we could come across. The first ones are those who make a hue and cry about purity of principles and unconditional adherence to deontic principles and duties but hardly pay attention to the totality of the consequences of their acts. However, there are also the second types: those who are concerned about maximizing the overall consequences of a choice for the whole of society without really caring about its effect on individuals. The merit of Sen's approach seems to lie in the fact that it offers the possibility of thinking about the importance of our moral acts and duties but at the same time puts those considerations into a larger context of thinking about all the different types of consequences.

 *b) Rights: Side-constraints or Goals?*

Instead of considering rights to be functioning as side-constraints on what others can or cannot do, Sen maintains the view that the fulfilment of rights should be included as among the goals to be pursued. We would certainly require inviolable rights as fundamental principles of social justice, but at the same time we cannot overlook the consequences of these rights and of the 'multilateral interdependence' between different rights and between rights and social goals. Moreover, thinking of rights-realizations as part of the goals to pursue makes it possible to think of rights not only as correlating to a 'single' duty, but also as generating a 'multiplicity' of duties. This can be illustrated with the following example (Sen 1982b). Ali, a shopkeeper is about to be beaten up by a gang of racist thugs, the Bashers. Donna has come to know about this and can prevent it by informing him beforehand, but she can get to know his whereabouts only by breaking into the room and inspecting the files of Ali's therapist Charles, thereby violating Charles' right to privacy. What should Donna do?

Sen suggests that if Donna adopts a morality in which rights are side-constraints, so that any action that would violate a right is removed from the set of eligible acts from which one chooses, then, her choice is to do nothing, violating no one's right but allowing the Bashers to beat up Ali. If, on the other hand, she adopts a consequentialist morality, then it would be permissible for her to 'violate' Charles' right to privacy in order to warn Ali and thereby prevent violation of his right not to be beaten. Sen believes that the best way to account for this fact is to take account of the very significant *negative* value of a state of affairs in which Ali's right not to be beaten is violated, and the *positive* value of preventing this state of affairs occurring.

Rights theorist Steiner (1990) does see the plausibility of a consequentialist ethics, such as Sen's, that attaches value to 'rights-realization' and correspondingly, attributes disvalue to the violation of rights. However, he points out that a consequentialist structure incorporating rights-realizations in a plural value system can do without 'trade-offs of some rights against others'. Steiner therefore notes that if Donna has a duty to help prevent Ali's right from being violated, then that same moral theory must also impose a similar duty on any other innocent third party including, and specifically, in this case, Charles. Hence, the moral theory that would obligate Donna would also obligate Charles to allow Donna to get the necessary information in whatever way feasible, and in particular would assign to him a duty to allow breaking into his own office. Therefore, in breaking into Charles's office, according to Steiner, Donna is not violating any right and there are no rights being traded off against any others, either.

Indeed, it is possible to characterize the above situation from two different perspectives. Like Sen, we can consider it as a trade off between conflicting rights, namely, the trade off between Charles's right to privacy and Ali's right not to be beaten up. Or, like Steiner, we can also look at it from the perspective of the 'multiplicity of duties' that rights might generate not only on the potential violators (the Bashers), but also on other agents (Donna, Charles and others) who can prevent or mitigate rights violation. Nonetheless, what seems to emerge is that Sen's theory not only offers the scope of recognizing rights for their intrinsic value, but also places rights in the larger context of a consequence-sensitive evaluation of issues at hand.[3]

---

3   Dworkin has suggested viewing rights as 'trumps' by concentrating on the role which rights ought to play in controlling the demands of 'general collective justification': 'Rights act as trumps over some background justification that appeals to collective welfare' (Dworkin 1977: 367). The kinds of collective goals that Dworkin has in mind are aggregative social benefits that institutional agents such as governments are likely to pursue: economic efficiency, equality of opportunity, international excellence and so on. The purpose of a right is to protect the individual from certain forms of treatment that promotion of such goals might require. Rights, so to say, literally 'triumph' over social goals. In an illuminating conceptual analysis, Pettit (1987) has pointed out that the metaphor of 'trumps' does not imply the absoluteness and extreme view implied in the metaphor of 'side-constraints'. As he puts it: 'Both [Nozick and Dworkin] agree that all rights must be privileged in some degree but they take different

The potential conflict between property rights on the one hand and the threat of famine and deprivation (or the right not to die of hunger) on the other can be one such instance where a consequence-sensitive approach rather than a side-constraints approach might prove to be closer to our moral intuitions. The right to hold, use and bequeath property that one has legitimately acquired is treated as inherently valuable. In fact, Locke's classical defence of property rights takes this form. For him, extensive property rights are supposed to have existed already in the state of nature, and the aim of the government is to protect these rights. This is because he advocates the idea that human beings have a 'natural right' to own their labour and by extension to what they mix their labour with. 'Every man has a property in his own person: this nobody has any right to but himself. The labour of his body, and the work of his hands, we may say, are properly his. Whatsoever then he removes out of the state that nature hath provided, and left it in, he hath mixed his labour with, and joined to it something that is his own, and thereby makes it his property' (Locke 2003: 111-112). Locke does foresee a 'proviso' that qualifies the exercise of property ownership subject to the condition that 'enough, and as good' resources are left for the common use. However, in practice Locke dispenses with or weakens this 'enough, and as good' proviso by his conviction that a strict regime of property rights would in fact add to common resources: 'he who appropriates land to himself by his labour, does not lessen, but increase the common stock of mankind' (Locke 2003: 116). As pointed earlier (§4.1), Nozick follows the footsteps of Locke, and goes even further to support property rights with an elaborate theory of entitlements system that makes it much more absolute and sacrosanct.

However, what seems to be missing in this sort of justification of property rights is the fact that property rights might have consequences which themselves might require assessment.[4] In fact, as in many parts of the world, the cause of hunger and

---

views of the extent of the privilege that is actually involved. For Dworkin it is such that the right trumps a certain unspecified number of collective goals; for Nozick it is such that the right trumps all' (Pettit 1987: 12). For our purposes here, the difference between Sen's and Dworkin's views lies in the fact that Dworkin depicts social goals ('general collective justification') as being independent of rights. If rights and social goals are two independent things, then, as Dworkin suggests, in order to take rights seriously, rights should have the force to override rights-independent social goals. Yet such a need does not seem to arise in Sen's view because social goals are constituted inclusive of rights considerations.

4   As Nagel (2003: 66f.) points out, Rawls's theory makes an important departure from the libertarian defence of property rights. Libertarians give significant moral weight to property rights – not just the right to possess some personal property, which Rawls includes among the list of basic liberties (§2.1), but extensive rights of accumulation and disposition of private property. According to Rawls, entitlement to what one has legally acquired or earned has a completely different status from free speech, freedom of conscience and freedom of the person. Property rights are valued not as an essential part of individual liberties, but as indispensable feature of economic system without which long-term planning, investment, production, and capital accumulation would not be possible. Moreover, the difference principle stipulates redistribution in favour of the least advantaged in society. In Rawls's justice as fairness therefore individual property rights are the consequences, and not the foundation, of the justice of economic institutions. In the case of Nozick, it is just the opposite.

severe deprivation as well as their prevention may materially depend on how property rights are structured and administered. If a set of property rights leads to starvation or severe deprivations, then we certainly need to question the absoluteness of having these rights regardless of the consequences. Sen, however, does not suggest that interference with property rights is the only way to avoid famines and deprivations. As illustrated in Chapter 3, since famines are caused by entitlement failures, the main economic strategy would have to take the form of increasing the entitlements of the deprived groups, and in particular of guaranteeing a minimum of entitlements for everyone. As a short term measure, transfer of income or food and commodities through various public policies may prove to be effective in overcoming famines. In the long run though, this might involve many different ways such as economic growth, increase of food supply and distributional adjustments. Some of these policies might also require that property rights and the corresponding entitlements of the more well-off groups be restructured. So, Sen advocates a social ethics that values both property rights and other goals such as overcoming famines and starvation, or fulfilment of people's right not to be hungry. Such a moral system can value property rights for their intrinsic importance, but at the same time recognize the importance of state interventions in property rights (through income tax, inheritance tax, etc) when that would lead to better overall consequences, including the negative consequences of rights violations (Sen 1982c). If one were to remain within the framework of rights as constraining the actions of others, then one could only insist that individuals are entitled to a restricted number of particular rights, say, a right to x, y and z. On the other hand, when one puts these rights in the context of general social goals that include other non-rights considerations (capabilities, values, and so on) then it lends the possibility to reinforce the idea that we require effective public policies such as p (x), p (y) and p (z), and social institutions such as s (x), s (y) and s (z) that pursue the goal of realizing these rights.

c) Promoting and Honouring Values

Pettit (1991; 1997c) suggests that the distinction between a consequentialist and constraints-based social ethics can be understood from their difference in attitude towards values: whether or not the proper response to values is to 'promote' or just 'honour' them.

> Consequentialism is the view that whatever values an individual or institutional agent adopts, the proper response to those values is to promote them. The agent should honour the values only so far as honouring them is part of promoting, or is necessary in order to promote them. Opponents of consequentialism [constraints-based deontologists], on the other hand, hold that at least some values call to be honoured whether or not they are thereby promoted. (Pettit 1991: 231)

This way of introducing the distinction between a consequentialist and a non-consequentialist approach seems appealing and brings some more clarity to the traditional opposition between the two theories. It reinforces the idea that all consequential theories such as Sen's are in fact concerned about not just honouring values but also promoting them. Why would this be so? The answer seems to lie in the direction of how we envisage morality, public morality in particular. Morality in some sense, as Pettit suggests, can be seen as a relation between agents and values. How does an individual or institutional agent situate herself and *respond* to a perceived value? In other words, at every instance, as it were, an agent seems to be confronted with two sorts of questions concerning a value: does my primary responsibility consist in honouring a value, by devoting myself to it? Or, does it consist in promoting that value? Take for instance the value of women's equality. What should I do regarding this value? The honouring-attitude seems to just require that I 'represent' this value in my life and behaviour. Maybe I could be nicer and more courteous to women; maybe I should realize how unjust and discriminating my prejudices are and do something about it. But this does not necessarily mean that I do anything more positively to see that more of this value is realized in society at large. At least two things seem to back up an honouring-attitude (Pettit 1988; 1997c). First, an honouring-attitude more or less assumes a perfect compliant world. I do my part in the best way I can and hope that others would also do the same. My honouring of a value might eventually help to promote the value in question but this comes more as a second instance than as a primary motivation. Second, the relation between the agent and a value is viewed as intrinsic. I, as a moral agent, am primarily called to respect a value, whether or not that will promote it.

The promoting-attitude, on the contrary, seems to motivate the agent not just to represent a value in his or her life but also be prepared to realize it in the world. The scope of morality would be too limited if we are keen on only keeping our hands clean but do nothing to realize the values that we believe in. In the actual and non-compliant world, we might have to 'dirty our hands'. If I value women's equality as something desirable, in addition to my representing that value, I might perhaps want to talk about it to my wife and children. Maybe I with a few like-minded colleagues would found a women's equality centre. Or, I might through politics or civil society groups lobby for proportional representation of women in university campuses and public office. Of course, for moral progress and a better realization of values I should subject to scrutiny whatever I do and how I do it – by a despotic or political approach, by force or persuasion – in order to promote my values. Also, if I only seek to promote values without caring to honour them in my own life and behaviour, then such promotion would not only lack integrity, but also will eventually lose its effectiveness.

Would promotion of values, then, also involve maximizing them? Even here, a broadly visualized consequentialism can be differentiated from other consequentialist theories. If one is attracted by the idea that one should always act according to and promote what is 'optimally the best' – as in the case of utilitarian consequentialism – then one cannot but insist on a maximization process leading to a total outcome (Slote 1985; Scheffler 1988). Sen by contrast insists that since the values that are important for human life are plural and incommensurable, public deliberation might have to settle for only what is feasible rather than aim at the optimal best.

> A consequentialist approach does involve the use of maximizing logic in a general form, but maximization does not require that all alternatives be comparable and does not even require that a best alternative be identifiable. Maximization only requires that *we do not*

choose an alternative that is worse than another that can be chosen instead. If we cannot compare and rank two alternatives, then choosing either from that pair will fully satisfy the requirements of maximization (Sen 2000a: 563-564, my emphasis)

This is a weak and 'satisficing' interpretation of what maximization would require in a consequential reasoning. For Sen maximization requires only that we do not choose an alternative that is *worse than* another. In Sen's broad consequentialist theory therefore, under circumstances where we cannot compare and rank two alternatives, then choosing either from the pair would satisfy the requirements of maximization. From the standpoint of real issues in social policies and public deliberation, even a weak interpretation of promotion of values and the improvement of social situations can have significant differences. Governments and policymakers often have to choose a balance between requirements of efficiency on the one hand and demands of equity on the other, and often this has to be done under conditions of scarce resources. Consider for instance three distinct ends that an institutional agent (like the state) should promote: education, health and protection of political liberties. Each of them is important and it is difficult to rank them *vis-à-vis* each other, thus generating a complete ordering that is required for optimization. But a broad consequentialism that relies only on 'no worse than the available alternatives' could still give ample guidance for public deliberation and choice: outcomes that lead to progress on three areas are better than outcomes involving setbacks on all three areas; outcomes involving progress on one area and *status quo* on two might be preferred to *status quo* in all three; and so on.

4.3 Rights, Consequences and the Market

When a broadly construed consequentialist ethics is closer to our moral intuitions and is found to be helpful in identifying and targeting policy areas for social progress, it is hard to deny its relevance in validating various social institutions and arrangements. As Sen puts it: 'Individuals live and operate in a world of institutions. Our opportunities and prospects depend crucially on what institutions exist and how they function. Not only do institutions contribute to our freedoms, their role can be sensibly evaluated in the light of their contributions to our freedom' (Sen 1999a: 142). More than ever before, among the institutions that require a close scrutiny is the market particularly because of the pervasive role it has come to play in determining people's freedom and their capability prospects. We do not normally produce all the things that we want and require and hence our life would indeed be impoverished without proper access to the market. Even for people who typically question the 'value' or the 'moral standing' of the market, what they intend is not a world without market transactions at all – in fact, it would be hard to imagine a world in which each one of us must produce every piece of goods and services that we can consume. Instead, what the critics of the market are concerned about is the effective functioning of the market: what are the 'freedoms' and 'un-freedoms' that are generated by the market? Do market norms undermine values and virtues such as respect, trust, equity, freedom and so on? How much of regulation and restraint, if any, should the state exercise on market mechanisms?

a) The Ethical Limitations of the Market

At the outset, the market can be assessed on the basis of the possibilities it offers towards the enhancement of basic capabilities (Sen 1985c; 1999a). One fundamental reason seems to be the freedom of market transaction *per se*. We have good reasons to produce what we want and are capable of, to buy and sell, and to seek lives that can flourish on the basis of market transactions. A denial of opportunities enabled by market mechanisms can itself be a source of unfreedom and be a constraint for the exercise of many capabilities related in this area. Furthermore, we have reason to value freedoms that are part of the market life such as the freedom to change jobs, to start a business or to move from place to place. As the Friedmans plainly put it, '[t]hat is the basic difference between the market and a political agency. *You are free to choose.* There is no policeman to take the money out of your pocket to pay for something you do not want or make you do something you do not want to do' (Friedman and Friedman 1980: 223, my emphasis). The all-encompassing presence of the market in modern societies can sometimes make us take this for granted. The absence of freedom to choose and to transact can be a serious issue in a variety of contexts. Free access to labour markets, for example, can be denied by legislations, laws and social customs. In the pre-Civil War period in the United States of America, the African Americans of the South may have had higher income and higher life expectancy than the wage labourers in the North. Yet we can say that there was a fundamental lack of freedom in the fact of slavery itself. A similar denial of freedom seems critical in the face of 'bonded labour' and 'child labour' and women's lack of access to jobs and public offices in some of the developing countries. Even Marx, a staunch critic of capitalism, saw the emergence of freedom of employment in a capitalist economy *vis-à-vis* the feudal labour arrangements as an important progress.

Also, a competitive market mechanism seems to possess the potential to achieve the type of efficiency that it may not be possible to realize in a centralized system with minimal or no market at all. However, the standard economic models have tended to view efficiency in terms of utilities, incomes and wealth. Efficiency is defined in terms of 'Pareto optimality' – a situation in which utility or welfare of no one can be raised without reducing the utility of someone else. Sen points out that efficiency should be accounted for in terms of individual freedom. The market may be considered to be efficient insofar as it generates freedom for individuals both in terms of freedom to choose 'commodity bundles' and in terms of 'capabilities to achieve valuable functionings' (Sen 1985c). Moreover, the capacity of the market to deliver efficiency should not be viewed only on the basis of efficient 'culmination outcomes', but also 'comprehensive outcomes'. The former implies that attention is given only to final outcomes disregarding the processes of getting there, including the exercise of freedom and agency. The latter indicates that careful thought is given also to the processes through which the culmination outcomes come about.

Opportunities and advantages that come through market efficiency are not without limitations. The market generates a number of negative consequences and hence, a complete evaluation of the market institutions also has to pay attention to their ethical limitations (Sen 1999a; Anderson 1993: 141ff.). First and foremost, achieving market efficiency need not particularly be sensitive to the resulting *inequalities*. A situation can be efficient in the sense that no one's utility or income can be enhanced without cutting into the utility or income of someone else, and yet there can be vast inequalities in the distribution of utility and incomes. Inequalities tend to get further aggravated when attention is shifted from income inequality to inequality in the distribution of substantive freedoms and capabilities. If one were to evaluate the market from the standpoint of antecedent rights, then the resulting income as well as capability inequalities need not be of concern, for the 'producer' or the 'owner' has the right to enjoy the fruits of his labour. In contrast, in a moral system where the market is also assessed on the basis of the consequences it generates, there is a compelling moral interest to assess it both in terms of efficiency *and* equity. Moreover, the logic of market mechanisms is geared to 'private' goods rather than to 'public' goods such as a clean and healthy environment, public transport, educational and cultural institutions. Since public goods are 'consumed' together rather than separately, there is not enough incentive for the private market to provide for these goods. Nonetheless, because the presence of public goods is so important for the enhancement of people's basic capabilities, we might require non-market institutions such as the state to provide public goods, going beyond what the private market mechanism would offer. Basic education is one pertinent area where the state and social institutions can play a crucial role rather than leave it to the uncertainties and vagaries of private market forces. Basic education is a 'mixture' of private and public good, benefiting the individual as well as the society at large. No doubt an educated person stands to gain personally in terms of knowledge acquired and in terms of future employment and life prospects. However, basic education can also have a public-good aspect in the sense that a general expansion of education and literacy in a region can facilitate social change, economic growth and political participation from which others too stand to gain. Therefore, an effective reach of basic education and related services might require cooperative activities and provisioning by the state and social institutions.[5]

The logic of market mechanisms has serious repercussions and ethical limitations with respect to the enrichment of capabilities related to the 'goods' of personal life as well (Anderson 1993: 150ff.; Vandevelde 2000). The goods exchanged or jointly cherished in the context of personal relations such as marriage, friendship, partnership, etc are expressions of trust, loyalty, affections, intimacy and commitment. One cannot buy them or produce them as if they were commodities. The goods related to personal relations are realized through gift exchange. The 'rules' governing a gift

---

5   When we look at the growth of basic education, it emerges that the state has played a major role in the expansion of basic education across the world. The rapid progress of literacy levels in the rich countries of today in Europe and Asia owes to a large extent to the low cost of public education combined with its shared public benefits. In this regard, Sen cautions those who recommend that developing countries should rely fully on an unrestricted free market even for basic education. See Drèze and Sen (2002: 143f.). Even Adam Smith who was generally against any type of regulation of the market was in favour of supporting education through public expenditure: 'For a very small expence the public can facilitate, can encourage, and can even impose upon almost the whole body of the people, the necessity of acquiring those most essential parts of education' (quoted in Sen 1999a: 129).

exchange are quite different from market exchange. Gift exchange establishes or reiterates the bonds of relationship between the giver and the receiver and aims to realize a shared good in the relationship itself. In contrast, market exchange focuses on distinct goods for each party, the buyer and the seller. A true gift is one where the giver does not expect anything in return, although there is invariably an implicit or unwritten understanding of reciprocity: the receiver is 'obligated' to respond to and reciprocate a gift in one form or another. However, the kind of reciprocity involved in gift exchange differs from the one entailed in market exchange. One does not calculate or weigh in order to see whether what one reciprocates is exactly the same as or proportionate to what one has received, and the form of reciprocity is not measurable in monetary terms. Also, reciprocity involved in a gift is informal and not time-bound, so that any delay would not call for legal action as in the case of market exchange. And finally, gift exchange is focused on the person and is responsive to his or her personal characteristics and individuality. Since gifts are meant to express and to symbolize ties of bonds and relationships, we seek to give gifts that in some form resonate with the existing interpersonal bond rather than those that are impersonal and generic. Exploration of these differences between gift exchange and market exchange helps to shed light on how goods relating to personal life will be commodified when the norms of market mechanisms are applied to them.

The ethical limitations of the market can also be seen in its inability to acknowledge and to enhance capabilities concerning the political sphere, particularly of democratic 'voice', 'participation' and 'forum' (Anderson 1993: 158ff.). The market is primarily a preference-regarding institution. It is responsive to people's preferences accompanied by their capacity to pay for the things they prefer. It is hardly interested in the reasons people have for their preferences. Furthermore, it does not discriminate between urgent needs and intense desire, and people's judgements *vis-à-vis* their preferences. Often individuals get to influence the exchange of commodities through 'exit' rather than through 'voice'. When a product or service does not conform to the consumer's preferences, he or she can just quit without being obligated to justify oneself. Since the market works under assumptions such as 'the consumer is the sovereign', 'the customer is always right' and so on, it cannot function as a *forum* for the justification of principles and values one stands for and of policies one supports. In contrast to the market, goods related to the political sphere are not just based on preferences and one's capacity to pay. Everyone, irrespective of one's economic status, is entitled to the good of democratic participation and citizens exercise their freedom through voice and not merely exit. Citizens state their opinions and express their judgements in view of justifying themselves to their fellow citizens. In this sense, the sense of respect that governs the marketplace is different from the political forum. To respect consumers is to respect their privacy by not looking more deeply into the reasons for their tastes and preferences. To respect a citizen, by contrast, is to show willingness to understand and to take seriously the reasons one might have in advocating a principle or a policy in public.

b) The Welfare State, the Minimal State and the Market

The above broad and many-sided evaluations of the market have shown that while the market offers many possibilities, it is also limited on many fronts. An unregulated market is therefore:

- indifferent to social and economic inequalities
- favourable to 'private' goods rather than 'public' goods
- limited in the enhancement of capabilities related to personal relationships and
- incapable of creating appropriate conditions for political capabilities.

Sen therefore insists on a balancing role between political and social institutions on the one hand and the market on the other, so that the market might be harnessed to the extent of realizing basic capabilities for everyone in society (Sen 1985c). Because a libertarian tends to justify market mechanisms on the basis of *a priori* rights to market exchange and transfer, any form of welfare state that aims to be more than a 'minimal state' would necessarily be antagonistic to people's rights. Sen however, realizes the need for acknowledging the 'interdependence' between the market and the state, how one needs the other for proper functioning (Sen 1985c). The successful functioning of market forces can be deeply influenced by the nature of different political institutions, particularly the state. It is a well-recognized fact that the market in general and the process of production and exchange in particular can hardly function in the absence of legal provisions that protect contracts, patents, copyrights and property rights, and of legal sanctions in the event of non-compliance and fraud. Furthermore, the agency of the government might be pertinent in initiating and facilitating market-based economic growth. Initiation and nurturing of market mechanisms by an active state can in fact pave the way for a robust and self-sufficient role of the market at later stages. The market benefits a great deal not only from the existence and proper functioning of a political entity such as the state, but also from its 'embeddedness' in culture and social norms. The 'social capital' that is part of the social ethos in a society enhances and stabilizes economic interactions between people. Values such as trust, work ethics, honouring of contracts and reciprocity play a crucial role in making market forces function and prosper.

The influence between the market and state works also in the other direction. It is difficult to think of a state achieving an acceptable social and political arrangement when citizens are prohibited from producing goods and services on their own initiative and from free exchange and transfer of goods and services. So, in principle a welfare state and its related social and economic institutions that aim to create better conditions for the enhancement of citizens' capabilities are not necessarily antagonistic to individual rights. In fact, as argued in Chapter 7, when interventions of the state for redistributive purposes are non-dominating, capabilities-promoting and under the purview of the law, and are linked to a process of public reasoning and discussion, they facilitate rather than hamper the exercise of individual liberties.

Nevertheless, Sen cautions that a plea for the recognition of the interdependence between the state and market should not be viewed as a suggestion for the suppression or elimination of market forces (Sen 1985c; Dréze & Sen 2002: 44ff.). Generally, we can distinguish two kinds of intervention by the state: market-excluding and market-complementary interventions. Economic and social arrangements brought about through the state intervention may be considered to be *market-excluding* in the sense that the market is not allowed to function freely or even operate at all. Or, they can also be in the nature of *market-complementing* in the sense of complementing those things which otherwise would not normally be provided by market mechanisms without eliminating the market. Coming back to the issue of famines, it is important to realize that famines have occurred in both non-market socialist economies and market-based capitalist systems. Yet when we particularly focus our inquiry on why a market system has not been able to avoid famines, the answer does not lie entirely in the distortion of the food market, although in some cases it does. Manipulations of the food market by organized traders have aggravated the crises associated with famines. Nonetheless, the threat of famines cannot be overcome by eliminating the market, but rather through an interventionist strategy by the state that would create incomes and purchasing power for the disentitled section of the population and then leave the supply of food to respond to the newly created demand through private trade.

Not only in the case of famines, but also in other areas of concern a hybrid of market-complementing approaches rather than market-excluding interventions works out to be beneficial. The need for a more active use of the market in industrial production and services, for example, does not do away with the requirement to provide basic education, access to primary health care, unemployment benefits and social security. In fact, these market-complementing provisions enable and equip people to make better use of the opportunities brought about by market transactions. Furthermore, paying attention to what the competitive market does not provide or typically leaves out need not be thought of as the exclusive domain of a 'political' entity such as the state. Almost every society has a rich tradition of 'cooperative' actions in the sphere of civil society such as exchange labour, micro-finances, farmers' cooperatives, protection of village commons, etc. Moreover, cooperative actions are not restricted only to economic activities. They have played and continue to play a pertinent role in public health, conflict resolution, cultural life and environmental protection.

4.4 The Moral Limits of Consequential Reasoning and Trade Offs

As the objective of realizing basic capabilities for all requires a series of policy priorities and rationing of scarce social resources between equally compelling claims, it is pertinent to link up the capability approach with a consequentialist ethics but understood in the broad sense. Yet oddly enough human rights and basic capabilities cannot be effectively protected in a moral system that leaves everything open and vulnerable. Despite the many valuable insights and guidelines that a carefully considered consequential reasoning can offer in the arena of public policy, its scope, we tend to think, cannot be so thorough, wide-ranging and comprehensive. There are indeed moral limits to the extent to which we may subject human affairs to a kind of consequential reasoning and trade offs between incommensurable values. When consequentialist theorists start off from the premise that all things considered some sort of ordering of states of affairs is possible, and hence, even the most difficult conflict could be resolved, they fail to sort out the different kinds of questions involved in moral dilemmas. As Nussbaum realizes (2001b; 2001c), in the domain of moral conflicts we need to distinguish two quite fundamentally distinct questions.

[I]n many situations of choice, there is not just one question to be asked, there are two. One is the obvious question: what should I do? But the other one, the one that I shall call the 'tragic question' is the question 'Is there any option available to me that is free of serious wrongdoing?' I am suggesting that the answer to the tragic question is sometimes 'no', and that it is important to ponder this fact. But what does this mean? Isn't it just moral squeamishness to say that there is an undefeated moral claim on the scene when an agent has chosen the best of the available alternatives? I would argue not. (Nussbaum 2001c: 114)

A consequentialist ethics might be best suited to address the first sort of question, namely, 'what is the best thing I should now do, all things considered?' One can pose this question to oneself even in the most difficult and trying situations and frequently one can arrive at some sort of answer, without serious culpability. However, it is doubtful whether a consequentialist ethics would be suited and capable of facing the second type of question, namely, the *tragic* question: whatever course of action the agent takes, it causes a serious and inevitable loss; there is always moral culpability. In their eagerness to solve problems and arrive at solutions, consequentialists fail to ponder over the complexities involved in tragic questions; they hesitate in taking a detour to notice all the claims that such a situation could put on individual and institutional agents.

Often tragic questions come up in the form of moral dilemmas that people face between spheres of values. Take for instance the characters of the Greek tragedy, Sophocles' *Antigone* (Nussbaum 1986: 51ff.). Creon makes it clear to the entire population of the city that anyone who offers burial to the traitor Polynices is an enemy of the city and will incur the death penalty. Antigone, however, cannot accept this ruling because it requires her to violate a fundamental (natural) religious obligation to give her beloved brother a decent burial. The point of this tragedy is to portray vividly a painful tension between the two worlds of values: the city (*polis*) and the family (*oikia*); civic and family obligations; the public and private sphere. In an interesting discussion of *Antigone*, Hegel speaks of the narrowness of both Creon and Antigone (Nussbaum 1986: 51ff.; Ricoeur 1992: 240ff.). Both seemed to have indulged in a simplification of the world of values. Creon thinks only of the city and its legal obligations without any regard for the 'unwritten laws' of family obligations. Antigone fixes her mind only on the family, without any consideration for the city. It is this simplification that blinds each protagonist from taking full cognizance of the tragic situation at hand.

What is perhaps interesting to note here is the offstage 'political' significance that Hegel thinks a tragedy like *Antigone* could have. Having presented to its viewers the deep conflict between different spheres of life in the drama, such a tragedy kindles their imagination to think of a possible world where such conflicts would not confront people: why should people face again and again tragic choices in their lives? Could individuals and the state do anything to prevent these? The problems of the drama, so to say, are resolved in real life. It is in this light that Hegel proposes a solution to *Antigone*'s conflict. The tragic conflict between the state and religion comes about only because they are defined in a particular way, one excluding the other. If instead a state thinks of protection of the free exercise of religious duties as among its most important duties, then citizens will not often be put under the strain of having to face such tragic choices. Nussbaum sees to a large extent eye to eye with Hegel: many tragic conflicts could indeed be avoided or minimized by better social and political arrangements. Yet she finds Hegel guilty of 'too much faith in human progress, too much pride in the controlling power of reason and order' (Nussbaum 1986: 77). Not all moral conflicts could be eliminated from human life; residuals of moral dilemmas always seem to be around the corner. Besides, *Antigone*'s main narrative mostly tells us about the moral dilemmas surrounding the conflict between the city and family. But moral dilemmas are pervasive in relationships within and surrounding the family. A person could quite often be torn between matrimonial and blood relationships, between parental and societal obligations and between familial and professional roles. All of these conflicts are in some sense reminders of an important human condition: a tragic dimension is structurally built into the conditions of human life. This is the reason why moral dilemmas have often been referred to as a 'secular analogue' of 'Original Sin': 'you can't live a fully pure life, a life in which you are false to no value' (Nussbaum 2001c: 117; 1990a: 133-135).

Consider the moral dilemma presented in the Indian epic, the *Mahabharata*, a case which is not entirely dissimilar to *Antigone* (Nussbaum 2001b; Sen 2000a). Arjuna, a warrior and the protagonist of the story, is told by Krishna, his friend and advisor, to obey his duty as a warrior and engage in a bitter battle. The battle is between the Pandavas to whom Arjuna belongs and the Kauravas, their cousins who have wrongly usurped the kingdom. Arjuna is therefore put in a dilemma: if he fights he will have to kill so many people, most of whom are his own kith and kin; and if he does not he will simply let the unjust cousins rule the kingdom. Despite Krishna's advice to fight, Arjuna hesitates thinking of the consequences that his action would bring about. The long debate that follows between the two is often seen as arguments for and against a deontological and consequentialist ethics. However, what might be more significant to note here is that the moral dilemma faced by Arjuna to fight or not to fight is not something chosen by Arjuna himself; it was, as it were, thrust upon him. Whatever decision (including inaction) he takes will inevitably result in some serious loss.

A consequential reasoning that begins with the idea that social progress is possible because we can put together all that might be regarded as valuable and then trade off between the most important and the less important can indeed be incognizant of the complexities of moral reasoning (Nussbaum 2001b; Barry 1991a). A typical consequentialist tends to hold the view that in any situation, however sticky, there is always a best thing to do. There cannot be a situation in which all alternatives are wrong. Even if every course of action seems to conflict with some non-tradable principles, there has to be one that is less bad than the others. That is the alternative which one ought to choose, all things considered.

The traditional cost-benefit analysis prevalent in economics can be one such type of consequential reasoning (Frank 2001). Cost-benefit analysis is a method of reaching decisions by comparing the costs of doing something with its benefits. Accordingly, the basic rationale behind this lies in the idea that things are worth doing if the benefits resulting from doing them outweigh their costs. The basic limitation of this approach is that almost everything is calculated in economic terms (willingness-to-pay) and market mechanisms. For example, in deciding to build a huge hydroelectric dam we would never be able to put a price on the destruction of an outstanding natural beauty and on the 'human costs' of displacement of villages and communities. Sen has certainly come far from cost-benefit analysis because the type of consequential reasoning he advocates embraces rights whose fulfilment or violation have intrinsic importance and hence cannot be subjected to any economic or market evaluation. However, insofar as Sen is unwilling to delineate a set of fundamental rights and basic capabilities that would not be traded off, he is much imbued with consequential reasoning.

As Nussbaum (1986: 318ff.; 2001c) has contemplated, we can relate our philosophical reflections on tragic questions and tragic choices to the capabilities list. The presence of tragic dimensions in human life is an invitation to constructive social and political thinking. This can take many forms. One urgent task would be to identify a core group of basic entitlements and try to guarantee them to everyone in society. No matter what society's goals are, individuals in society should be secured of a minimum threshold of capabilities in order to live a flourishing human life. Nussbaum thus adopts the 'principle of each person's capability' for judging the normative effectiveness of social, economic and political institutions. Furthermore, she also envisages the list of basic capabilities as a 'moral constraint' on consequential reasoning and trade offs (Nussbaum 2000a: 198ff.). A moral approach that starts out with a set of basic entitlements seems better poised to address issues of justice in the face of tragic choices, than the one that leaves everything open and unspecified. A set of fundamental rights and basic capabilities would be a constant reminder that there are indeed moral limits to consequential reasoning involving trade offs and maximization.

Yet endorsing a heterogeneous list of non-tradable basic capabilities cannot itself disregard the interconnections and the human condition of conflict between different capabilities. It seems that one of the best ways of empowering and promoting a fuller political participation of women and the underdogs of society is to attend to the opportunities they have for literacy and higher education. People can live with self-respect and human dignity only when basic political liberties are in place and when there are at least minimum protections against discrimination on the basis of race, caste, sex, sexual orientation, religion and so on. Indeed, these interconnections cannot be overlooked.

Nevertheless, sometimes due to scarcity, bad political planning, or simply the condition of being human with its attendant mixture of capabilities and vulnerabilities, conflicts can occur between different values. As we have pointed out earlier, conflicts can occur between family and civic obligations, as in Sophocles' *Antigone*. Governments sometimes have to face the dilemma of respecting citizens' religious liberty and at the same time preventing the abuse of human rights in the name of religion. Policymakers are often confronted with the difficult choice of rationing resources between education, health care and other urgent requirements. In all of these, one can like the hedonist or utilitarian compress different components of the good life into one or a few items and pretend that such conflicts do not exist. Or, one might view moral conflicts and tragic choices as an invitation to social and political planning so that, as far as human and material resources would allow, avoidable and unnecessary vulnerabilities and reversals can be overcome. In addition, setting limits on consequential reasoning and trade offs has another significance in view of tragic choices: they remind us of the responsibility that we owe to each other in making good the loss incurred in tragic choices; the unavoidable loss brought about by a tragic choice does not just disappear from the moral scene, but rather places important claims on our future actions. Often moral theorists who rely on broad-based evaluation and decision procedures seem to efface the phenomenon of tragedy. Their confidence can sometimes generate an unfortunate attitude that once a suitable method is found in arriving at the decision the losing claims in tragic choices cease to exert concern.

4.5 Neither a Prole nor an Archangel

R.M. Hare (1981: 44ff.) presents two prototypes of agents deliberating in situations of moral conflicts: the *Archangel* and the *Prole*. The Prole (Proletariat) is one who is endowed with ordinary, everyday rationality. He cannot but see moral dilemmas as real and indissoluble and is continuously weighed down by remorse and reparative actions. The Archangel, on the contrary, is one who is gifted with a critical rationality, a 'god's-eye view' perspective. She can rise above the mundane complexities of moral dilemmas and deliberate in such a way that moral dilemmas in fact disappear. We need not pretend to be Hare's Archangel in our approach to social ethics. At the same time we do not have to be also like the Prole, either – swinging to the other extreme of expressing disbelief in the possibility of social progress because it involves difficult and hard choices.

　　The theory of broad consequentialism to political morality does offer the possibility of making progress on different fronts of social justice because it seeks to overcome the traditional opposition between rights-based and goals-based approaches. In a broad consequentialist perspective not only rights but also capabilities are taken to be fundamental principles of social ethics. Capabilities are what people would require to make effective use of certain fundamental rights. Although some capabilities – the most urgent and pressing ones – can be formulated in terms of rights, not all of them can be formulated in the language of rights. Simultaneously, a broad consequentialist theory does not have to go to the extent of suggesting that all capabilities have a claim on justice. For example, we can consider love and recognition to be important for human well-being, but we cannot as a matter of justice, claim that there is an unconditional right to love and recognition.

　　On account of its consequentialist moral reasoning, in the capability paradigm society's major economic and political institutions and in particular market mechanisms are justified not on the basis of some unqualified antecedent rights to free exchange and transfer but rather in terms of the consequences they generate for the realization of fundamental rights and basic capabilities for all. Even though the market might offer many opportunities and possibilities, it cannot be considered as a panacea for all social ills. In fact, many market institutions turn out to be ethically limited and are unsuitable in the areas of personal relationships, social interactions and political participation. Any effort to apply market norms to these areas only 'commodifies' the goods related to these respective realms. Hence, complementing what is and cannot be provided by the market requires a balancing role between the state on the one hand and the market on the other. Contrary to this, we cannot but recognize a certain ambiguity in the extreme libertarian view that upholds market freedoms and rights as mere side-constraints and privileges the market over any form of welfare state.

Chapter 5

The Question of Individual Responsibility

By becoming the source of morality, other people are promoted to the rank of the object of concern, in respect of the fragility and vulnerability of the very source of the injunction. The displacement then becomes a reversal: one becomes responsible for harm because, first of all, one is responsible for others.

Paul Ricoeur, *The Just*

When men are thus dependent on one another and reciprocally related to one another in their work and the satisfaction of their needs, subjective self-seeking turns into a contribution to the satisfaction of everyone else ... The compulsion which brings this about is rooted in the complex interdependence of each on all, and it now presents itself to each as the universal permanent capital which gives the opportunity, by the exercise of his education and skill, to draw a share from it and so be assured of his livelihood, while what he thus earns by means of his work maintains and increases the general capital.

G. W. F. Hegel, *The Philosophy of Right*

Consider Alice and Ben who start off with equivalent capability sets with regard to education and health. While Alice squanders them and ends up with a life of bad functionings, Ben makes use of them responsibly thus leading to an outcome of a much better off life. Should society in the name of justice make good Alice's ensuing position relative to Ben? Normally we tend to think that Alice should be made to bear the consequences of her choices. Consider again Alice and Ben, but now in a somewhat different scenario. If it were the case that Alice's relatively worse off position is not the result of her prodigal behaviour but due to circumstances and factors beyond her control, what should society do? Our appraisal here would most probably be in the opposite direction. We do seem to think that society has some obligations not only to restore Alice to a baseline of education and health as far as possible, but also to design the basic structures of society so that recurrence of such cases can be prevented in the first place or their impact can be minimized.

As this simplified case brings out, one of the litmus tests for a theory of justice is to give a coherent account of two conflicting intuitions: about individual responsibility and agency on the one hand and about obligations of redistribution with a view to compensate for people's shortfalls on the other; the illegitimacy of certain compensations on account of the fact that people should be made accountable for their choices and the legitimacy of certain compensations owing to the fact that people's well-being and standing in society can be made worse off because of chance, vulnerability and circumstances.

These two ideas require no detailed explanation. As far as adult citizens are concerned, a theory of justice must regard people as 'agents' because of their capacity to critically reflect, act and pursue a plan of life. The nurture and exercise of this capacity of course depend on internal factors such as the person's genetic endowment and history. It is also contingent on external factors such as the social, political and economic opportunities that are available to the individual. Yet acknowledging the influence of internal and external factors on individuals need not lead to a determinist view that human beings are just puppets or machines. A theory of justice thus should see persons as 'agents', who can act and bring about change, and who can take responsibility for their choices and actions, rather than as 'patients' to whom welfare benefits will be dispensed irrespective of whether or not they assume responsibility. But along with the idea of agency, a theory of justice must also embody the idea that it is objectionable for some to be worse off than others because of pure bad luck (brute luck) – factors and circumstances beyond a person's control and the individual concerned could have done nothing to avoid them. If that were to be so, society then has some obligations to make good the loss or shortfalls of the individuals in question in some form or other.

When especially the stated objective of the capability approach is construed as realizing basic capabilities for all and creating the greatest possible condition for it, the onus then is on the capability theorist to justify and to spell out how this vision would take the issue of individual responsibility seriously while holding the view that justice demands redistribution for compensating people's capability shortfalls. Are individuals unqualifiedly entitled to material and social resources that would enhance their capabilities irrespective of their contribution and participation? What conditions, if any, can discount individual responsibility? For example, can we say that under situations as varied as accidents, duress, ignorance and 'bad upbringing' an agent has no or diminished responsibility? Based on what criteria can we decide that some capability shortfalls of individuals deserve to be compensated and not others? Should drunken drivers, willing drug addicts and dangerous sports lovers be subsidized for their medical care? Sen, Nussbaum and other leading capability theorists have not written extensively on the issue of responsibility and are yet to address this theme in a substantial way.[1] Nevertheless, from a closer analysis of their writings and from the general 'ethos' of the capability approach, we can try to derive their position.

The capability approach espouses what can be called a reciprocal view of responsibility wherein individual responsibility is seen as embedded and nurtured in the context of social responsibility (§5.1). While it is important to uphold the idea

---

1   Anderson does address the issue of individual responsibility in the article 'What is the Point of Equality?' (1999). Here, she criticizes the 'luck egalitarian' theories for failing to address issues of basic capabilities required for a regime of 'democratic equality' under the pretext of promoting individual responsibility. However she has yet to develop a complete account stipulating what principles would be relevant in meeting different ranges of complex capabilities.

that the outcome of people's lives should be sensitive to the choices they make, it is equally important to stress that society – individuals in the collective sense – should consider it as its duty to create appropriate conditions and institutions for making worthwhile choices. Personal responsibility and agency, in other words, are not to be thought of as divorced from or opposed to social responsibility. The liberal accounts of justice such as those of Rawls and Dworkin do acknowledge the importance of a suitable social base for personal responsibility (§5.2; §5.3). They also recognize that it is part of justice and not just humanity or benevolence to adopt some levels of redistribution to the worse off in society to compensate them for their unfavourable circumstances and factors. Yet the liberal preoccupation to make the responsibility condition as strong as possible leads these accounts to embrace what can be called a control view of responsibility by which individuals are thought to be totally in control of their life and circumstance. Moreover, these accounts try to extend the scope of individual choice to such an extent that it leaves very little room for human vulnerability and reversals.

5.1 Freedom, Opportunities and Responsibility

Sen (1992: 148-51) claims that the capability approach can be closely allied with a commitment to individual responsibility. One important reason for this claim is the idea that the capability approach as a theory of justice proposes that people's benefits and standing in society should be judged in terms of their *capabilities* and not in terms of their *achieved functionings*. Hence he says:

> In dealing with responsible adults, it is more appropriate to see the claims of individuals on the society (or the demands of equity or justice) in terms of *freedom to achieve* rather than *actual achievements*. If the social arrangements are such that a responsible adult is given no less freedom (in terms of set comparisons) than others, it is possible to argue that no unjust inequality may be involved. (Sen 1992: 148)

One thing that seems clear at this point is that the capability approach is not an equality-of-outcome (or -result) theory, thus creating a space for individual responsibility. What an advocate of the equality-of-outcome view tends to recommend is that society be organized, and social policies be designed, in such a way as to make all individuals equally successful in some stipulated forms of outcome such as income, welfare or resources. All individuals in society should be equal in some respect, regardless of their active involvement and contribution. On an equality-of-outcome view therefore individuals are not effectively held responsible for their choices. The capability approach by contrast considers individual choice to be central by advocating that society is required to offer people as far as possible only equal prospects of capabilities ('*freedom* to achieve') rather than their actual achieved functionings. The capability theorists would therefore say – provided opportunities for education and health are available, the way in which individuals make use of their education and health belong to the sphere of individual responsibility; while society should try to ensure that jobs are available, professional careers would be an exercise of individual choice and actions; provided voting rights, freedom of speech and freedom to participate in public protest are in place, the manner in which each citizen will make use of these in order to politically participate would be a matter of personal responsibility, and so on. On account of this distinction between freedom and opportunities on the one hand and the actual achieved functionings on the other, the capability theorists are in tune with Rawls and other liberal philosophers who criticize and reject an outcome-based approach to justice.[2]

The idea that from a justice point of view it is more reasonable to concentrate on what people are able to do and be rather than what they actually come to achieve not only offers individual agents the space to choose the type of life they have reason to value, but also does not obligate society to insure against bad results, when they are the consequences of individuals' choices. This choice-centred view of responsibility, as Nussbaum (1990b: 234ff.) realizes, is so reminiscent of the different dimensions of responsibility that emerges in Aristotle's discussion.[3] In *Ethics*, Book III, Aristotle says that *voluntary actions* are the only ones for which a person could be held responsible. In attempting to characterize what a voluntary action is, Aristotle says that a voluntary act is the one in which 'the originating cause lies in the agent himself, who knows the particular circumstances of his action' (*Ethics* III, 1: 115). He contrasts this with *involuntary acts*, actions which are 'performed under compulsion or through ignorance' (*Ethics* III, 1: 111). Discussing compulsion and ignorance at some length, Aristotle comes to the conclusion that under such conditions a person cannot be held responsible. In cases of compulsion, such as when a sea captain is overpowered by men or carried off course by wind, the cause is external to the agent, and the agent himself contributes nothing to it. Similarly, an act done through inculpable ignorance is involuntary, particularly when the agent shows subsequent regret and pain.

Aristotle seems to come up with cases such as compulsion in order to show that responsibility would indeed be empty of content, if it can be shown that the agent who chooses to act in a particular way did not have sufficient opportunities to choose and did not have eligible alternatives to deliberate a course of action. In other words, Aristotle seems to be of the opinion that, at an initial approximation, the presence or absence of individual choices is a right way to determine an agent's

---

2   As demonstrated in Chapter 2, on the issue of individual responsibility, Rawls's theory and the capability approach share a common ground. Roemer for example, holds the opinion that since Rawls's and Sen's theories are not outcome-based theories, they are to be seen as responsibility-sensitive theories. 'Neither [Rawls's or Sen's] theory advocates a distribution of final outcomes; both primary goods and functionings are inputs into what a person can accomplish by his own volition. Thus both theories reserve a space for personal responsibility' (Roemer 1996: 164).

3   Unfortunately, Nussbaum does not discuss elaborately the link between the capability approach and Aristotle's discussion of responsibility. Aristotle's account of responsibility that I present here follows Glover's textual reading and interpretation of *Ethics*, Book III. See Glover (1970: Chapter 1). Also, see Broadie (1991: Chapter 3); Hardie (1968: Chapter 9); Meyer (1993). For a more recent but a sophisticated account of responsibility that appropriates Aristotle's discussion in Book III, see Scanlon (2000: Chapter 6). As I try to show here, Scanlon's exegesis of Aristotle's discussion of responsibility gives the required link to examine the account of individual responsibility embraced by the capability approach.

responsibility. Yet a fuller account of responsibility cannot stop there. It also needs to inquire, to investigate and to take note of the background conditions of freedom that go to determine whether or not an agent's choice is a 'genuine choice'. Indeed, in Aristotle's account, responsibility requires different forms of freedom: physical, economic and political, among others. The capability theorists echo Aristotle's view in as much as they too like Aristotle insist that incrimination of responsible or irresponsible acts and behaviour should be proportionate to the conditions of freedom and choice available to individuals. Attribution of responsibility should look into whether or not individuals were coerced into choosing a particular course of action or a way of life.

If external coercive conditions can lessen or do away with an agent's responsibility, what about acts occasioned by anger or desire? Can we say that an agent acting under the impulse of intense anger (rage, for instance) or intense desire (such as craving) has a diminished responsibility? After all, these seem to share some similarities with coercive actions in the sense that the agent did not have the necessary preconditions of (internal) freedom. Aristotle does not seem to think so. For him, actions done in a fit of anger or passion cannot be considered as involuntary actions. These actions may lack the clear deliberative character associated with genuine choices, but that does not entitle them to be classified as involuntary actions. 'Actions due to temper or desire', says Aristotle, 'are also proper to the human agent. Therefore it is absurd to class these actions as involuntary' (*Ethics* III, 1: 115). In other words, Aristotle who thinks coercion can diminish or absolve an agent's responsibility to varying degrees does not deem that discrepancies in character or personality traits warrant any excuse of responsibility.

This also seems to be the impression we get when we read Aristotle's discussion of *akrasia* (weakness of will) in Book VII, Chapters 1-10.[4] People of weak will, says Aristotle, are those who tend to experience some degree of psychological counter-pressure, after they have made a certain kinds of decisions. Their rational resolve is opposed by an appetite for pleasure or anger or some other emotion, and so they experience a troubling internal tension. In contrast, one of the accomplishments of a virtuous person is that he has so mastered himself that such counter-pressures do not occur. Virtues, so to say, free the virtuous person from irrationalities that so often afflict ordinary people. Aristotle therefore holds the ethical view that agents are responsible for their character and cannot arbitrarily excuse themselves because of intense emotion, bad upbringing or *akrasia*.[5] However, it is somewhat puzzling to learn that Aristotle who advocates a rather 'perfectionist' view on individuals being

---

4   Aristotelian scholars agree that Aristotle's treatment of *akrasia* is notoriously difficult to interpret. Here I follow the conclusions found in Broadie (1991: Chapter 5).

5   Aristotle, who shows leniency in holding agents responsible in conditions of coercion, seems to be stringent in holding individuals responsible for their character. This can be partly attributed to his 'perfectionist' position: however difficult or favourable one's environment, individuals should strive towards excellence of virtues. However, his general classification of human actions into voluntary and involuntary actions, and treating actions of anger or passion as a subclass of voluntary actions and *not* as involuntary actions seems illuminating. Aristotle's moral psychology suggests that voluntary actions must be further classified on the basis of whether or not they have a clear *deliberative* character.

responsible for their character, also acknowledges that human actions are quite often complex, defying a neat distinction of actions that are performed 'voluntarily' and 'involuntarily'. Aristotle gives the example of sailors who in a life-threatening storm throw the cargo overboard in order to save the ship and themselves. He also gives the example of the person at the mercy of a tyrant who threatens to kill his parents unless he does something very dishonourable. Aristotle says that such actions are 'mixed' because in some sense they are like voluntary actions and in others like involuntary ones. These are voluntary actions since 'the origin of the action is within' the agents. But they are also involuntary actions since the agents concerned did not have the opportunity to choose an alternative course of action.

As Scanlon (2000: 280, 290-293) has shown, Aristotle's insights on the 'mixed' nature of human actions can be exploited to derive two concepts of responsibility: responsibility as *attributability* and responsibility as *accountability* (substantive responsibility). To say that someone is responsible in the first sense is to ask whether an action can be *attributed* to the agent and whether the agent is subject to *moral criticism* for having acted in that way. We would not, for instance, attribute an offensive remark to the agent if it turned out that it was uttered whilst sleepwalking or produced by someone else by stimulating the agent's brain with electrodes. Yet if the same offensive remark is uttered out of (even intense) envy or anger we would still attribute that to the agent. On the other hand, to say that someone is responsible in the second sense is to ask whether it is proper to make the agent bear the consequences of the action. Responsibility as accountability is substantive conclusion about 'what we owe each other'. Consequently, in Scanlon's reading, the sailors in Aristotle's example are responsible in the first sense since it is appropriate to attribute those actions to them, but they are not responsible in the second sense because it may not be proper to make them pay for the cargo they threw overboard. Also, these two senses of responsibility can illuminate our reasoning with regard to social policies and public deliberation. Scanlon puts forward the following example:

> We can imagine a person who, as a result of generally horrible treatment as a child and the lack of proper early training, is both undisciplined and unreliable. If this person lies to his employers, fails to do what he has agreed to do, and never exerts himself to get a job done, he is properly criticized for these actions and attitudes. But if they render him unemployable it would not be permissible to deny him welfare support on the ground that this unemployability is due to actions for which he is responsible. He is responsible (that is to say, open to criticism) for these actions, but he cannot be simply be left to bear the consequences, since he has not had adequate opportunity to avoid being subject to them. (Scanlon 2000: 292)

It is true that the judgement we may make regarding unemployment benefits cannot be generalized to other issues such as drunken driving, drug addiction, dangerous sports, harmful smoking, etc. Whether or not something would fall under the range of social responsibility and the level of welfare assistance that would be extended to such people must be decided on a case-by-case basis. Often judgements on these matters depend on social norms and the communal context of the particular society in question.[6] Nevertheless it drives home the point that failure to distinguish substantive responsibility from moral attributability and blameworthiness leads a disputable view that if people are found to be morally blameworthy for their actions then they are not entitled to any assistance in restoring back to a life of decent functionings and that they can be left to suffer the consequences for their actions.

The account of responsibility underlying the capability approach shares a number of resemblances to what Scanlon gets out of Aristotle's choice-focused view of responsibility. Most capability theorists advocate that an argument for holding people responsible for their choices should be accompanied by certain conditions of freedom in the first place. One of the obvious conditions is related to 'uncertainties' resulting from brute luck.[7] Here, the capability theorists are in agreement with what most other egalitarian philosophers would also endorse. When a person's standing in society is worse off in terms of crucial functionings such as levels of education, health, employment and others due to factors and circumstances beyond her control, society then has some obligations to make good these shortfalls as far as possible. The predicament of the person arising from brute luck cannot be overlooked on grounds of individual responsibility.[8]

But, what about 'uncertainties' which arise not from brute luck, but from people's own choices (option luck)? Here the capability theorists seem to hesitate to advocate a rigid formula. On the one hand, they think that when the person himself willingly takes the risk and ends up losing the gamble, there is then more scope for invoking the person's own responsibility. Theoretically, this means that individuals should be made to bear the cost of their choices and society has no obligation in the name of justice to compensate them for the capability shortfalls they suffer. People like Alice of our earlier example should be made to realize the consequences of their prodigal, unwise or risky behaviour. Such a stance might seem a bit harsh on people like Alice, but that is the price one must be willing to pay for making freedom central to a theory. Freedom otherwise is empty; the cost of freedom is responsibility.

On the other hand, the capability theorists, somewhat similar to Scanlon, seem to doubt whether the idea of 'moral desert' – the idea that when an agent does something morally wrong, it is morally better that he or she should suffer some loss in consequence – should be the basis of public morality. They seems to hesitate because of the difficulty of getting adequate information in order to make intelligent decisions, particularly when it concerns individual choices that are deeply tied to institutional failures. As Sen (1992: 149) reminds, even well-known insurance companies and well-regarded banks collapse. In such cases it would indeed be

---

6   In section §5.4, we shall take up this issue for further exploration.

7   The term 'uncertainties' is mostly used in economic literature as an equivalent to what in Aristotelian and other philosophical literature is referred to as 'luck'. Sen speaks of uncertainties in the sense of both brute luck and option luck (Sen 1992: 148ff.).

8   Barry (1991b) for example, considers compensation for brute luck as one of the important principles of justice. He states the demands of this principle in the following terms: 'It [the principle of compensation] says that the institutions of a society should operate in such a way as to counteract the effects of good and bad fortune. In particular, it says that the victims of ill luck should as far as possible be made as well off as those who are similarly placed in all respects other than having suffered this piece of bad luck' (Barry 1991b: 142).

unfortunate that the victims are made to bear the consequences on grounds that those victims themselves 'chose' the insurance company or the bank. Agents' actions here seem to resemble what Aristotle called 'mixed' actions: they are both voluntary and involuntary. According to the ethos of the capability approach therefore even though there is more scope for invoking individual responsibility in the case of bad option luck than brute luck, that question needs to be separated from the issue of whether a society has some obligations to compensate the individual as far as possible in such unfortunate circumstances too. Especially when people's loss touches such crucial functionings as nutrition, shelter, health and employment prospects, capability theorists refuse to make access to these entitlements conditional on moral desert. As it is now often done in many places, in order to discourage free-riding attitudes and ever-dependent behaviour, the beneficiaries of social security can be made to give back something to the community either in cash or in kind such as higher insurance premiums, community work and so on.

5.2 The Web of Individual and Social Responsibility

Responsibility in a theory of social justice is best seen not as the ability of the individual to take a complete control of oneself and the environment, but rather as a reciprocal relationship between the individual and society. The individual as an agent who can critically reflect, act and follow a plan of life should assume responsibility for her choices and actions. On the part of the individual, this might involve, among other things, overcoming external barriers and internal limitations that may or may not be conducive to the exercise of agency. Society, as a collective entity of individuals, in turn takes responsibility for providing circumstances and opportunities that would encourage rather than hamper the individual's initiative and agency. This means that social responsibility may require not only a supportive role of compensating for citizens' capability shortfalls, but also an active role of designing economic and political institutions that would be favourable to citizens' nurture and exercise of agency. Also, this implies that social responsibility is not merely backward-looking in order to determine the responsibility lapses of individuals and regulate compensation accordingly, but also forward-looking where individual freedom would be part and parcel of social commitment.

Most notably Rawls is among those who took the lead to bring to the forefront these two related dimensions of individual and social responsibility to inform and to shape a conception of justice. He calls this 'a social division of responsibility' and considers it as part of the justification for primary goods – the reason why a fair distribution of primary goods can fulfil the demands of social justice.

> The preceding account of primary goods includes what we may call 'a social division of responsibility': society, citizens as a collective body, accepts responsibility for maintaining the equal basic liberties and fair equality of opportunity, and for providing a fair share of the primary goods for all within this framework; while citizens as individuals and associations accept responsibility for revising and adjusting their ends and aspirations in view of the all-purpose means they can expect, given their present and foreseeable situation. This division of responsibility relies on the capacity of persons to assume responsibility for

their ends and to moderate the claims they make on their social institutions accordingly (Rawls 1993: 189).

Rawls in the first place talks about society's responsibility in guaranteeing citizens both basic rights as well as material (income and wealth) and non-material (opportunities and self-respect) resources required for pursuing their life plans. As part of society's duties, he also envisions a redistribution of resources stipulated by the difference principle in order to compensate for the disadvantages of society's worse off. However, this is only one half of the social division of responsibility. The other part comes from the individual: individuals are expected to assume responsibility for their life plans, and when required, to 'moderate', 'adjust' or 'revise' their life plans such that these fall in line with the share of primary goods they can reasonably expect. Rawls, for instance, would not recommend that people with 'expensive tastes' be compensated or subsidized by society in order to fulfil their life plans (§2.1). To a large extent, the social division of responsibility between citizens and society that Rawls advocates seems appealing, particularly because it works with a simple and straightforward idea that citizens as agents can take charge of their lives and are owed compensation only for those things that they can do little or nothing about. Even from the viewpoint of a political conception, Rawls's account of responsibility seems appropriate because a society modelled on Rawls's theory would recommend neither a minimalist government nor a full-blown interventionist state, but rather a skilful and satisfactory combination of both. Against an argument for a minimalist state, Rawls would point out that under a society of *laissez-faire* economy, for instance, there is always the danger that citizens' basic rights and opportunities are not respected. Concern for the promotion of individuals' agency may therefore require on the part of the state and its social responsibility the protection of human rights and the guarantee of equal opportunities. Thus Rawls would distance himself from the libertarian views of Nozick and his proposal for a minimal state (§4.1). While Nozick would treat redistributive programmes required by the difference principle as interference in the freedom and lives of people, Rawls would justify them as part of the demands of justice. Simultaneously, against an argument for a fully-fledged interventionist state where the state is thought to be responsible for everything, Rawls would say that such arrangements condone paternalism and undermine citizens' ability to act as responsible agents.

However, when viewed from the perspective of the capability approach, Rawls's social division of responsibility does not seem to go deep enough to capture the disadvantages that typically arise from low levels of basic capabilities. The capability theorists find that not all capability shortfalls of citizens are addressed by a fair share of primary goods and by the redistribution required by the difference principle. For example, Sen expresses his dissatisfaction as follows:

Indeed, the criticism of Rawls's theory of 'justice as fairness' from the capability perspective arose partly from our attempt to take direct note of a person's difficulties – naturally or socially generated – in converting 'primary goods' into actual freedoms to achieve. A person less able or gifted in using primary goods to secure freedoms (e.g. because of physical or mental disability, or varying proneness to illness, or biological or conventional constraints related to gender) is disadvantaged compared with another more favourably placed in that respect even if both have the same bundle of primary goods ... It is for this reason that the [capabilities] approach presented here draws on and criticizes Rawlsian theory – it draws on Rawls's illuminating analysis of fairness and responsibility to criticize his theory's particular dependence on the holding of primary goods (as opposed to the freedoms and capabilities the person respectively enjoy). (Sen 1992: 148)

It is not quite that Rawls's theory does not pay attention to the disadvantages accruing from people's capability shortfalls. Instead, what Rawls wants to emphasize is that there are indeed limits to what society can do to compensate for people's disadvantages. He is not so sure that all or most of society's resources should be spent on extremely unable and sick people who nevertheless can be restored only to insignificant levels. This is the reason why in *A Theory of Justice* (*TJ*, 100ff.) Rawls remarks that justice as fairness rejects the traditional 'principle of redress' for it obligates society to compensate handicaps and shortfalls without setting any boundaries. He says:

Now the difference principle is not of course the principle of redress. It does not require society to try to even out handicaps as if all were expected to compete on a fair basis in the same race ... [A]lthough the difference principle is not the same as that of redress, it does achieve some of the intent of the latter principle. It transforms the aims of the basic structure so that the total scheme of institutions no longer emphasizes social efficiency and technocratic values. We see then that the difference principle represents, in effect, an agreement to regard the distribution of natural talents as common asset and to share in the benefits of this distribution whatever it turns out to be. (Rawls 1971: 101)

Rawls believes that because his theory downplays 'social efficiency' and 'technocratic values', an institutional order satisfying his difference principle would treat the poorly endowed much better than they have been treated historically and in other conceptions of justice. As discussed in Chapter 3, this is precisely the point of difference and disagreement between Rawls's theory and the capability approach. Sen, Kittay, Nussbaum and other capability theorists point out that the scope of the difference principle and its underlying social responsibility should indeed be extended if especially the special needs and additional social and material resources that disabled people, dependency workers and some of the socially disadvantaged people would require. Moreover, the capability theorists find that Rawls's liberal concern for 'agency', 'autonomy', 'self-respect' and so on, leads him to advocate a control view of responsibility – a view that sees responsibility more as the ability of an individual to take control of oneself and the environment than as a reciprocal relationship between the individual and society. Rawls's theory assumes that persons do not take their wants and desires as determined by happenings beyond their control (Rawls 1980: 545ff.; 1993: 185ff.). A fuller account of responsibility will have to take note of fact that the institutions and circumstances under which one lives shape and influence one's wants and desires.

What conclusion then can be drawn regarding the account of responsibility supporting the capability approach with respect to Rawls's? Since the capability approach, more than Rawls's theory, stresses the importance of the background conditions of people's freedoms and basic capabilities, it assigns a broader scope for social responsibility, without of course replacing or diminishing individual's responsibility. A broader affirmation of social responsibility need not be viewed as reducing the space of individual responsibility. When it is stated that it falls within the purview of social responsibility to target economic policies so as to provide widespread employment opportunities, it does not rule out that it is ultimately individual responsibility to decide what skills to acquire and work option to choose. When it is said that the denial of opportunities for basic education and health care is a failure of social responsibility, it is not denied that the educational or health achievements are a matter of personal responsibility. An affirmation of social responsibility can also be seen as advancement of individual freedom and agency. At the level of a political conception, this implies that the capability theorists favour a conception of democracy and welfare state where social responsibility would include not only the protection of human rights and a fair distribution of primary goods, but also the promotion of people's basic capabilities.

One might indeed come to see and appreciate the effort of the capability theorists to anchor individual agency and responsibility in a broader social base and interdependence. Yet what remains somewhat incompletely developed in the capability theory's account of responsibility is the lack of criteria in order to determine which capability shortfalls should merit the attention of social responsibility and which capability shortfalls should be considered as individual responsibility. Up until now Sen, for example, has promoted the view that before holding people responsible for their capability shortfalls, we have to look at whether the individuals concerned had sufficient opportunities to choose, and whether their choices were 'genuine'. He has not attempted to provide a theory of what capability shortfalls are really beyond a person's control, and what capability shortfalls are within the realm of a person's genuine choice. Even Nussbaum and Anderson who work with a list of capabilities fail to define the threshold level of partitioning between social and individual responsibility for each of the items on the list. Sen's answer in this regard has been to refer to the democratic process: each society through public discussion makes a list of capability shortfalls that it judges to be beyond a person's control and thus merit compensation from society in some form or other. One can argue that this answer is incomplete particularly because the participants in a democratic deliberation – politicians, policymakers and the public – are themselves looking for some theoretical insights to confirm or correct their ethical intuitions.

5.3 Dworkin's Account of Responsibility

While the capability theorists basically accept Rawls's idea of the social division of responsibility, they want more scope for social responsibility so that appropriate social base can be created to address capability inequalities as well. But their suggestion to broaden social responsibility suffers from a lack of delineation as to what would come under social responsibility and how much compensation can an individual claim against society. The legal philosopher Ronald Dworkin (2000: ch. 2) thinks that a different distributive scheme suggested by his 'equality of resources' can overcome not only the limitation of Rawls's theory but also the vagueness of the capability approach. A government's political ideal of treating all citizens with 'equal concern', Dworkin points out, can best be realized not when the government tries to make its citizens equal in terms of welfare or primary goods, but rather in terms of *resources*. As part of resources, Dworkin includes two kinds of things. The first one is *social* (impersonal) resources such as civil and political liberties, education, health care, employment, and claims to personal property and public goods. The second is *internal* (personal) resources such as an individual's physical abilities and talents.[9]

Obviously, Dworkin's definition of resources is more inclusive than Rawls's primary goods because, besides all the items on Rawls's list (§2.1), Dworkin's resources also include what Rawls leaves aside: 'natural primary goods' such as 'health and vigour, intelligence and imagination' (Rawls 1971: 62). Dworkin's intention to include as part of resources what Rawls leaves out makes sense, since we tend to think that people who are worse off than others due to low levels of endowments and capacities should be compensated for these shortfalls. Dworkin of course realizes that physical abilities and talents cannot be equally divided like material resources such as property or wealth. Nevertheless some *indirect* ways can be devised for compensating their shortfalls – some physically disabled people for instance, can be made mobile by providing them with wheelchairs and by making public spaces such as schools, public transport and cinemas accessible and disability-friendly. Dworkin's resources theory therefore seems to be a good response to the problems in Rawls's theory.

What is the relationship between Dworkin's and the capability theory? As Dworkin (2000: 300ff.) himself points out, his resources theory is close to the capability approach for the reason that both share the idea that a society must stipulate (re)distribution of resources so as to compensate for the disadvantages in internal resources. Not surprisingly, then, Dworkin, in defining resources, comes to use similar vocabularies that are by now more familiar in the capability approach literature: 'People's powers [capabilities!] are indeed resources, because they are used, together with material resources, in making something valuable out of one's life' (Dworkin 2000: 80). Yet these two differ in *how* they want to fix and justify the correct amount of compensation. As pointed out earlier, the capability theorists particularly suggest that justice requires that society should channel additional resources to those with capability shortfalls insofar as this is required for a life of valuable human functionings. Nevertheless, when asked how to go about this, Sen for example, alludes to a circular answer of democracy and public discussion, without critically investigating the issue further.

---

9   I use the term 'internal resources' to refer to what Dworkin calls 'personal resources', because in ordinary usage my house, car and bicycle are also referred to as personal resources or property. Similarly, the term 'social resources' seems to capture much better what Dworkin means by the term 'impersonal resources'. Although Dworkin does not give a precise definition in the essays where he lays out his theory of equality of resources, we can find one in his essay 'Foundations of Liberal Equality' (1985b). Here he says: 'Personal resources are qualities of mind and body that affect people's success in achieving their life plans and projects: physical and mental health, strength, and talent. Impersonal resources are parts of the environment that can be owned and transferred: land, raw materials, houses, television sets, computers and various legal rights and interests in these' (Dworkin 1985b: 224).

In that respect, Dworkin's theory attempts to go a step further than the capability approach, although bringing with it its own difficulties. Dworkin advocates that some measure of *what* and *how much* should be compensated can be arrived at through the thought-experiment of a hypothetical insurance market. At the outset, the hypothetical insurance that Dworkin suggests should not be equated with the actual insurance scheme of the welfare state or social security. It is a counterfactual exercise to justify his equality of resources. For this reason, Dworkin's hypothetical insurance is similar to Rawls's original position. We are to imagine participants behind a modified 'thinner' veil of ignorance in the sense that they do not know their place in the distribution of natural talents.[10] Assuming that each of them has an equal share of resources, and each of them is equally vulnerable to various physical handicaps and low talents, we can try to answer a hypothetical question: how much of their resources would the participants be willing to spend on insurance against being handicapped or otherwise disadvantaged in the distribution of natural endowments? It is highly likely that none of them would spend all their resources on buying insurance, because they would then have nothing remaining to pursue their life plans with. Instead, everyone would buy some insurance for the different disadvantages they are likely to suffer.

Dworkin suggests that depending on the kind and the level of insurance people are willing to buy, we can use the tax system to make parallel calculations. The real-world income tax can be a way of collecting the premiums that people hypothetically agreed to pay. The various welfare, healthcare and unemployment schemes would be the different ways of paying the coverage to those who turned out to suffer from the natural disadvantages. Also, Dworkin thinks that the measure of compensation suggested by the hypothetical insurance would be something in between nothing and everything: some individuals' disadvantages genuinely require compensation and therefore we cannot say that no compensation whatsoever is required; at the same time, we cannot take the position that every disadvantage should be compensated, since this will lead to undermining individual responsibility and agency. Dworkin's equality of resources theory suggests a 'middle ground' between compensating nothing and everything. Of course what this middle ground would be will be determined by the insurance market.[11]

Perhaps Dworkin is able to invoke a stronger sense of agency and individual responsibility than other theories because of his well-articulated and uncompromising stance on two issues that underpin his theory: (a) the distinction between brute luck

---

10 The veil of ignorance in Dworkin's hypothetical insurance is thinner than Rawls's original position because Dworkin's insurers know their conception of the good, namely, what they think is valuable in life. See Dworkin (2000: 112-119) for more details about the difference between these two theories.

11 As a more practical outcome, Dworkin claims that his equality of resource theory and hypothetical insurance would recommend much more redistribution in Britain and the United States: 'The arguments become compelling, I think, well above the level of income presently used to trigger transfer payments for unemployment or minimum wage levels in either Britain or the United States' (Dworkin 2000: 97). However, Dworkin does not mention about welfare states such as Sweden or Belgium which might not only fulfil the requirements of his theory, but also implement more redistribution for social solidarity.

and option luck and (b) the responsibility-test. The capability theorists find these to be problematic and unhelpful especially for a capabilities-oriented reasoning about what we are obligated to each other.

a) Capability Deprivation and Failure to Insure

A very important weapon in the armoury of contemporary theorists of justice is the institution of insurance (Barry 1991b). By invoking the possibility of insuring oneself against different misfortunes, these theorists point out that it is possible to construct an argument that marginalizes the principle of compensation for many cases. The idea behind it is that if your house, for example, burns down due to causes beyond your control, then this is undoubtedly an instance of bad luck. However, whether you will suffer financial loss from the destruction of the house will depend on your prior decision to insure it fully, inadequately or not at all. Hence many theorists of justice tend to advocate the idea that someone who loses everything in a fire can legitimately be left to suffer the consequences because the option of insuring against the loss was available and not taken.

Dworkin fully exploits the idea of insurance. He draws a clear distinction between brute luck and option luck, and recommends compensation *only* for the shortfalls suffered by victims of brute luck. The misfortunes suffered by the victims of bad option luck do not have any claim for compensation. Furthermore, Dworkin's insurance market suggests that persons are indeed agents who can take charge of their lives and decisions, and can convert most of the foreseeable instances of brute luck into some form of option luck. Therefore, any outcomes due to voluntary choices whose consequences can be reasonably foreseen should be borne by the agent. The shortfalls these choices may create do not warrant any claim for compensation.

> Option luck is a matter of how *deliberate* and *calculated* gambles turn out – whether someone gains or loses through accepting an isolated risk he or she should have anticipated and might have declined. Brute luck is a matter of how risks fall out that are not in that sense deliberate gambles. If I buy a stock on the exchange that rises, then my option luck is good. If I am hit by a falling meteorite whose course could not have been predicted, then my bad luck is brute ... Insurance, so far as it is available, provides a link between brute and option luck, because the decision to buy or reject catastrophe is a *calculated* gamble. (Dworkin 2000: 73-74, my emphasis)

Dworkin's recommendation that the *victims of bad option luck* should be differentially treated from the *victims of brute luck* seems to make sense, because otherwise society would end up subsidizing people's bad choices. More importantly, it gives expression to and supports an important ethical experience that most adult citizens would endorse. None of us would like to be seen as objects of pity or compensation by our fellow citizens. Nor would we like to think that our deliberated actions and judgements are causally determined by a set of genetic and circumstantial factors. We see ourselves and others as agents because we can not only choose between different alternatives, but also take responsibility for what follows from these choices. So, Dworkin's equality of resources theory gives a clear institutional shape to people's ethical experience of being agents and wanting to take consequential responsibility for their choices. Sen himself alludes to this ethical experience when he emphasizes the importance of agency and reciprocity even in famine relief and poverty reduction programmes. Instead of just distributing food and welfare, it is more dignified to link these to some public work and employment. Indeed, beneficiaries would be resentful and feel humiliated, if the welfare compensation dispensed to them is condescending and involves absolutely no reciprocity on their part (Sen 1999a: 177-178; Drèze and Sen 1989:122ff.).

However, it is also important to realize that the ethical experience of a person acting and being seen as an agent can be in tension with the idea that distribution of health care, unemployment benefits, family welfare or any other forms of compensation should be regulated by fault and moral desert: the agent after all has chosen it, and therefore he or she should suffer some consequence for it. We tend to say that destitution and basic capabilities deprivation are too high a penalty for failure to insure or insuring inadequately (Barry 1991b; Phillips 2004). Surely, the victims of bad option luck do stand open to moral criticism in the way that the victim of brute luck do not, but that need not lead to the view that because they have chosen these outcomes, society has no obligations to compensate them. Anderson (1999) argues that the stance of 'luck egalitarians' such as Dworkin refusing to come to the aid of the victims of bad option luck expresses a failure to treat these unfortunates with 'equal respect' and 'equal concern': 'Luck egalitarians tell the victims of very bad option luck that, having chosen to run their risks, they deserve their misfortune, so society need not secure them against destitution and exploitation ... Even the imprudent don't deserve such fates' (Anderson 1999: 301). To illustrate this, Anderson gives the example of a person who is given the opportunity to insure against injury but chooses not to and is subsequently seriously injured in a car accident. She points out that luck egalitarians such as Dworkin will leave such persons unattended. Similarly, those who choose to undertake hazardous work or live in hazardous areas without insurance will be refused assistance in the event of misfortune on the ground that they failed to insure. As shown in Chapter 3, Anderson's alternative recommendation is to move away from luck egalitarianism to a regime of 'democratic equality' which guarantees to all citizens a set of basic capabilities, and distinguishes it from those capabilities whose loss may not generate any claim for compensation: 'Democratic equality does not indemnify individuals against all losses due to their imprudent conduct. It only guarantees a set of capabilities necessary to functioning as free and equal citizen and avoiding oppression. Individuals must bear many other losses on their own' (Anderson 1999: 327).

b) Responsibility-test

A second complex issue which the capability theorists find problematic is with regard to Dworkin's stance on whether individuals are responsible for their character. Dworkin advocates the view that individuals are fully responsible for their character particularly for the formation of their 'ambitions and preferences' irrespective of whether those were formed or induced by factors over which they had no control. Dworkin also offers a 'responsibility-test' that he thinks can help to determine the borderline between individual and social responsibility. According to this, so long as a person *identifies* with his or her preferences, the choices that follow from them fall within the realm of individual responsibility. Dworkin of course understands that there are some categories of preferences such as 'cravings' which should not be viewed as part of an individual's responsibility. A craving, Dworkin says, is a preference one wishes not to have, and therefore, does not form part of the individual's personality. Except for cravings, Dworkin thinks that a person should be considered responsible for all preferences, because he or she identifies with them.

Dworkin's responsibility-test has the advantage of advocating a stronger sense of individual agency. However, as Cohen (1989) points out, Dworkin's responsibility-test turns out to be inadequate for determining the requirements of justice with regard to certain basic capability shortfalls, even when the individual concerned identifies with the situation. Cohen, therefore, argues that in order to find out what obligations of distribution and compensation we have, the right question to ask is *not* whether the individual 'identifies' with his preferences or not, but rather whether the individual could have avoided the disadvantage and whether that disadvantage can now be overcome.

> When deciding whether or not justice (as opposed to charity) requires redistribution, the egalitarian asks if someone with a disadvantage could have avoided it or could now overcome it. If he could have avoided it, he has no claim to compensation from an egalitarian point of view. If he could not have avoided it but could now overcome it, then he can ask that his effort to overcome it be subsidized, but, unless it costs more to overcome it than to compensate for it without overcoming it, he cannot expect society to compensate for his disadvantage. (Cohen 1989: 920)

Dworkin's responsibility-test also seems rather paradoxical in cases that capability theorists have been highlighting. Consider a child who grows up in a poor family. Her parents are illiterate and hardly care about exposing the child to any books at home, or sending her to school. As a result, the child develops preferences in which education has a very low priority. When she grows up she does not care to become educated, and believes that education will not make her life successful. She identifies with these preferences, and considers them as intrinsic to who she is. How would Dworkin approach such a case? Because of his responsibility-test, we believe Dworkin would have to say that such a child or the adult that she becomes does not require any social support and solidarity for the low level of education she has acquired, and the consequentially low income that she is likely to earn.

Among other things, this response only understates the fact that the aspiration that shape our choices regarding education, social involvement, career and so on are themselves framed by our 'social location', most notably and persistently by the impact of social class. Phillips (2004), for example, brings to light the persistent correlation between class of origin, educational achievements and class of destination in Britain, despite all the changes of the last hundred years. One can attribute this phenomenon to reasons such as genetic inheritance, educational standards between fee-paying and state schools, and between state schools in rich and poor neighbourhoods. Along with these, the educational experts have also highlighted another important factor: the transmission of aspiration from parents to children, and the way our perceptions of what we might wish to do and achieve do reflect what our parents have done before us. Our choices are enhanced or constrained not only by the resources available to us, but also by the ways in which our preferences and ambitions are formed. Dworkin's responsibility-test might easily bypass these social realities.

5.4 Social Norms and Policy Imperatives

Whether one approaches the issue of responsibility from the perspective of the capability approach or from the viewpoint of the liberal egalitarian theories of Rawls and Dworkin, a pre-institutional determination of the borderline between individual and social responsibility turns out to be a difficult affair. One might try to settle this on the basis of 'empirical' evidences about human behaviour and action. How much of awareness and choice is involved in drug addiction, injurious smoking, drunken driving and aversion to education and career, for example? Yet one must also be aware that social norms and communal settings play a crucial role in public judgement about these matters. They represent and embody an understanding about what is to be regarded as matter of collective responsibility and what is to be treated as a matter of individual responsibility. For example, although western Europe and the United States seem to have a number of things in common, when it comes to certain fundamental social norms concerning social solidarity and related issues of income inequality, unemployment, health care and so on they emphasize contrasting principle of social ethics (Sen 1997b). By now it is quite well known that in American public policy priorities, there is very little commitment to providing basic health care for all, and there is likely to be no radical change in the near future. And it appears that more than 40 million people are without any kind of medical coverage or insurance in the United States. A comparable situation in Europe would not be acceptable, socially and politically. Not only is the basic medical coverage seen as a basic right of every citizen, but also the provision of various public facilities ranging from health care to education is considered to be a social responsibility of the welfare state.

However, when we shift our attention to social norms about unemployment, the scenario seems to be rather different. In recent years, unemployment seems to have increased to different degrees in the countries of western Europe. Studies have shown that unemployment brings with it not only economic loss to individuals and an additional fiscal cost of unemployment benefits, but also negative psychological and social consequences in the well-being of individuals and society. Yet there seems to be a reluctance to confront this problem head on. On the contrary, the level of unemployment that is currently tolerated in Europe would be socially and politically unacceptable in America. A double-digit increase of unemployment, for instance, would be politically risky for any government in the United States.

How does one account for this difference in social values between Europe and America? Sen ponders over the contrast in the following terms:

The contrast between western Europe and the United States raises another interesting – and in some ways a more general – question. The American social ethics finds it possible to be very non-supportive of the indigent and the impoverished, in a way that a typical western European, reared in a welfare state, finds hard to accept. But the same American social ethics would find the double-digit levels of unemployment, common in Europe, to be quite intolerable. Europe has continued to accept worklessness – and its increase – with remarkable equanimity. Underlying this contrast is a difference in social attitudes towards social and individual responsibilities – an issue that would call for some comment. (Sen 1997b: 160)

Sen suggests that the contrast can partly be explained by the fact that individual responsibility and the value of being able to 'help oneself' is much stronger in America than in Europe. The American self-help culture seems to show much more commitment against unemployment than against being medically uninsured or against falling into deep poverty. It is believed that providing different welfare benefits would make the citizens more and more dependent. On the contrary, offering opportunities to be employed, it is thought, can facilitate helping oneself. That seems to be the reason why there is more public engagement for 'workfare' than for 'welfare'.

A similar contrast of social values can be also noted between India and the United States concerning affirmative action.[12] Both India and the United States share a history of entrenched social prejudice and inequalities. While social discrimination in India was largely based on the Hindu hierarchical caste system, in America it was based on race. However, when tackling these historical inequalities, India and the States have shown contrasting approaches. The founding fathers of the Indian Constitution were quite convinced that the transition from a rigid hierarchical Hindu society to an egalitarian India would not be possible without affirmative action in politics, public employment and education. They were well aware that these are indeed a digression from a *formal* interpretation of equality in terms of equality of opportunity for all based on merit or competition to a more *substantial* interpretation that advances the position of the underdogs of society. True, at various times in the past, the affirmative measures have been a source of violence, tension and reinforcement of caste identities. But for the past fifty years and more, the Indian State and civil society have upheld these policies and programmes. The justification for affirmative action was partly backward-looking, considered as a rectification for historical inequalities. But as historical events become remote in time and the identification of the target group becomes more and more difficult, a backward-looking justification becomes less convincing. Moreover, affirmative action was envisaged only as a transitional measure. However, what still provides an acceptable justification is a forward-looking and capabilities-oriented reasoning.

Contrary to India, the general disposition of the American public does not seem to be in favour of affirmative action, but rather any policy or programme favouring the racial minority has been looked at with scepticism and even with some amount of phobia (Nussbaum 2002). It is not that American society does not think a fair competition based on merit requires a 'levelling of the playing field'. In fact, the American judiciary and some of the political class have been very supportive of

---

12 See Nussbaum (2002) for a more elaborate discussion of the differences between Indian and American social norms. Also, see Alexander (2003b) for details about social attitudes and consensus regarding India's affirmative action.

private initiatives of universities and business enterprises for racial diversity policies in recruitment and employment. Yet these private sympathies have so far not translated into any official legislation and programmes to the extent experimented within India. On the whole, the state and civil society in America seem to think that any deviation from equality of opportunity *per se* would be detrimental to efficiency and incentives.

The point of highlighting the differences of social norms between Europe and America or between India and America is not so much to say that the United States is a more individualistic society than western Europe or India. Nor should we come to an easy conclusion, that while Dworkin's account of responsibility would be suitable to societies with competitive economies, the capability approach would provide a theoretical justification to societies of social solidarity and welfare states. One can dispute these differences and come up with different arguments and conclusions. What is perhaps more important to stress is the complexities and difficulties involved in advocating a pre-institutional overarching theory of individual responsibility. It is important to recognize that social values and communal practices do play a considerable role in determining the borderline where social responsibility ends and individual responsibility begins. A theory of justice cannot be indifferent to the dynamics of communal embeddedness and public discussion.

5.5 The Art of Attaining Equilibrium

Alms giving can sometimes turn out to be an unpleasant experience. When someone knocks at your door asking for help you might willingly help. But if it turns out that the person concerned has lied to you and in fact was not a deserving case to be helped, you feel cheated, let down and perhaps even a sense of resentment. But from this it is difficult to draw an overall conclusion that every person who knocks at the door should be turned down. An analogical lesson can be drawn to highlight the obligations that we may owe to each other as a matter of justice. The capability theorists are indeed perceptive to think and suggest that a broader base of social responsibility and social security can tackle issues of injustice that are not normally addressed in other dominant theories. Yet the potential dangers of such an extension are abuses and wastage of social resources. When more and more people become dependent on and beneficiaries of the social welfare system or when it turns out that people are overcompensated for what they do not truly deserve, it even becomes difficult to maintain the already existing institutional forms of solidarity for people who are genuinely affected by vulnerability and misfortune. Yet whether the potential dangers of abuse would warrant the effacement or retrenchment of the social safety net meant to support the poor and the vulnerable is a complex question for every society to answer. The challenge for a political morality is indeed to reach a reasonable balance between individual responsibility and collective accountability that could be acceptable to everyone.

As a theory of social justice, the capability approach can be considered responsibility-sensitive particularly because it gives importance to the agency aspect of the person and does not recommend compensation for the capability shortfalls that are the consequences of individual choices. However, the capability approach is also somewhat different from other contemporary theories because it advocates a reciprocal view of responsibility and places emphasis on the interdependence between individual and social responsibility. It stresses the idea that appropriate conditions of freedom and choice offer a much better environment for individuals to act as agents and assume responsibility. The capability theorists also distinguish themselves from others to the extent they refuse to make capabilities related to the achievement of such crucial functionings as nutrition, health, education and employment conditional on moral desert and retributive social ethics. Moreover, a comparison of the capability approach with the liberal theories of Rawls and Dworkin brings to light the fact that the strength of the capability approach lies in envisioning a broader scope for social responsibility, without at the same time replacing or diminishing the individual responsibility condition. A broader scope of social responsibility may require a new form of social democracy that would not only protect human rights and provide citizens with equal access to material and social resources, but also promote basic capabilities for all citizens.

Chapter 6

Aristotle and Nussbaum's Hybrid Theory of Capabilities

When Aristotle praised justice as the first virtue of political life, he did so in such a way as to suggest that a community which lacks practical agreement on a conception of justice must also lack the necessary basis for a political community. But the lack of such a basis must therefore threaten our own society.

Alasdair MacIntyre, *After Virtue*

It was its direct relation to political life which determined the orientation and scope of classical political philosophy. Accordingly, the tradition which was based on that philosophy, and which preserved its orientation and scope, preserved that direct relation to a certain extent. The fundamental change in this respect begins with the new political philosophy of the early modern period and reaches its climax in present-day political science. The most striking difference between classical political philosophy and contemporary political science is that the latter is no longer concerned at all with what was the guiding question for the former: the question of the best political order. On the other hand, modern political science is greatly preoccupied with the type of question that was of much less importance to classical political philosophy: questions concerning method. Both differences must be traced to the same reason: to the different degree of directness in which classical political philosophy, on the one hand, and present-day political science, on the other, are related to political life.

Leo Strauss, *What is Political Philosophy?*

It is quite common among the capability theorists to identify Aristotle and Aristotelianism as the philosophical foundations and a source of inspiration for the capability approach. More than any other capability theorist, it is Nussbaum who clarifies this conceptual connection and develops a hybrid theory of capabilities that blends Aristotle's focus on valuable human functionings with the liberal doctrines of moral equality and universal human dignity. In doing so, Nussbaum places herself in the company of a wider group of philosophers who want to rejuvenate Aristotelian insights to confront contemporary problems. As far as Nussbaum's hermeneutical trajectory is concerned, a close textual study of the relevant parts of Aristotle's *Ethics*, *Politics* and *On Rhetoric* reveals at least three areas to be important points of reference for the capability approach.

First, Aristotle derives and justifies ethical and political principles not on the basis of any contractual notion that came to be prevalent among the seventeenth and eighteenth century philosophers and later revived by philosophers like Rawls, but on the basis of the 'political' nature of human beings to come together in a political community called the polis. Although the polis would not constitute the finality of the good life, the good life cannot, however, be conceived of and pursued outside the polis. Hence the political community needs to provide both the required level of material resources, education and social conditions for the pursuit of the good life (§6.1).[1] In contrast to some contemporary 'laissez-faire' and even 'political' liberals, Aristotle does not have any qualms about imposing a moral imperative on the state to enhance the capability prospects of citizens. For example, Aristotle (*Politics* II, 9: 149) supports the practice of citizens eating together and heartily approves the custom of funding the common meals from a common fund as in Crete; he however, disapproves of and criticizes the Spartan way of relying on individual contributions for this practice since it disadvantages the poor and keeps them out of participation.

Second, according to Aristotle, justice construed in a broad sense consists in being lawful and in acting in conformity with the laws, rules and conventions of the political community in question. And when it is specifically a question of distributive justice, Aristotle shows distaste for *pleonexia*, the tendency to hoard and to take more than what is one's due, and favours the idea that citizens should receive goods in proportion to their needs and in view of what they are able to do and be. Thus, Aristotle (*Ethics* II, 6: 100; *Politics* VII, 16: 442) points out that a professional wrestler needs more food than a child, and a pregnant woman needs to take more nutrition than a nonpregnant woman (§6.2).

And finally, Aristotle recognizes a cognitive structure in emotions and assigns them a normative role in the pursuit of the good life. Emotions are not just brute animal forces, but intelligent and discriminating parts of the person intimately linked to ethical beliefs and actions. For capability theorists such as Nussbaum, Aristotle's theory of emotions becomes a point of departure for envisaging compassion as a 'social emotion' and providing the essential link required to discern the obligation of justice in the political community (§6.3). While most liberal philosophers would prefer to avoid any reference to compassion as being among the motivations for social cooperation, Nussbaum proposes certain institutional forms of compassion as indispensable for sustaining a just society.

Despite these points of convergences between Aristotle and the capability approach, there are serious difficulties in appropriating Aristotle for contemporary political argument. Aristotle held the view that slaves, women and menial labourers such as craftsmen, farmers and metics (resident foreigners) were not eligible for full citizenship either because they are poorly endowed and are incapable or because the type of harsh and demeaning labour they do does not make room for the leisure and education that are required for a life of virtue and true human happiness. Recognizing these anti-egalitarian dispositions as major drawbacks in Aristotle, Nussbaum attempts to resolve them by modifying and revising Aristotle's theory, moderating especially the threshold requirements of leisure, wealth and education.

---

1   Arguments and materials for this chapter, particularly for §6.1, are drawn from my article 'Non-Reductionist Naturalism: Nussbaum between Aristotle and Hume', *Res Publica: A Journal of Legal and Social Philosophy* (2005a). I have benefited from a number of commentators on Aristotle's *Ethics* and *Politics*. Among others, see Hardie (1968), Broadie (1991), Annas (1993), Vandevelde (1994), Miller, F.D. (1995) and Kraut (2002).

Moreover, she sees in Aristotle a philosopher who is unwilling to acknowledge the unfairness and contradictions in his own view. As Nussbaum (1988a: 171) expresses it, Aristotle 'fails to look our issue in the eye'. Hence her argument is that if Aristotle is seen as committed to the view that the state should provide the conditions for the good life of certain individuals (all free males, in Aristotle's time), there is no reason, except bad faith and an easy acceptance of the prevailing customs, not to extend these conditions to all without any discrimination. By a similar line of reasoning, Nussbaum (1997b: 118ff.) suggests that it amounts to 'descriptive chauvinism' when some contemporary ethical and political theorists insist on seeing Aristotle as anti-democratic and anti-liberal, unwilling to recognize the possibility of liberating his thoughts for constructive political purposes.

6.1 Aristotle's Naturalism Revisited

a) The Two Concepts of Nature in Aristotle's Ethics and Politics

Aristotle's ethics and political philosophy can be called naturalistic because of the central role that Aristotle gives to the concept of nature (*phusis*) in justifying ethical and political principles (Annas 1993; 1996; Miller, F.D 1995; Kraut 2002).[2] Hence some of his more famous claims: 'human beings are by nature political animals' (*Ethics* IX, 9: 305; *Politics* I, 2: 59); 'the polis or the political community exists by nature' (*Politics* I.2: 59); 'polis is by nature prior to the individuals which constitute it' (*Politics* I, 2: 60). These and other related claims all seem to affirm a hallmark Aristotelian tenet: political life is deeply rooted in human nature, and human nature in turn requires political life for its fulfilment.

Yet while exploring such claims more closely, we begin to see that Aristotle does not have one singular, uniform understanding of nature. Rather, Aristotle seems to use the concept of nature, particularly in *Ethics* and *Politics*, in two different ways. In the first understanding, nature is considered as 'mere nature', that which is the source or origin (*arche*) of things that are 'given' from the start. In the second

---

2   It is important to note that Aristotle uses a naturalistic approach both for his ethical and political argument and envisions a sort of continuity between the two. An indication to this effect can already be found at the beginning of *Ethics* (I, 2: 64) where Aristotle announces that the subject matter he has chosen to examine, namely the good life, is one that belongs to the science of politics. He holds the view that understanding the nature of the good life is of crucial importance to the way we conduct our lives and that since politics is the science that controls all other practical disciplines, it is appropriate for it to inquire into the nature of the good life and to come up with suggestions on the basis of its inquiry. Further on, as Aristotle proceeds in *Ethics*, not only does he remind his audience of the political character of his discussion, but also conducts a detailed discussion on justice in Book V. Finally, in the concluding chapter in *Ethics*, he refers to the importance of a detailed examination of laws, constitutions, political systems and the proper arrangement of the polis which are treated in *Politics*. Yet Aristotle also makes a distinction between ethics and political philosophy insofar as while in the former he is generally concerned about the study of human well-being, character and virtues, in the latter he is specifically concerned about the study of constitutions (*politeia*) and cities. For further details see Kraut (2002: 16ff.).

understanding, however, nature is referred to as the goal or the proper end (*telos*) towards which a growing thing moves. One of the paradigmatic places where these two meanings of nature come to the fore is the trichotomy that Aristotle appeals to: nature (*phusis*), habit (*ethos*) and reason (*logos*). The development of human beings, says Aristotle, requires not only nature, but also habit and reason (*Politics* VII, 13: 429-430; *Ethics* II, 1: 91). Nature, left on its own, can be developed for better or worse depending on how human beings use their reason to cultivate or control nature through habit.

At least three observations can be made regarding this three-fold scheme of Aristotle. First, Aristotle seems to distinguish rather starkly between 'nature' on the one hand, and 'habit' and 'reason' on the other. Nature is not the same as habit or – even less so – reason. So, 'nature' here refers to 'mere nature', or potentiality: those basic materials of human beings that can be developed in different ways through habit and reason. Indeed, human beings begin with some tendencies and impulses. However, it is also true that human beings consequently develop these tendencies and impulses through habit and reason into what is usually referred to as 'second nature'.

Second, Aristotle says that for the development of human beings nature, habit and reason, all three 'work harmoniously': 'human being alone has reason, and so needs all three working concertedly [harmoniously]. Reason causes people to do many things contrary to nature and habit, whenever they are convinced that this is the better course' (*Politics* VII, 13: 430). Aristotle, here, seems to invoke a dynamic, perhaps an unusual explanation of what it means to 'work harmoniously'. The harmonious working of nature, habit and reason that he has in mind is not one of peaceful co-existence. Instead, harmony is quite compatible with conflicts and differences between reason, nature and habit.

The third observation, related to the second, concerns the place of reason in Aristotle's moral psychology. Reason, for Aristotle, is not an intellectual quality that is apart from and external to habituation. A virtuous person or a person 'brought up well' is not like a well trained pet obeying some external dictates of reason. Nor are the products of habituation to be treated as motivational inclinations that are independent of conceptual thought. On the contrary, reason (*logos*), for Aristotle, is *practical* reason (*phronesis*) – embodying the 'perceptual' capacity to discern and to pursue a true conception of the good. It is a *perceptual* capacity because one possesses it, as it were, not through scientific reasoning; instead, one acquires it through experience and reflection.[3]

Putting these observations together gives us a complex picture of Aristotle's use of the idea of nature. On the one hand, he suggests that we can distinguish between mere nature (or, we might call it the 'first nature') and the second nature that is the result of practical reason. On the other hand, he also seems to think that these two are interlocked to the extent that in order to know and determine what human nature *is*, we need to constantly engage in an ongoing inquiry of what human beings *ought* to be. Consider for example what Nussbaum on her list calls the capability to use

---

3   See Aristotle (*Ethics* V, 8: 215). For further details on the 'perceptive' nature of practical reason in Aristotle, see Nussbaum, 'Discernment of perception' in *Love's Knowledge* (1990a).

one's senses, imagination and thought (§3.2, number four on the list). Every human being, except perhaps some severely disabled people, is endowed with impulses towards this capability. In the beginning of the *Metaphysics*, Aristotle himself refers to this as an impulse or desire that every human being is born with. In that sense, this capability can be considered as mere nature. However, the nature of this capability cannot be further understood except in relation to its development through literacy and education in mathematics, science and philosophy. Obviously, a human life with opportunities for the development of this capability would be considered *better* than the one without it; it is indeed *desirable* and *valuable* for every human being to possess and to develop the capability to use one's senses, imagination and thought. Aristotle's use of nature, therefore, contains both a 'natural' component referring to the impulse or impetus that propels human beings towards a particular orientation or goal *and* a 'normative' content alluding to what is good and worthwhile for human beings.

Once we understand the interlocked, dual sense of nature at the background of Aristotle's moral psychology, it becomes a little easier to unravel some of his fundamental claims regarding the nature of human beings and the necessity of political principles and institutions that would nurture this. Consider first Aristotle's claim that 'a human being is by nature a political animal'. By this, Aristotle, on the one hand, wants to point out that human beings have within them right from the beginning a political impulse or impetus that moves them towards a life in the polis. As Arendt (1958: 22ff.) has argued, the political impulse that Aristotle has in mind is not only the general desire of human beings to escape isolation and to form social ties of the kind we find in the household and the village, but also the more specific desire to live in a political community, a unit which offers possibilities for living a more complex and richer life than in the household. The desire for recognition and excellence may be fulfilled only in a public sphere that transcends the private sphere of the family and clan. However, Aristotle, in calling human beings political animals, is referring not only to the natural psychological make-up that propels them into the polis, but also to the goal, the kind of life that human beings ought to live. Just as the absence of health, education, friends and family would impoverish our lives in a serious way, so too would it be a serious loss, if we did not have opportunities for recognition and excellence in a political community.

Similarly, Aristotle's thesis that 'every city exists by nature' can also be seen to contain both descriptive and normative elements. Its descriptive element rests on the presupposition that human beings are born with certain desires and needs that motivate them to found a political community called the polis: it is natural for human beings to come together in the household and the village in order to secure access to food, protection against enemies and to nurture future generations. But once these needs are ensured, or along with these, it is also natural for human beings to look for a larger community called the polis in order to satisfy their desire to live the good life. However, this descriptive claim is intertwined with Aristotle's normative claim that the process which leads from the primitive household to villages and finally polis is a process of the most *appropriate* (how it ought to be) development. In fact, participation in the polis, for Aristotle, becomes a distinguishing hallmark of human beings in contrast to nonhuman animals or gods: 'Whatever is incapable of participating in the association which we call the state [polis], a dumb animal for example, and equally whatever is perfectly self-sufficient and has no need to (e.g. a god), is not part of the state at all' (*Politics* I, 2: 61).

b) *Nussbaum's Appropriation of Aristotle*

Nussbaum's theory of capabilities would surely endorse the thesis that Aristotle uses the idea of nature for ethical and political arguments in its interlocked dual sense: that in order to know what human nature is, we need to look at what human beings are intended for. Not surprisingly, then, Nussbaum herself, like Aristotle, is of the opinion that 'to find out what our nature is seems to be one and the same thing as to find out what we deeply believe to be important and indispensable' (Nussbaum 1995c: 106). In fact, Nussbaum's claim that a list of (ten) capabilities should provide the basis for fundamental political principles can be seen as a revival of Aristotle's naturalistic approach incorporating within it the required corrections and revisions. Nowhere is the connection between Aristotle's naturalism and the capability approach clearer than in Nussbaum's idea of 'combined capabilities' (Nussbaum 2000a: 84-86). By this idea, Nussbaum suggests that human beings can be seen as having certain innate (*basic*) capabilities. A newborn child for example, has the capability for speech and language, love and gratitude, practical reason, etc in this sense. Yet these basic capabilities invariably require appropriate external conditions both for their full development (as *internal capabilities*) as well as for the ability to exercise and realize different functionings (*combined capabilities*).

True, some combined capabilities such as the ability to eat, to move around and to be capable of sexual functions may require just time and bodily maturation with a minimum of supporting conditions. But others such as the ability to speak a language and to creatively use one's thought and imagination may require more intensive and elaborate supporting conditions. Therefore the gap between basic capabilities and combined capabilities, for Nussbaum, is the locus of political goals and puts a moral pressure on governments, non-governmental organizations and international institutions to raise the capabilities of human beings above a certain minimum threshold. In other words, just like Aristotle – who appeals to an interlocked dual sense of human nature exemplified in practical reason in order to support his ethical and political judgements – Nussbaum too points out that the transition from basic capabilities to combined capabilities of citizens should be the focus of ethical and political reflection.

Furthermore, Nussbaum substantiates her position that requirements of justice are best known on the basis of a plural conception of the good life through a persistent inquiry and interpretation of Aristotle's 'human-function argument' found in *Ethics* I, 7. Aristotle here raises the question of whether human beings *as such* have a function or activity (*ergon*) that typically can be called their own:

> But is it likely that whereas joiners and shoemakers have certain functions or activities, man as such has none, but has been left by nature a functionless being? Just as we can see that eye and hand and foot and every one of our members has some function, should we not assume that in like manner a human being has function over and above these particular functions? What, then, can this possibly be? (*Ethics* I, 7: 75)

Aristotle's answer to this question is not straightforward. The prelude to the answer, starting already in *Ethics* I, 5, consists in the rejection of different possible candidates. He argues against the view that human function can be identified with the seeking of physical pleasure or wealth or honour and so on. In contrast to this, Aristotle's own answer to the question is a life of practical reason (*Ethics* I, 7: 75-76). Following Aristotle, Nussbaum (1988a: 181) envisages practical reason both as an *architectonic* principle that organizes the whole life, providing for its many activities, and as an *infusing* principle that makes each activity human rather than merely vegetative or animal. She holds the view that a flourishing human life and well-being should have many components, some of which will certainly be basic functionings related to being nourished, healthy, educated and so on. However, what makes them distinctively human functionings is the fact that they are done as parts of a life organized and infused by practical reason. Consequently, Nussbaum ascribes two interrelated roles to practical reason: ethical and political. It has an ethical role in as much as practical reason is the embodiment of an individual's virtuous life: through a continuous interaction of the first and second nature a human being discerns what it means to live the good life. But, for Nussbaum, an ongoing inquiry into what can and ought to be the components of the good life, and more particularly, what it means to live a life in accordance with practical reason, will also have a political role.

> The central task of the city [polis] will, then, be to give its people the conditions of fully human living: living in which the essential functionings according to practical reason will be available. This means don't just give food and allow people to 'graze': make it possible for people to choose to regulate their nutrition by their own reason. Don't just take care of their perceptual needs in a mechanical way, producing a seeing eye, a hearing ear, etc. Instead, make it possible for people to use their bodies and senses in a truly human way. And don't make all this available in a minimal way: make it possible to do these things well. (1988a: 183).

Not only does Nussbaum underscore the political import of the human-function argument, but also revises and reworks Aristotle's antidemocratic stance of excluding the slaves, women and menial labourers from full political participation. Nussbaum's task in this regard is to show the inconsistencies in Aristotle's position and to point out that Aristotle's thought can still be used for constructive political purposes. Here is how she expresses her dissatisfaction withAristotle's lack of radicalism:

> Aristotle at times shrinks back from what might be the *revolutionary implications* of some of his statements into the position that we owe this treatment only to those who have already managed to get a certain part of the way towards capability. But it seems to me that a political theory that developed the implications of these statements without shrinking could justifiably call itself Aristotelian. (Nussbaum 1988a: 184, my emphasis).

Nussbaum is hopeful that by deploying an 'Aristotelian argument' the kind of elitism that Aristotle himself seemed to have easily accepted can be effectively counteracted. Given the fact that the general thrust of Aristotle's ethics and political philosophy is to find out the valuable human functionings and seek out appropriate conditions to promote them, it is only legitimate that an appropriation of Aristotle for today's purpose focuses on the capabilities of every citizen in the political community rather than just on the capabilities of those who are already better off in terms of social position and education.

Paradoxically, an effort to revive Aristotle in the way Nussbaum's theory of capabilities attempts might seem to be out of step with certain 'modern' predispositions. As a preliminary groundwork, it would therefore be necessary to show how not to read Aristotle and to reject a reductionist understanding of human nature. As for example, MacDowell (1998b) realizes, during the intermediate historical gap between Aristotle and our generation, modern science and its allied philosophical thought have bequeathed to us a demystified and disenchanted view of the natural world.[4] The ancients and even medievalists were mostly inclined to look at nature with awe, wonder and with a certain amount of fascination. On the contrary, the moderns tended to look at it as an 'object' for dispassionate and value-free investigation. So much so that today, a proper approval and appreciation of science and its parasitic philosophical thought may be presumed by many to entail that we look at human nature as an uncontroversial scientific fact, and bracket out from its study all normative aspects of inquiry.

It is possible to read Aristotle's naturalistic approach to moral and political philosophy through such a modern reductionist lens, forgetting that for Aristotle the natural and normative elements of human nature come in a single package. T.H. Irwin (1980), for instance, seems to pursue a reading of Aristotle that is reminiscent of modern predispositions. The ethical arguments of Aristotle, according to Irwin, are validated not so much by the common beliefs of Aristotle's audience, but rather by independent metaphysical doctrines which seem to go 'beyond' common beliefs.

> He [Aristotle] is sometimes supposed to regard ordinary language and ordinary beliefs as the final arbiter of the correctness of an ethical theory; the theory should begin from the difficulties raised by common beliefs and try to make the beliefs coherent, pronouncing all or most of them true. This conception of Aristotle's ethical method is at best a half-truth... The argument of the *Ethics* depends upon more than common sense. It depends on the whole view of natural substances outlined in Aristotle's metaphysics and psychology. (Irwin 1980: 50-51)

Irwin is well aware that Aristotle, as he makes it clear in *Ethics*, Book I, Chapters 6 and 13, is generally 'reluctant' to bring in metaphysical doctrines to justify his ethical positions. He also concedes the fact that Aristotle 'does not advertise' the connection between his ethics and metaphysics. Nevertheless, Irwin insists that the general ethical method of Aristotle cannot be justified without appealing to certain 'external natural facts' which are 'more than' people's common beliefs.

Also, Bernard Williams seems to attribute to Aristotle an 'absolute understanding of nature' that can provide an external foundation for ethical and political judgements (MacDowell 1998b; Nussbaum 1995c). He thinks that questions about human

---

4   In similar terms, Charles Taylor also comments on the effects of modern science on the way we look at nature. In fact, he traces back the prevailing tendency to 'objectify' nature to modern scientific and philosophical outlook. See Taylor (1993).

nature, for Aristotle, are first and foremost, natural scientific facts which should be distinguished from ethical values. Whatever human beings do, believe or choose cannot alter the status of some undisputed elements in human nature. Furthermore, Williams also points out that since issues concerning human nature, for Aristotle, have to do primarily with scientific facts and not with human beings' doxastic states, they are not controversial in the way that ethical questions are, and hence provide us with fixed points, without which we would be carried to atrocity.

Nussbaum, however, rejects such a reading of Aristotle, pointing out that it goes against the very aim of Aristotle's approach:

> There is nothing anywhere in Aristotle's work precisely corresponding to a modern distinction between fact and value; and furthermore, science, as well as ethics, is 'internal' for Aristotle in the sense that it is the attempt to give an intelligent account of human experience of the world. Aristotle explicitly announces that his method in ethics is just the method he uses in all other areas: to preserve the greatest number and the most basic 'appearances' – human perceptions and beliefs – on the subject. (Nussbaum 1995c: 102)

In Nussbaum's view then, Aristotle is innocent of the modern 'fact/value dichotomy', and so is exempt from the reading that imposes on him the tendency to base ethical judgements on value-neutral scientific facts. The concept of human being, for him, is thoroughly an evaluative concept; the first nature and the second nature, the natural and the normative components of human beings are so intertwined with one another that it is impossible to pursue an inquiry about one without the other.

From the perspective of the capability approach a non-reductionist reading of Aristotle's naturalism is important for a deeper understanding of the nature and character of capabilities that are proposed to be important for public policy and state intervention. As Hilary Putnam (2002: 46ff.) points out, capabilities are not value-neutral concepts – and neither might an ethical approach that is centred on them be so. It works out that the number of 'valuable human functionings' and its related vocabularies such as 'well nourished', 'premature mortality', 'bodily integrity', 'self-respect' and 'being able to participate in a community life' that both Aristotle and Nussbaum speak of are 'thick ethical concepts', concepts that cannot be simply split up into an 'empirical part' and a 'normative part'. Just like ethical terms such as 'brave', 'temperate' and 'just', a number of capabilities found on Nussbaum and Anderson's list are 'thick' concepts in the sense that when one invokes them in public discourse and tries to justify them, one has to necessarily assume a certain evaluative point of view. This is further confirmed by the Human Development Reports (§3.1) which use the theoretical underpinnings of the capability approach to appraise and rank the performances of the countries in the world based on three capabilities of life expectancy, education and standard of living (Fukuda-Parr 2003). What is significant to note here is that even though the Human Development approach tries to use such fundamental empirical criteria as 'calories intake', 'years of schooling', 'freedom of the press' and 'cultural freedom to speak one's mother tongue and practice one's own religion' to measure people's well-being and their standing in society, it cannot but assume certain normative positions on the priorities to be assigned to different capabilities and to the different aspects within each of these capabilities.

Aristotle's Conception of Justice

Some preliminary observations might be helpful before commenting on the specific points of convergence and divergence between Aristotle's conception of justice and the capability approach. At the outset, Aristotle's conception of justice in many respects can be viewed as a critique of Plato's theory of justice, although Aristotle does not explicitly admit this in Book V of *Ethics*, where the treatment of the virtue of justice receives a detailed inquiry (Broadie 1991; Kraut 2002). In *Republic* (IV-V: 112ff.), Plato holds the view that justice is a relationship one has with oneself, a relation among the parts of the soul: reason rules, spirit acts as its ally and the appetite obeys. One can preserve the justice of one's soul only by remaining aloof from day-to-day social and political affairs and this can be achieved only by philosophers in an ideal society. Reflective of his hierarchical conception among different parts of the soul, Plato also envisages justice as the establishment of hierarchical order internal to society. This implies that in the just society everyone (farmers, merchants, soldiers, philosophers, etc) performs his own function. Aristotle criticizes Plato and develops a more complex conception of justice by distinguishing different types of justice. He, first and foremost, advocates the idea that justice requires an active participation in the matters of one's political community. Justice is not a relation of the parts of one's soul – as Plato conceives it to be – but rather a relationship among separate individuals in society. Justice requires that one does not harm others and that one has to treat them in accordance with the rules, customs, norms and laws of one's political community. Aristotle does envisage a sort of 'contemplative' life which might in certain circumstances require withdrawal from the affairs of the city, but nevertheless the image of the just person that Aristotle wants to project is not that of a philosopher king contemplating the eternal order of abstract objects. Instead, he is an expert on constitutional and legal matters, who knows how to reform political structures or prevent bad political systems degenerating into worse, and who is keen to use his proficiency and skill to promote the good of citizens. Aristotle's keenness to portray justice as being relational and being involved can also be seen in *Politics* (IV, 8: 235-238) where he emphasizes that a political theorist or philosopher must investigate not only the best possible city, but also cities of every possible variety, including those that have degenerated to the extent that they offer very little possibility for transformation. Thus, one of the ways to lead a worthwhile life is to promote justice in highly defective regimes, however small the effect might turn out to be.

As a further preliminary, it is important to be aware that in *Ethics*, Book V, Chapters 1-2, Aristotle advocates two notions of justice, one in a broad sense and the other in a narrow sense. In the broad sense, justice is equated with 'lawfulness': 'since the lawless person is ... unjust, and the law-abiding person just, it is obvious that all lawful things are in some sense just' (*Ethics* V, 1: 173). In the narrow sense, Aristotle characterizes justice as three types: (i) distributive justice (criterion to be followed for the distribution of goods), (ii) corrective justice (rectification for crime, transgression, etc), and (iii) commercial reciprocity (norms governing commercial activities such as buying, selling, lending, etc). Nevertheless, for Aristotle, these two conceptions are related because a person who is lawful in the broad sense would also search for the appropriate criteria in the distribution of goods, commercial activities and corrective justice, and adhere to them (Kraut 2002: 105ff.; Broadie 1991).

a) Justice as Lawfulness

Under the broad conception, by stating that justice consists in being lawful, Aristotle is not merely expressing the idea that 'respect for the law' is one of the components – although it might be an important one – of justice. Such an idea seems to have been already quite prevalent in the classical world prior to Aristotle. Plato for example, portrays Socrates as a person who has a great respect for the law, so much so that he would rather die than perform an unlawful deed. In contrast, Aristotle makes a more fundamental proposal by 'equating' justice with lawfulness: lawfulness is exactly what justice consists in.

One immediate and apparent objection to this proposal would be that there are such things as bad and unjust laws in which case lawfulness cannot provide the required standard of what amounts to justice. If the law happens to be bad and unjust, even if we obey the law, we might be doing what is unjust, since the law itself may be unjust. By similar reasoning, we might also say that when we disobey the law, our actions might still be just. Does Aristotle not take into account this possibility? Both in *Ethics* and *Politics*, there are a number of indications that Aristotle is indeed aware of this problem. As pointed out below, Aristotle refers to another kind of justice besides legal justice, one that is based on 'natural laws' and not dependent on human conventions or legislations in particular political communities (*Ethics* V, 7: 189-190). This implies that for Aristotle there is a standard of justice which can be used to discern whether or not the enactments of a ruler or legislature are just. Furthermore, in *Politics,* Aristotle laughs at the 'old' and 'uncivilized' laws of archaic societies (II, 8: 137-138) and points out that every defective regime has many unjust laws (III, 11: 206). Although he admires the education of Sparta, he criticizes the Spartan militarism, since a regimented life cannot be the whole of the good life. Aristotle therefore, is well aware that legislators can be wrong about what justice is and that laws can be unjust. If Aristotle was indeed aware of the possibility of unjust laws, how can he still equate lawfulness with justice? The following elements may provide the key to understanding Aristotle's conception of justice as lawfulness.

i) 'Nomos' is what the people as a whole regard as a valid and binding norm
First and foremost, we should take note of the fact that the Greek word 'nomos' that is translated as 'law' covers not only the enactments of a lawgiver or legislature, but also the customs, norms, and unwritten rules of a community. Furthermore, the noun '*nomos*' is related to the verb '*nemein*', of which one sense is 'to believe'. This implies that whatever conduct a community believes to be appropriate constitutes the *nomoi* (plural of *nomos*) of that community. There would be no such thing as *nomoi* in which no one believes. In other words, for a *nomos* to exist is to be recognized, acknowledged and observed by a group of people. As Aristotle in *On Rhetoric* points out, even though there are certain 'unwritten laws' that scem to be accepted in all communities, a *nomos* requires that it be accepted by *one* community and not by all: 'Law is either specific [*idion*] or common [*koinon*]. I call specific the written law

under which people live in a polis and common whatever, though unwritten, seems to be agreed to among all' (I, 10: 88). So, when Aristotle under the broad conception of justice says that a just person is a lawful person (*nomimos*), he is ascribing a certain relationship between the person concerned and the laws, norms and customs generally accepted by the community. Thus justice has to do not only with the written enactments of a community's legislators, but with the wider set of norms that govern the members of that community. In a similar line of thinking, we can also point out that an unjust person is one who not merely violates the written code of laws, but one who trespasses the rules accepted by the community in which he lives.

ii) Laws should be distinguished from 'decrees'
In *Ethics* (V, 10: 199), Aristotle makes a distinction between *nomoi* (laws) and *psephismata*, which could be translated as 'decrees' (MacDowell 1978: 43ff.; Kraut 2002: 105ff.). The latter refer to legal enactments directed specifically to present circumstances, and set no precedents that would apply to similar cases in the future. The former, by contrast, are meant to have a general character and scope, since they apply not only to cases at hand, but also to a general category of cases that are likely to occur in the future. If the legislature awards citizenship or a particular honour to one person on account of some distinguished services to the city, it has then passed a decree because it does not commit itself to any general principle. On the other hand, if it comes to a conclusion that the child of a citizen is himself a citizen, then it has adopted a law, since the general scope of that norm makes a commitment to a definite way of proceeding in future cases.

Aristotle's distinction between the law and a decree and his insistence on the necessity of laws for the ideal polis are clarified in the context of his analysis of different types of regimes (*Politics* IV, 4: 250; IV, 6: 256). Aristotle points out that it is characteristic of tyrannical regimes to rule by a series of 'decrees' rather than by a stable system of law and he compares the worst forms of oligarchy and democracy to tyrannies. In all deviant forms of governance such as tyranny by a dictator, democracy by demagogues, and oligarchy by the wealthy elite, the rulers do not provide the city with a general and stable legal structure. In these systems, it is individuals who rule who have authority and not the law. Such rulers show concern neither for consistency over time nor for commitment to long-term principles.

iii) A just person is not merely a passive follower of rules
According to Aristotle, in order to be a just person, it is not enough to know the norms of one's community and abide by them. He finds this to be an easy task for any adult to accomplish. What is however difficult to achieve is any real virtue that requires practical wisdom (*phronesis*). In this sense, for Aristotle, the virtue of lawfulness is not a mere matter of being law-abiding.[5] Instead, it also consists in actively being involved in things such as distributive justice, corrective justice and commercial exchange. A lawful person will be one who is skilful in distributing

---

5   In order to reflect the active sense of being lawful, Irwin's translation of *nomimos* as 'lawful' seems more suitable than Thomson's translation as 'law-abiding' in the passage (*Ethics* V, 1: 173) we have quoted above.

goods and resolving disputes. He strives to play an active role by contributing to decisions in matters of distributive issues and juridical questions in the city. Thus, a fully just person in Aristotle's thinking, is not merely a passive follower of laws, but is also an active maker and arbitrator of the law.

Furthermore, Aristotle also envisages laws to be connected to and supported by a 'science of legislation' (*nomothetike*) – a study that prescribes a system of laws and legislation on the basis of a proper understanding of human well-being and political institutions. Laws, by their nature, are universal and broad in scope: they are generalizations and for that reason they are valuable. Yet this advantage comes at a price, because it is impossible for legislators to foresee all complications and exceptions that might become relevant in particular instances, although some legislators are more capable than others in anticipating the future so that the laws they enact are less in need of revision or supplementation. In these instances, a judge will exercise his 'fairness' to correct those deficiencies of the laws that result from their over-generality. The correction undertaken by the judge is not an expression of contempt for those who made the law, but instead it is based on the reasoning that the legislators themselves *would* have intended if they had encountered such circumstances. The virtue of lawfulness, consequently, does not require casting a blind eye to the deficiencies of the law, and mechanically abiding by it. One requires considerable attention to discern what lawfulness calls for in particular circumstances. Ironically, lawfulness might sometimes even require 'violating' the law.

The above characteristics offer a wider perspective for understanding why Aristotle thinks that justice under the broader conception can be defined as lawfulness. His definition incorporates the idea that every community requires the stability that comes through a body of established norms and customs, rules and laws which are not changed unpredictably and frivolously. His definition also points out that the legislators in determining what is lawful are not only looking at the existing laws, but are also exercising the virtue of justice as lawfulness.

b) Criteria for Distributive Justice

Along with the broad conception of justice that leads Aristotle to identify justice with lawfulness, he uses an accompanying idea of justice in the specific sense of relating to distributive justice, corrective justice and commercial reciprocity. Under this specific sense, Aristotle is particularly concerned about identifying the appropriate norms, criteria and guidelines that would govern the just distribution of various goods among citizens. The following considerations suggested by Aristotle become points of reference for the capability approach, even though Nussbaum's hybrid view tries to purify and relativize Aristotle's elitist and illiberal properties.

i) Arithmetic and proportionate equality
Aristotle does not recommend one uniform criterion of justice when it comes to corrective justice *vis-à-vis* distributive justice. In the case of corrective justice which is concerned with the rectification of wrongs done either in transactions that are voluntary among all parties (sales, promises, loans, etc) or in exchanges in which one party has participated involuntarily (theft, poisoning, adultery, assault, etc),

Aristotle suggests that the most appropriate criterion to follow is *arithmetic* equality (*Ethics* V, 4: 179ff.). When a court for example, faces the question whether one person has stolen from another, and if so, what the relevant punishment should be, it does not take into consideration how the complainant and the defendant should be compared in terms of merit. The law treats the two parties as 'arithmetically' equal, and examines only whether the defendant has done the wrong he has been accused of. As Aristotle puts it: 'For it makes no difference whether a good man has defrauded a bad one or vice versa ... all that the law considers is the difference caused by the injury; and it treats the parties as equals, only asking whether one has committed and the other suffered an injustice, or whether one has inflicted and the other suffered a hurt' (*Ethics* V, 4: 180). In the case of distributive justice, by contrast, Aristotle proposes that the most appropriate criterion will be not arithmetic but *proportionate* or *geometrical* equality. Therefore, Aristotle points out that the question that has to be faced in the realm of distributive justice is: how do the potential recipients of various goods compare with each other? (*Ethics* V, 5: 182-184). According to Aristotle, the generally accepted criterion of distribution of goods, particularly the goods of public offices, and positions of power and honour, is merit (*axia*) and hence, a just distribution is one based on merit (*kat'axian*).

At this point, Nussbaum raises the question as to whether Aristotle, besides the criterion of merit, considers also some other criteria such as 'needs', 'individual capability variations' and 'equality of opportunity' as relevant for distributive justice. In *Ethics*, Book V, although Aristotle thinks merit would be the right criterion for distributive justice especially when it comes to the distribution of political offices and honours, he leaves open the question of how exactly 'merit' should be understood. He is also aware of the fact that different people understand merit differently: the democrats in terms of 'free birth', the oligarchs in terms of 'wealth' and the aristocrats in terms of 'excellence' (*Ethics* V, 3: 178). Moreover, Aristotle sometimes sets aside the criterion of merit when especially it is a matter of considering people's needs and potential talents relative to their capability variations. As pointed out in the beginning of this chapter, we can recall here the examples of the wrestler and the pregnant women. Aristotle in these cases insists that it is the responsibility of the legislators to take care of the additional needs of these people. As a further example (*Politics* III, 12: 207-208), in the analogy of finding out who should receive the best flutes, Aristotle sets aside the criterion of beauty or inferior birth as relevant for this judgement. The best flutes should go not to those of noble birth or who are beautiful but to those who can perform better. Nussbaum wishes to exploit this openness in Aristotle:

> The Aristotelian recognizes wide individual variation in the functional role of the instrumental goods. In Aristotle's famous example, the right amount of food for Milo the wrestler, given his activity level, size, and occupation, is an amount that would be too much for most people. On the other hand, Milo would be very badly off, from the view point of functioning, if he had an amount of food that is just right for a small sedentary philosopher. Again, as Aristotle prominently recognizes, the needs of pregnant women for food and other goods associated with health are very different from a nonpregnant woman. (Nussbaum 1990b: 211)

Nussbaum extends Aristotle's examples to contemporary scenarios:

> We might add that ... a person with mobility problems, or a missing limb, will require a much larger subvention in order to be mobile than will a person with no such deficiency. If we look further into social context, still more variety appears. Children from minority groups need more money spent on them: we can see this by looking at what they are able to do and to be. All this is one more reason why the Aristotelian wishes to make the central question not, 'How much do they have?', but rather, 'What are they able to do and to be?' And she wishes to say that government has not done its job if it has not made each and every one of them capable of functioning well – even if it has not given them many things. (Nussbaum 1990b: 211)

My intention in citing these passages is to show how Nussbaum reconstructs Aristotle's understanding of 'proportionate equality' for a capabilities-oriented understanding of justice. Aristotle rightly recognizes that in matters concerning the distribution of goods relevant for a valuable human life we should be guided by proportionate rather than arithmetic equality. However, he was inclined to understand this largely in terms of merit with an elitist bias. Nussbaum's contribution in this regard is to illustrate that along with merit we must also take into consideration other principles such as needs, fairness and equality of opportunity for developing one's potential talents.[6]

ii) Against the vice of 'pleonexia'
One fundamental intuition that stands out in Aristotle's conception of distributive justice is the *instrumental* nature of material goods. Wealth, income and possessions are not valuable in themselves, however much people might be obsessed with gathering or amassing them. They are merely means of achieving different doings and beings in human lives. This implies that in order to answer any of the relevant questions concerning the distribution of these goods – e.g. how much to give, to whom, under what conditions, etc – we should first and foremost look at the ways they promote or prevent different human functionings. In fact, Aristotle believes that a failure to recognize this priority of 'human functionings' over 'material goods' can lead to an excessive obsession with wealth, distracting citizens from valuable things such as social interaction, friendship, knowledge, arts and virtue.

Moreover, as pointed out earlier, justice, in the Aristotelian paradigm, is basically a relational virtue. Hence, Aristotle (*Ethics* V, 1: 171ff.; Kraut 2002: 136ff.) directs his criticism towards *pleonexia*, which literally means 'desiring to have more than one's due share'. Accordingly, he defines the unjust person as *pleonektes,* meaning

---

6   In this regard, Nussbaum points out two kinds of approaches to political thinking in the ancient world. The first one insists that the main problem for human happiness is bad thinking and feeling. Hence, it recommends that human beings can be made to flourish by learning to think differently, without really paying attention to any material and institutional changes. The second one, advocated by Aristotle, admits that human flourishing requires appropriate material and institutional conditions. Nussbaum therefore highlights Aristotle's deep and urgent interests in questions such as hunger and scarcity, property and its distribution, the funding for common meals, and population control and its relation to scarcity. See Nussbaum (1988a: 171-172).

a 'grasping' or 'greedy' individual. He also points out that *pleonexia* can express itself in the excessive desire to increase one's share of goods such as money, wealth, honour and so on. When someone is avaricious for wealth that is more than his due share, he turns out to be an unjust person. Similarly, someone claiming honour which he does not deserve is greedy for honour. The gain or profit that is sought after in this injustice is not material wealth, but the good opinion of others. What makes *pleonexia* a distinctive vice and an act of injustice is that it involves a desire to have more at the expense of others. The unjust person does not merely want to have a greater amount of goods such as money, wealth or honour, but he is also not displeased that others will be harmed or deprived of their goods on account of his greed. In fact, such a person takes pleasure in his gains and part of what pleases him is his profiting at the expense of others. It is this interpersonal and communal dimension of injustice – desiring to have more at the expense of others – that makes *pleonexia* into a part of injustice in the broader sense of being unlawful. When someone exercises the vice of *pleonexia*, he does this by violating a law or principle that is generally observed in the community or *could* be observed in an ideal political community. He regards such rules as unnecessary restrictions on his behaviour and disregards those fellow citizens who in fact follow the law. His injustice, in other words, expresses contempt for the law and those who respect the law. For capability theorists such as Nussbaum the basic intuition of Aristotle about the instrumental nature of material goods serves as a platform to criticize those theories of justice that try to assess people's well-being either fully or partly on the basis of income and material goods. Income and wealth are no doubt useful in achieving valuable human functionings, but they are only the means to worthwhile activities and goals in life. When it concerns the issue of restraining people's myopic behaviour and promoting the virtue of justice, the capability theorists distance themselves from the type of perfectionist state that Aristotle wishes to realize (§3.2). Nonetheless, the capability theorists also think that having the right type of economic and political institutions in place would be very supportive of just behaviour among citizens.

6.3 Compassion as a Social Emotion

Most contemporary liberal theories have been rather careful to avoid talking about compassion and other related emotions as having a role in understanding the demands of justice. These theories hold the view that what we owe to each other in the name of justice is one thing, and what we, like the Good Samaritan, might be motivated to do for others by compassion or pity is totally another. Arguments from the standpoint of justice should be differentiated from obligations of humanitarianism, altruism or compassion. It is best that we do not mix these different intuitions.

Yet Nussbaum's hybrid theory of capabilities endorses the idea that although we do not have to mix up justice with compassion, the latter can be made to play a crucial 'public' role in informing and shaping the reasoning and judgements of individuals and political communities in recognizing the obligations of justice. Compassion provides the required link between the individual and the community, and hence, can be thought of as our species' way of hooking the interests of others to our own personal goods' (Nussbaum 1996: 28). While many contemporary moral and political theories dismiss compassion as an irrational force in human affairs, one that has no use, or is likely to mislead or distract us when we try to think about the nature and scope of just social institutions and policies, Nussbaum thinks of it as an emotion entailing a complex 'cognitive structure' and 'reasoning', and therefore having normative influence in public life.[7] As she puts it: 'Compassion is not the entirety of justice; but it both contains a powerful, if partial, vision of just distribution and provides imperfect citizens with an essential bridge from self-interest to just conduct' (Nussbaum 1996: 57).

a) Nussbaum and Aristotle on Compassion

In trying to enunciate the content of compassion, Nussbaum basically adopts the analysis of pity followed by Aristotle in *On Rhetoric.*[8] Aristotle defines pity as follows:

> Let pity be [defined as] a certain pain at an apparently destructive or painful evil happening to one who does not deserve it and which a person might expect himself or one of his own to suffer, and this when it seems close at hand; for it is clear that a person who is going to feel pity necessarily thinks that some evil is actually present of the sort that he or one of his own might suffer and that this evil is of the sort mentioned in the definition or like it or about equal to it. (*On Rhetoric* II, 8: 152)

---

7   Similar to Nussbaum, Hume has suggested that the 'passions' are closely connected with the realm of morality, giving us clues and indications as to how we ought to conduct ourselves. Consider for instance, how Hume understands sympathy (Hume 2000: 179ff.). For him, sympathy is a general capacity of humans to know and to experience as their own the sentiments or opinions of others; it is a principle of 'communication' (Hume 2000: 273) and that which not only 'corresponds' to the operations of human understanding, but also 'transcends' them. In this connection, Hume says: 'Sympathy is exactly correspondent to the operations of our understanding; and contains something more surprising and extraordinary' (Hume 2000: 208). Here, Hume on the one hand seems to emphasize the idea that sympathy is 'correspondent' to understanding in the sense that sympathy makes use of the same associative principles such as resemblance, contiguity, and cause and effect that are involved in understanding. On the other hand, Hume is also keen to point out that sympathy has something 'more' than understanding in the sense that sympathy has the capacity to 'transform' ideas into lively and dynamic impressions. Despite this similarity between Nussbaum and Hume with regard to sympathy and compassion, there are important differences between their approaches. For details on how Hume too can be seen as an inspiration for a non-reductionist reading of human capabilities and how Nussbaum's position can be situated as a mid-way between Aristotle and Hume see Alexander (2005a); De Dijn (2003).

8   A note about the use of terminology: when I use the terms 'compassion' and 'pity' I am speaking about the same emotion. I shall use the term 'pity' when particularly analysing Aristotle's definition, because that is the term that is normally used in English to translate Greek *eleos*. However, since the Victorian era the term 'pity' has acquired the tone of condescension and superiority to the sufferer that it did not have formerly. Hence, it seems more appropriate to use the term 'compassion', which is closer to the German expression 'mitleid' (or 'medelijden' in Dutch).

Following Aristotle's definition, Nussbaum identifies three characteristics to be essential for compassion. First, compassion arises in the context of 'serious' matters, matters that obstruct, jeopardize or destroy a person's life and well-being severely or in a serious way. As pointed out in the above definition, Aristotle calls it a 'destructive or painful' evil in someone's life. The occasions that Aristotle thinks would evoke compassion on the part of observers are the following: death, torments, disease, old age, lack of food, lack of friends, separation from friends, ugliness, weakness, mutilation and serious reversals from sources thought to be good (*On Rhetoric* II, 8: 153). These kinds of events do indicate that people are not normally moved to compassion by matters of a trivial nature. For example, the loss of a shoe lace or a coat button or even a valuable thing that can eventually be replaced would not be appropriate matters for compassion. In other words, internal to the emotional response of compassion is the judgement that what is at issue is indeed serious, involving life and death, livelihood and well-being.

Second, compassion arises in the instances of 'undeserved' misfortune. When a person suffers on account of his or her neglect or fault, we tend to reproach or blame rather than expressing sentiments of compassion. On the other hand, we tend to sympathize when we find the person to be without blame for the loss or impediment, and even when there is some fault, if the suffering turns out to be out of proportion to the fault in question. Expressions of compassion on such occasions are motivated and supported by a particular worldview, namely that there are indeed serious things that may happen to people through no fault of their own and that things near and dear to one's life and well-being are not always safely under a person's own control, but can be turned topsy-turvy by misfortune.

Third, compassion is a judgement of 'similar possibilities'. As Aristotle in the above cited definition reminds us, it concerns those misfortunes 'which a person might expect himself or one of his own to suffer' (*On Rhetoric* II, 8: 152). He also adds that it will be felt only by those with some experience and understanding of suffering; and one would not have compassion if one thinks that one is above suffering and has everything (II, 8: 152-53).[9] This implies that, for Aristotle, compassion requires the acknowledgement that one has possibilities and vulnerabilities similar to the sufferer. One makes sense of the suffering by recognizing that one might oneself encounter such situations and one tries to estimate its significance by thinking what it would mean to face that oneself. Nussbaum, however, does not want to narrow down compassion only to a judgement of 'similar possibilities' as Aristotle portrays

---

9   This aspect of compassion is very much emphasized in Rousseau's *Emile*. Rousseau, like Aristotle, points out that an awareness of one's own weakness and vulnerability is a required quality for compassion (*pitié*). He writes: 'Why are kings without pity for their subjects? Because they count on never being human beings. Why are the rich so hard toward the poor? It is because they have no fear of being poor. Why does a noble have such contempt for a peasant? It is because he never will be peasant ... Do not, therefore, accustom your pupil to regard the sufferings of the unfortunate and the labours of the poor from the height of his glory; and do not hope to teach him to pity them if he considers them alien to him. Make him understand well that the fate of these unhappy people can be his, that all their ills are there in the ground beneath his feet, that countless unforeseen and inevitable events can plunge him into them from one moment to the next' (quoted in Nussbaum 2001a: 315-316).

it. It turns out that even when we can reasonably be sure that we ourselves will not go through similar weakness and vulnerabilities, we can still make the well-being of the sufferer as part of our own. Hence, Nussbaum characterizes compassion as a 'eudaimonistic' judgement implying that the person must consider the suffering of another as a 'significant part of his or her own scheme of goals and ends' and as 'affecting her own flourishing' (Nussbaum 2001a: 319).

Since Nussbaum envisages compassion to positively inform and influence individuals and communities in understanding the obligations they may have in the name of justice, she refers to some of the following roles that this emotion can play in public life (Nussbaum 2001a: 401ff.).

i) Moral and civic education which cultivates compassion and humanity should be supported

When we believe the capacity to imagine the misfortune and sufferings of others to be an important part of our personal and social life, we find ways and means of cultivating and expanding the sentiments of compassion. Although much of this would and should be done in families, and by far parents and families ought to shoulder this responsibility, every society would have to complement this by teaching its members ideals of civic judgement, duties and citizenship. One crucial step in fulfilment of this aspiration would be public education of the young – although not only the young – so as to cultivate their ability to imagine the experience of others and participate in their struggles, hardships and sufferings. This is likely to create the possibility of rising above 'ethnocentrism' and of recognizing and respecting fellow citizens no matter what class, gender, group, clan, or race they belong to. Motivated by this, Nussbaum is led to suggest a larger place in education for Humanities and Arts especially because they have the potentiality to enlarge the moral imagination of future citizens.

ii) Compassionate imagination should inform and shape economic thought in the direction of enhancing human capabilities

A basic contribution of the capability approach to economic thought and the measurement of human well-being in particular has been to highlight the inadequacies of traditional well-being indicators such as income or wealth. As illustrated in Chapter 3, an increase in the level of GDP per capita does not necessarily mean improvement in the quality of life. Against such traditional economic approaches, the capability approach has always been insisting on investigating people's quality of life in terms of capability indicators such as infant mortality, access to health care, life expectancy, the quality of education, the actual possibilities for political participation and the situation of gender relations. Nussbaum notes that, although it is appropriate to think of requirements of justice in terms of basic capabilities, a thought experiment in compassion can lead us towards it.

iii) We require both compassionate individuals and institutions

Nussbaum argues that political leaders, lawyers and judges, besides their expertise in their respective fields, should be persons who show the ability for compassion. Because political leaders and public officials have the responsibility to deliberate and take pertinent decisions that affect the lives and well-being of people whom they are asked to represent, they ought to possess the willingness to understand the plights and situations of people. The capacity for compassion that is expected from political leaders and public officials however should not be envisaged as something opposed to the role of neutrality and non-partisanship that is often required of them, but rather as something that will aid in performing their public tasks more effectively. Furthermore, Nussbaum also realizes that some matters of compassion are so pertinent that we cannot rely only on the goodwill of individual leaders and officials. We need to design and keep in place structures of public institutions such as a just welfare system and a system of taxation to support it. Institutions and individuals often reinforce each other. When compassion, to a certain extent, can be made to embody public institutions, it influences the behaviour of individuals.

b) *Justice versus Compassion*

In endorsing Aristotle's analysis of compassion and referring to it as a basic 'social' virtue, Nussbaum implicitly takes the virtue of compassion beyond personal morality and into the realm of the 'social' and even 'political' – thus claiming that compassion is intrinsic to, or at least instrumental to justice rather than distinct from it. Similar to Aristotle's, Nussbaum's analysis of compassion includes laying out specific ways in which the emotion can and should play a 'public' role in moral and civic education, economic planning and policies, political leadership and public institutions. Nussbaum's concrete proposals and political applications regarding the virtue of compassion can be criticized for reasons of perfectionism, a trait that is reminiscent of Aristotle's concern for the virtuous life of citizens in the polis. People come together in a specific entity called the polis not only to meet their commonplace needs for food, health, security and social intercourse, but also for living a virtuous life including a life of compassion towards their fellow citizens. Nussbaum might address such an objection by saying that some 'minimal' and 'acceptable' forms of perfectionism might be required and might even be necessary for sustaining society's major social and political institutions.

On a more fundamental level one can also object to Nussbaum's Aristotelian project for failing to adequately embody the distinctive character of justice on the one hand and compassion on the other. Her idea that we can envisage justice and compassion as related virtues, and deploy compassion in order to know and understand claims of justice runs the risk of conflating 'politics of pity' with 'politics of justice' (Boltanski 1999: 3ff.; Ricoeur 1996). One distinctive characteristic of justice is the notion of reciprocity. We can meaningfully talk about justice and the obligations implied thereof only when there are certain forms of interaction and reciprocity between parties involved. Traditionally, such reciprocity has been understood in 'political' terms in the sense that questions of justice arise between people who are subject to the same coercive sovereign authority or between citizens who are subject to a common set of coercively imposed laws and institutions (Nagel 2005). In modern times, particularly after Rawls's influential justice as fairness theory (§2.3), reciprocity has also been understood more broadly to include 'economic' interactions and interdependence. Consequently, obligations of justice would arise not only because the concerned parties are under common political institutions, but also because they are more generally engaged in 'cooperative ventures' for mutual advantage. In contrast to this, compassion or pity arises in the context of non-reciprocity. In fact, the vulnerability and weakness of the sufferer or victim makes it inappropriate to invoke any form of reciprocity. Of course, when displaying compassionate feelings or translating them into action, one can do it keeping in mind the dignity and agency of the sufferer. But even then it is not the same type of reciprocity that would be required for justice. Neither the people with capability shortfalls themselves nor a capability theorist who argues in their favour would be cheered that their grievances are addressed on grounds of compassion alone. Hence, if and when the issues are raised as demands of justice, some kind of reciprocity should be involved in order to obtain a wider moral and political endorsement, although the kind of reciprocity envisaged need not be direct, immediate and purely economic.

Connected with reciprocity is the idea of justification. A politics of justice invariable requires justification in the sense of giving reasons for a particular course of action one pursues. Justifying one's action with reasons that other reasonable people could recognize and endorse is a necessary condition for justice. A politics of pity however, starts off from the premise that the situation at hand is an evident case for compassion. We do not normally pose questions of justification to a victim of misfortune as we might do to a claimant of justice. In fact, we would find it indecent to raise these questions when confronted with incredible displays of suffering. In matters of compassion, the urgency of the action to be taken prevails over considerations of justification.

Furthermore, justice invariably invokes the idea of desert (Baker 1987: 53ff.; Miller, D. 2001: 131ff.). An act or gesture may be said to be unjust only if it can be shown that the person concerned has been denied what he deserves. There would be of course different criteria of desert, depending on the types of goods distributed. For example, the criterion of desert is different for academic positions, political offices and athletic honours. Nonetheless, demands of justice involve some form of desert judgement. Compassion in contrast works not on the basis of desert, but rather on the idea of 'luck'. Instances of (bad) luck can make the life and well-being of some people exposed and vulnerable. Thus, while compassion focuses on the opposition between the fortunate and unfortunate, justice concentrates on the distinction between the deserving and the undeserving. Recognizing this distinction requires on the part of the capability theorists further thinking as to what sort of specific principles and patterns of distribution are required in realizing basic capabilities for all.

6.4 A Public Conception?

The capability theorists have often pointed out that the intellectual structure and the philosophical linkages for a capabilities-oriented theory of justice need to be sought in Aristotle. Nussbaum deserves the recognition for having made very significant contributions along these lines, particularly by elucidating the connections between Aristotle and the capability approach. First and foremost, she has shown that an ongoing inquiry into the nature of 'valuable human functionings' and a search for the appropriate political forms and social arrangements which would be congenial to citizens' capabilities were central to Aristotle's ethics and political philosophy. Prompted by this fundamental Aristotelian principle, Nussbaum has always insisted that people's benefits and standing in society should be evaluated on the basis of a list of (ten) basic capabilities.

Furthermore, Nussbaum has contributed in a major way by developing a hybrid theory of capabilities by reinterpreting and revising Aristotle's doctrines so as to align them with liberal sensibility about the worth of each and every individual. Hence she corrects Aristotle's elitist reading of what 'proportionate' equality and the 'human-function' argument imply for a political conception. Quite convincingly she argues that a political conception centred on capabilities should focus on appropriate basic economic, social and political structures that would promote capabilities not merely of citizens who are already better off in terms of noble birth, social position and qualification, but of everyone in the political community. Finally, Nussbaum's hybrid view also envisages compassion as a social emotion, demonstrating how compassion can play a crucial public role in discerning the basic capabilities that citizens are obligated to provide one another as a matter of justice.

Despite these valuable contributions, what seems to receive a less forceful attention and articulation in Nussbaum's hybrid view is the idea that the capability approach is primarily a 'public' conception of justice that could be recognized and endorsed by reasonable citizens for political purposes (Ackerly 2000; Pogge 2002b; Jaggar 2006). The lack of emphasis as to the public character of the approach may partly originate from the fact of having to come up with a predetermined list of basic capabilities, even when one might claim such a list to be open-ended and ecumenical. It is true that Nussbaum (2000a: 69, 76) often alerts both the critics and fellow capability theorists that the list is not evolved on the basis of being 'dictatorial about the good', but instead on the basis of years of 'cross-cultural discussions' and the 'input of other voices'. Also, the later Nussbaum (2000a; 2000b) no longer refers to the earlier metaphor of 'the thick vague conception' of the good (1990b) that is to provide inspiration for drawing up the list of basic capabilities, but claims to make use of the 'overlapping consensus' in the Rawlsian sense. Yet the public character of the capability approach will be more forcefully expressed when it is bound up with the idea of public reasoning and reinforced by the laws of the political community rather than just producing a list of valuable items which may lack the required legitimacy. A clue might in some sense be found in Aristotle himself, although he considered this to be the privilege of a few wise legislators and the prerogative of the science of legislation.

Chapter 7

Which Freedom? What Sort of Public Reasoning?

A complete political morality must include a doctrine of justice. But any plausible view of justice rests on principles and doctrines which are neither uniquely liberal nor derivable from specifically liberal principles. The specific contribution of the liberal tradition to political morality has always been its insistence on the respect due to individual liberty. To the extent that liberal theories of justice present a distinctive conception of justice, this is due to the way their principles of political freedom feed into and shape their conception of justice.

Joseph Raz, The Morality of Freedom

Everyone who wanted to speak did so. It was democracy in its purest form. There may have been a hierarchy of importance among the speakers, but everyone was heard, chief and subject, warrior and medicine man, shopkeeper and farmer, landowner and labourer. People spoke without interruption and the meetings lasted for many hours. The foundation of self-government was that all men were free to voice their opinions and equal in their value as citizens ... Majority rule was a foreign notion. A minority was not to be crushed by a majority.

Nelson Mandela, Long Walk to Freedom

7.1 Some Unanswered Questions

Before laying out the final argument, it is good to briefly take stock of what we have been doing until now and look at the remaining issues from that angle. While the first three chapters situated the capability approach and assessed its contributions with respect to utilitarianism and Rawls's theory, the next three expounded and examined the principles and philosophical foundations for a plausible capabilities-focused vision of a just society – particularly when such a vision can be construed as aiming at the greatest possible condition for the realization of basic capabilities for all. As it has emerged at different points of the discussion so far, both in their critique of other dominant theories of justice and in developing their own versions of the capability approach, the capability theorists appeal to and attach great importance to democracy and the related idea of public reasoning. This is so very true especially of Sen who in comparison to others is keen on elevating the capability approach as a public conception. For instance, it can be recollected that in order to resolve the issue of selection of the relevant capabilities for policy priorities, Sen alludes to democracy: every society through public discussion and democratic deliberation might decide on the list of basic capabilities and on the threshold of each of these capabilities. Unlike Nussbaum or Anderson, Sen does not think that the reach and relevance of the capability approach will be minimized or make less forceful by not embracing a predetermined universal list of capabilities. Also, on the issue of which capability shortfalls of individuals have a claim on justice and social responsibility and to what extent the warranted compensation should be done without at the same time undermining agency and personal responsibility, Sen again, recommends that these are matters for public judgement and social ethos.

For some familiar reasons Sen's unwavering faith in the potential of public reasoning and of a robust and well-functioning democratic government to promote citizens' capabilities comes as less of a surprise. In the context of his study of the causes of famines (§3.1), Sen highlighted the fact that the practice of democracy and public discussion plays a crucial role in avoiding famines and other societal failures, and more constructively in the identification and realization of even people's most basic 'entitlements' or 'capabilities' of nutrition, health and education. In addition, Sen (1999c) has argued democracy to be a 'universal value' that people everywhere may have reason to see as significant. However, going beyond these rather abstract and general appreciations of democracy, when we press further on to the question of the relationship between capabilities and democracy, Sen seems to leave a number of conceptual and philosophical issues unexplored and unscrutinized. Instead of just saying that democracy rather than despotism would be more congenial to the promotion of people's capabilities, should we not more specifically explore what form of democracy might be more suitable to promote a free and equal society? Instead of just saying capabilities are notions of positive freedom, should we not further explore the possibility of how capabilities and positive freedom might help us rethink and accordingly reshape our democracies to preserve or create as genuinely free a society as possible?

As pointed out in Chapter 2, in contemporary political philosophy, liberal democracy particularly the variety advocated by Rawls has apparently gained an impressive ascendancy, often presenting itself as the only legitimate base for representing freedom and equality. Voices of discontent against liberalism and liberal democracy have no doubt been coming forth from different quarters: a 'communitarian' discontent that the liberal stress on individual freedoms and rights encourages egotism, and refuses to acknowledge communal embeddedness and political participation (Sandel 1982; Taylor 1985a; §2.1); a 'leftist' discontent that the liberal priority on 'political' equalities overlooks or even aggravates substantial economic and social inequalities (Gray 1989; Baker 1987: 41ff.); a 'feminist' discontent that the liberal separation of public and private spheres leaves many gender-related discrimination and inequalities unaddressed (Nussbaum 2000a; Kittay 2003; Okin 1989); and a 'cultural' discontent that the liberal insistence on neutrality underestimates the values of identity and recognition in a multicultural political community (Phillips 1994; Fraser 1997; Baker et al. 2004). Important as they are as critics of a liberal mode of theorizing about social justice, until now, hardly any of these voices of discontent have developed to the stature of providing a fully-fledged alternative approach to social justice. Can we say that the capability approach is just another voice of discontent against liberal democracy?

On account of certain characteristics and convictions, the capability app
can quite comfortably be fitted into the liberal landscape. It embraces both the .
moral worth of each and every individual and the priority of human rights that
are by now considered to be foundational pillars of every liberal democracy. Yet
because of other features and principles the capability approach also breaks with the
liberal conception of justice. In the realm of public morality, as it has been argued
thus far, the capability approach involves broad consequentialism and a reciprocal
view of responsibility. Moreover, owing to the fact that the capability approach is
embedded among the good-based theories it starts off from an inquiry into the plural
components of the good life and does not have to rely on the idea of social contract
that is so crucial to most liberal theories for deriving and justifying claims of justice.
To take this differentiating argument a step further, it can now be illustrated how
the capability approach entails a notion of positive freedom (§7.2) – in the sense of
what people are *actually* able to do and be, and advocates certain basic capabilities
as a substantive content that can inform and shape democracy and public reasoning
(§7.3). Nevertheless, it will also be suggested that in order to develop the capability
approach as a more radical ideal of social justice, its theoretical framework needs to
be extended in order to incorporate the republican idea of freedom as non-domination
(§7.4). Capabilities are necessary but not sufficient for overcoming conditions of
domination. Conditions of domination can be effectively overcome only when
people possess the required capabilities and when these capabilities are reinforced
by constitutional provisions so that the possession and exercise of these capabilities
do not arbitrarily depend on the favour and the good will of others.

7.2 Capabilities as Positive Freedom

Sen (1987b; 1988b) distinguishes 'positive' freedom from 'negative' freedom, and
claims that capabilities are the best candidates to represent the notion of positive
freedom. He also claims that the fundamental aim of the capability approach is not
merely to guarantee freedom in the negative sense, but rather to promote freedom in
the positive sense.

> There are two ways of viewing freedom each of which has been fairly extensively
> explored over a long time. One approach sees freedom in 'positive' terms, concentrating
> on *what a person can choose to do or achieve* [capabilities], rather than on the absence of
> any particular type of restraint that prevents him or her from doing one thing or another.
> In contrast, the 'negative' view of freedom focuses precisely on the *absence of a class of
> restraints* that one person may exercise over another, or indeed the state may exercise over
> individuals. This contrast, which has been discussed particularly by Isaiah Berlin is quite
> important since the two ways of characterizing freedom may yield different results. (Sen
> 1988b: 272, my emphases)

Sen's proposed linkage between capabilities and positive freedom, and his
invocation of Berlin to buttress this linkage might not be as evident and straightforward
as Sen assumes it to be. In fact, if we do not explicate Sen's association of capabilities
with positive freedom, it could lead to some misleading conclusions. It would

therefore be helpful first to inquire into what Berlin meant by positive freedom, and consequently, try to suggest in what way Sen's identification of capabilities with positive freedom can be understood.

In the classic essay *Two Concepts of Liberty* (1969), Berlin made a distinction between two concepts of freedom, negative and positive. Under the negative concept, he points out that freedom requires the absence of interference by others: 'I am normally said to be free to the degree to which no man or body of men interferes with my activity. Political liberty in this sense is simply the area within which a man can act unobstructed by others' (Berlin 1969: 122). So, according to Berlin, the negative conception of freedom refers to the absence of interference by others – the state or fellow citizens. That the negative conception of freedom *is* about the absence of interference becomes clear when we look at the question involved: 'What is the area within which the subject – a person or group of persons – is or should be left to do or be what he is able to do or be, without interference by other persons?' (Berlin 1969: 121-122). As Taylor (1985b: 213) has explained, Berlin's negative conception of freedom is an opportunity concept in the sense that absence of interference by the state or fellow citizens makes it possible or creates an 'area' for the individual to do certain things which the individual may *eventually* come to do. This is opposed to the exercise concept where freedom consists not just of having the opportunity to do, but of *actually* carrying out a certain action.

In contrast to the negative conception of freedom, under the positive concept, Berlin points out that freedom requires not merely the absence of interference or having the opportunity to do, but rather the presence of self-mastery and actually *doing* certain things: 'The 'positive' sense of the word 'liberty' derives from the wish on the part of the individual to be his own master. 'I wish my life and decisions to depend on myself, not on external forces of whatever kind' (Berlin 1969: 131). Consequently, the questions, according to Berlin, that are relevant to a positive conception of freedom are: 'what, or who, is the source of control or interference that can determine someone to do, or be, this rather than that?'; who controls me?; who governs me? (Berlin 1969: 122, 131ff.). These questions, in other words, are basically concerned about 'authority' – whether it is I or someone else who controls my life.

Having distinguished negative and positive freedom in this way – negative freedom as the absence of interference and the opportunity to do or be something, and positive freedom as self-mastery and actually carrying out a certain action – Berlin in that classic essay goes on to point out that positive freedom would 'logically' lead to or degenerate into authoritarianism. In its softer form it degenerates into paternalism because it involves discrimination between 'higher' and 'lower' nature and determination of what is the 'true' or 'authentic' self. This gives the possibility for persons other than the individual *himself* to claim to know what is good for the individual and to interfere in his life in order to 'make him free' against his will. In its extreme manifestation it can degenerate into totalitarianism, or as Taylor (1985b: 214-215) calls it a 'Totalitarian Menace' because it involves not only determining the 'true' self, but also stipulating the right canonical form of society where the life of a true self can be realized.

a) Authoritarianism or Real Freedom?

Owing to the ascription of authoritarianism to positive freedom or the possibility of a perversion of positive freedom into authoritarianism in Berlin, Sen's claim that capabilities are notions of positive freedom might be misleading and misrepresent Sen's own position. Sen (1993: 42-46) hardly intends capabilities to acquire an authoritarian connotation. He, as highlighted in Chapter 3, introduces the concept of capabilities to emphasize the idea that a person may be said to be free when he or she has the relevant capacities *as well as* the required opportunities to develop and exercise the capacities to achieve certain valuable functionings. In other words, when Sen refers to capabilities as positive freedom he does not mean to deny the necessity of negative freedom, namely, the absence of interference from the state or fellow citizens. It would hardly be possible for an individual to possess and exercise certain capabilities if others (for paternalistic or other reasons) constantly interfere with his life. Nonetheless, Sen (or for that matter Nussbaum and other capability theorists) would not reduce freedom to mere absence of interference from others.[1] That Sen does not intend capabilities to take on Berlin's authoritarian connotation becomes even clearer when we look at his arguments for switching attention away from 'control freedom' to 'effective freedom' (§3.1). Advocates of control freedom tend to think that an individual is free only insofar as the person herself directly exercises control over all that pertains to her life. Sen by contrast, insists that individual freedom is enhanced not only when the individual concerned directly exercises control, but also when other agents, family, community and the state play a crucial role in creating an environment for individual freedom. Here Sen and other capability theorists particularly think of the effective freedom brought about by public goods such as a safe and healthy environment, public infrastructure, education, culture and language. The opportunities created by these public goods are hardly the outcome of direct exercise of control by individual persons. Nevertheless, the public goods play an indispensable role in enhancing individual freedom.

Hence, instead of an authoritarian interpretation, Sen's use of positive freedom and the linkage that he envisions between capabilities and positive freedom can be interpreted in the sense of *real* freedom (Sen 1992: 41, 64-69).[2] Such an interpretation

---

1   Among the vast amount of literature that followed Berlin's distinction between negative and positive freedom, MacCallum (1967) had illuminatingly showed that all debates about negative and positive freedom, in fact, involve explicitly or implicitly a *triadic* relationship between agents, constraints and ends: 'X is (is not) free from Y to do (not do, become, not become) Z.' Accordingly, what MacCallum wishes to emphasize is that it does not make sense to define negative freedom exclusively in terms of '*freedom from* some obstacles' and positive freedom as '*freedom to* do certain things'. Although depending on the context one might emphasize the 'obstacle' side or the 'exercise' side of freedom, a full account of freedom would have to include both aspects. Sen's understanding of positive freedom resonates with MacCallum's explanation insofar as the presence and exercise of capabilities presuppose the absence of non-interference.

2   For the interpretation of Sen's positive freedom in the direction of real freedom, we can draw support from a number of contemporary philosophers who have discussed the capability approach. Among others, see Korsgaard (1993); Pettit (2001); Nussbaum (2000a). In fact,

can draw valuable resources from a variety of traditions in the history of political philosophy. As Nussbaum (1988a: 183) has pointed out, the idea of real freedom can be found in the early writings of Marx, although not the 'authoritarian' interpretation of Marxism that Berlin is concerned about; it is central to the Aristotelian tradition that assigns a moral obligation on the state to facilitate valuable human functionings and the good life. The idea of real freedom has also been a favourite theme of some of the earlier egalitarian thinkers who were critical of capitalism.[3] In contemporary political philosophy, Philippe Van Parijs (1995; 2000), in a somewhat similar, and yet a different theory from the capability approach, has argued for the ideal of 'real-freedom-for-all' (or real libertarianism) and suggests that a universal basic income for all citizens would be the best way of achieving this ideal. What is interesting to note here is that despite the differences between these two theories, both Sen and Van Parijs advocate not only negative freedoms (understood mainly in terms of non-interference and formal rights), but also positive freedoms (understood in terms of capabilities and real opportunities to lead the kind of life one has reason to value) as legitimate political objectives.

b) Basic Income and the Capability Approach

At first, like most traditional libertarians, Van Parijs advocates that a society might be considered to be free and just only when there is a well-enforced structure of rights, particularly *property rights*. In the absence of a proper definition and enforcement of property rights including an effective system of sanctions, Van Parijs points out, it is difficult to give shape to a free society. Instead, we can only expect chaos and triumph of the strongest over the weakest. In the libertarian framework, therefore, there can be no liberty without property. Furthermore, along with property rights, like the traditional libertarians, Van Parijs also affirms the importance of *self-ownership*. This is because it is possible that in a society the property rights are absolutely respected, but the members do not own themselves, as in the case of slavery for instance. Therefore, in a libertarian framework, no society might be deemed to be free, if its members can constantly be prevented from what they might want to do by the arbitrary use of threat or coercion.

However, Van Parijs, unlike the traditional libertarians, also adds a third condition for a free society – the condition of real freedom in which people are not only free to do what they might want to do with themselves and with the property

---

Sen himself uses this term 'real freedom' in *Inequality Reexamined* (1992). He writes: 'The elimination of these [epidemics, pestilence, famines, chronic hunger, etc.] unloved things ... can be seen as an enhancement of people's *real freedom*' (Sen 1992: 62, my emphasis).

3   Tawney (1952: 228), for example, invokes a distinction between 'real' and 'nominal' choices in understanding the significance of freedom: 'there is no such thing as freedom in the abstract ... whatever else the conception may imply, it involves a power of choice between alternatives, a choice which is *real*, not merely *nominal*, between alternatives which exist in fact, not only on paper'. In a similar pattern of thinking, Norman emphasizes that freedom is more than non-coercion and includes various things – wealth, power and education, among others – that enable us to make choices. For thinkers who belong to this tradition of thought, see Van Parijs (1995: 240-241).

they legitimately own, but also have the 'greatest possible opportunity' to do what they might want to do. In other words, Van Parijs points out that although property rights and self-ownership as advocated by the traditional libertarians are extremely important and even necessary to freedom, they are not sufficient for it. For instance, it is perfectly possible for a society to have a well-enforced system of property rights and self-ownership, but individuals in such a society might lack the means and opportunities to do the things they might want to do. In such instances, according to Van Parijs, the members of that society are only 'formally' free; they lack the means and opportunities they require in order to be 'really' free. Therefore, the real-libertarian conception of justice advocated by Van Parijs combines two ideas: first, the members of the society should be *formally* free, particularly, by ensuring that a well-enforced system of property rights that includes self-ownership is in place; second, besides being formally free, the members should also be *really* free by a distribution of opportunity (understood as access to the means that people need for doing what they might want to do) in such a way as to offer the greatest real opportunity to those with the least opportunities.

As an institutional implication of the ideal of real-freedom-for-all he advocates, Van Parijs proposes that all citizens should be paid an 'unconditional' and 'universal' basic income at a level sufficient for subsistence. So goes his definition of the basic income proposal.

> A *basic income* ... is an income paid by the government to each full member of society (1) even if she is not willing to work, (2) irrespective of her being rich or poor, (3) whoever she lives with, and (4) no matter which part of the country she lives in. The choice of the expression is meant to convey the idea that, owing to its unconditional nature, we here have something on which a person can safely count, a material foundation on which a life can firmly rest, and to which any other income, whether in cash or in kind, from work or saving, from the market or the State, can legitimately be added. (Van Parijs 1995: 35)

The institutional arrangement of basic income that Van Parijs proposes is a species of 'guaranteed minimum income' that has been prevalent in many European welfare states (e.g. Belgium, The Netherlands and Denmark) for a number of years in the form of various benefit schemes from state social security. But it differs from such traditional schemes in some important respects. Universal basic income is primarily unconditional in the sense that a basic income is given to all including people who choose not to engage in paid work such as housewives, househusbands, students and even 'idle surfers'. The traditional and most existing benefit schemes are restricted to the 'involuntarily unemployed', and put in place a number of conditions such as that the beneficiary should be actively searching for a job, willing to undergo suitable training, and should not have access to a sufficient income from other resources. Van Parijs' basic income places no such restrictions. Also, while the traditional benefit schemes take into account the household situation, Van Parijs' basic income proposal is strictly individual, since it is given to all citizens on an individual basis irrespective of their household situation.

As Van Parijs himself realizes, the ideal of real-freedom-for-all that he advocates is conceptually 'very close to Amartya Sen's approach'; he also admits that he 'could have followed his [Sen's] suggestion that the category of capabilities is the natural candidate for reflecting the idea of [positive] freedom to do' (Van Parijs 1995: 240, n. 45). However, when viewed from the capability perspective, Van Parijs' concept of real freedom and his suggestion that the best way to achieve real freedom is an institutional arrangement that would provide a universal basic income to all citizens seem counterintuitive in certain respects.

1. Since basic income is a monetary amount, given as cash to everyone, it is likely to leave those with capability deprivations disadvantaged. People with a low-level capabilities might need more income to achieve a similar level of human functionings like others: disabled people require more income to achieve equivalent freedoms to move around and to do other things than able-bodied; people who do unpaid dependent care work might need more income to achieve equivalent freedoms than those who do not engage in such work. Or, sometimes, instead of more income, these might directly require 'in-kind' distribution of certain specific goods such as education, health and social respect to enhance their capability prospects. Robeyns (2001), for example, has argued that the basic income proposal does not do justice to women in western societies under certain circumstances.[4]

2. As Sen (1992: 44-46) and Anderson (1999) have pointed out, at a more 'political' level, whether we like it or not, we need to make certain 'social priorities' for some capabilities over others: we might, for instance, assign a higher priority to education than leisure, even if some would prefer surfing to schooling. The basic income proposal refuses to make such social priorities. It appears that in a regime of basic income the idle surfer will be paid as much as any hard-working citizen.

3. When a basic income is given to everyone irrespective of whether they are willing to work or not, make a social contribution or not, it promotes real freedom without requiring agency and reciprocity. It is likely to undermine social solidarity, the foundation for a system of welfare democracy: people who work hard and pay taxes might be embarrassed and even resent the fact that they are supporting the undeserving poor. Moreover, the assurance of a basic income without any obligation to work would not positively promote a work-ethic in society.

Besides the above mentioned problems of the basic income proposal, even conceptually, there are some differences between the capability approach and Van Parijs' theory of basic income. Van Parijs (1995: 22-24), instead of the term 'capabilities', prefers to use a broader term 'opportunity-set'. This is because 'opportunities' can refer to a wide range of 'means' that are available to a person for doing what she might want to do; although 'capacities' can be an important component of the 'means', it is not the only means that people require to realize what

---

4   It is not that Van Parijs does not foresee a conditional extra-income for the disabled people, for example. However, the criterion for getting this would be strict. One of the reasons for this is that all expenditures for conditional income would diminish the amount of money available for basic income.

they might want to do. In other words, capabilities, in Van Parijs' theory, are only a subset of opportunities available to a person. Also, Van Parijs thinks that since a theory of justice should basically be concerned with the 'institutional' character of a free society, it has to concentrate on the just way of distributing 'mays' (opportunity sets broadly understood), and not 'cans' (capacities). Stretching the concept of real freedom, as Sen tends to do, to encompass both the opportunity dimension and the capacity dimension might be unnecessary. Notwithstanding these conceptual and institutional differences, what is important to realize is that since Sen emphasizes the idea that we cannot effectively guarantee liberty without guaranteeing people certain basic capabilities, his appeal to the notion of positive freedom to do and to achieve certain valuable human functionings can be interpreted in the direction of real freedom. Sen, we can now say, deploys a richer positive conception of freedom than Berlin. An inquiry into Van Parijs' theory has only strengthened the grounds for such interpretation. In fact, in line with the objectives of the capability approach, Van Parijs' theory has even helped to generalize Sen's argument: real freedom involved in the capability approach should not only be exclusively concerned with people's 'capacities', but also more generally be concerned with the 'opportunity-base' for the enhancement of capacities.

7.3 Capabilities, Value Construction and Public Reasoning

Any proposal about social justice and the criterion by which people should be treated as equals in society might be assessed from at least three different points of view (Korsgaard 1993). We can, first and foremost, assess them as a philosophical proposal about what constitutes the good life. The inquiry here will largely focus on whether the proposed criterion – be it of utilities, primary goods, basic income, capabilities, virtues or whatever – is the sort of thing we would want our life to be enhanced by. But we can also assess a proposal about social justice for its legitimacy as a political objective, in the sense of whether or not we as a political community would like to realize this through political means and institutions. And finally, we can also look at a proposal about social justice for the influence it exerts on policy implications – whether it provides accurate measures for designing or evaluating economic and social policies. The distinction that is drawn between these perspectives need not however deny their interrelatedness. If we, for instance, do not think capabilities to be important features that enhance human life, we are also less likely to think of them as desirable political objectives that we as a political community should strive to realize in our society. Similarly, however attractive and legitimate a philosophical or political ideal may turn out to be, if it cannot be made to show some differences in social institutions and policies, it will eventually lose the confidence and support of citizens. And yet, an assessment of a proposal about social justice as a political conception should look for distinctive elements of legitimacy.

The capability approach, at the outset, derives its legitimacy as a political ideal from the fact that it seeks to promote citizens' conditions of real freedom reflected in their capability sets. Accordingly, the state – citizens as a collective body – as a moral agent ought to create appropriate conditions for the realization of real freedom.[5] Such a political vision is different from the one based on classical utilitarianism which seeks to draw its legitimacy from satisfying citizens' preferences and advocates that the ultimate aim of the state should be to devise efficient means – particularly market mechanisms – to maximize preference-satisfaction. This is also different from forms of liberalism which try to ground their legitimacy in protecting citizen's basic liberties, but do not explicitly address citizens' capability requirements – or 'worth of liberty', to use Rawls's term – for effectively making use of basic liberties. Furthermore, the capability approach also derives its legitimacy from the fact that public reasoning rather than 'technical', 'aggregative' or 'private' reasoning plays a central role in conceptualizing, determining and prioritizing capabilities.

a) The Features of Public Reasoning

To begin with, public reasoning must be differentiated from 'technical' reasoning. As Sen (1987a: 2ff.) realizes, technical reasoning is what is involved in an 'engineering approach'. It would be inappropriate to deploy this as a central method in reasoning about human affairs in the political sphere, mainly because technical reasoning is 'concerned with primarily logistic issues rather than with ultimate ends' and because 'the ends are taken as fairly straightforwardly given, and the object of the exercise is to find the appropriate means to serve them' (Sen 1987a: 4). From the viewpoint of the capability approach what seems more suited is a wider 'ethical' reasoning involving public debate and discussion. The wider ethics-related reasoning takes into account the 'plurality of human motivations' in commitments and political actions, a number of intrinsically valuable goals, and above all, the process of public discussion and reasoning by which a community of citizens living together comes to recognize and endorse a set of important basic capabilities.

Another familiar misconception of public reasoning is the aggregative model. Young (2000), for example, describes the aggregative model in the following way:

> Individuals in the polity have varying preferences about what they want government institutions to do. They know that other individuals also have preferences, which may or may not match their own. Democracy is a competitive process in which political parties and candidates offer their platforms and attempt to satisfy the largest number of people's preferences. (Young 2000: 19)

In an aggregative conception, citizens are seen as consumers having various preferences including political ones. Accordingly, a popular 'show of hands' or a more

---

5   An important issue that might arise at this stage is the necessity and the legitimacy of state coercion and intervention in bringing about conditions of real freedom and thus the greatest possible condition for the realization of basic capabilities for all: Is the state, in the name of justice and for redistributive purposes, justified in 'interfering' in the lives of citizens? If so, to what extent? This issue is taken up in §7.4 of this chapter. It is demonstrated that certain (non-arbitrary, non-dominating, capabilities-promoting) forms of coercions and interventions are compatible with, and might even be necessary to promote conditions of effective freedom and basic capabilities for all citizens.

formalized methods of voting is used as the mechanism for aggregating individual preferences; the outcome is legitimate and just, provided it reflects the preferences of the majority of people. The kind of public reasoning entailed in this model is different from, and might even be considered more 'democratic' than technical reasoning on two grounds: first, the ends are not taken to be straightforwardly given or predetermined, but are decided on the basis of aggregative results; and second, instead of just professionals and technocrats, every citizen gets the opportunity to vote and to participate. Yet the aggregative model can be problematic because it makes individual preference-satisfaction the 'central' concern of the polity, and voting the 'primary' political activity. Sen rejects the idea that social and political institutions are to be exclusively evaluated depending on their contributions to individual preference-satisfaction. He by contrast, advocates the idea that 'open discussion, debate, criticism, and dissent are central to the processes of generating informed and reflected choices' and that we cannot 'take preferences as given independently of public discussion' (Sen 1999a: 153).[6]

Sen therefore seems to search for something more fundamental than the technical or aggregative model of public reasoning in democracy. He ponders on the type of public reasoning that is required for an effective democracy:

> What exactly is democracy? We must not identify democracy with majority rule. Democracy has complex demands, which certainly include voting and respect for election results, but it also requires the protection of liberties and freedoms, respect for legal entitlements, and the guaranteeing of free discussion and uncensored distribution of news and fair comment. Even elections can be deeply defective if they occur without the different sides getting an adequate opportunity to present their respective cases, or without the electorate enjoying the freedom to obtain news and to consider the views of the competing protagonists. Democracy is a demanding system, and not just a mechanical condition (like majority rule) taken in isolation. (Sen 1999c: 9-10)

Sen envisions a more demanding role for public reasoning in democracy by exploring the diverse ways in which democracy and its institutions can enrich and promote citizens' capabilities. First and foremost, democracy is *intrinsically* valuable

---

6   Elster (1986) has described the 'aggregative model' as an 'economic theory of democracy' that largely operates on the basis of social choice theory. An economic theory of democracy advocates the idea that 'the political process is *instrumental* rather than an end in itself, and the view that the decisive political act is a *private* rather than a public action, viz. the individual and secret vote. With these usually goes the idea that the goal of politics is the optimal *compromise* between given, and irreducibly opposed, private interests' (Elster 1986: 103). Like Sen, Elster too rejects the view that a political theory should be based on the aggregation of individual preferences because it assumes that 'the forum [politics] should be like the market, in its purpose as well as in its mode of functioning' (Elster 1986: 127). Elster also rejects the idea that politics – as some theorists of deliberative and participatory model tend to advocate – should be completely divorced from the market. Similar to Sen's position elaborated in Chapter 4, Elster advocates a mixed model where the state should regulate markets for redistribution and equity purposes: 'one can argue that the forum should differ from the market in its mode of functioning, and yet be concerned with decisions that ultimately deal with economic matters' (Elster 1986: 128).

(Sen 1999a). This implies that people's basic capabilities for social and political participation are in themselves valuable for human life and well-being – they need not be justified in the utilitarian fashion for their usefulness to something else (§1.1). Some argue that political and civil liberties are conducive to economic growth and prosperity. Others, however, point out that the connection between the two is only coincidental or at most weak (Roemer 1999). Whatever may be the degree of causal linkage between political and economic freedom, political capabilities have their independent worth and merit. That is to say that when people are prevented either from participating in such elementary things as elections and public criticism, or more generally are unable to effectively take part in their social and political community, these should indeed be treated as major deprivations on their own terms.

Second, democracy and its associated capabilities of social and political participation are also *instrumentally* important for preventing major societal failures such as acute famines and deprivations (Sen 1999a). Moreover, an unrestrained freedom of speech, possibilities for political protest and dissent, free and fair elections, critical press and media – all these empower and give a certain amount of leverage to citizens to express their 'needs' and 'values', and demand attention from their rulers and governments. At the same time, these create political incentives on the part of the leaders to listen to what people want, since they have to face their criticism and get their support in elections.

Third, democracy has a *constructive* role as well. At a more fundamental level, the exercise of political freedoms particularly by way of public criticisms and protests are not only useful in demanding a policy response towards urgent economic needs, but also the public debates and discussions that accompany them play a 'formative' or 'educative' role even in conceptualizing and prioritizing these economic needs: 'It can indeed be argued that a proper understanding of what economic needs are – the content and force – requires discussion and exchange' (Sen 1999a: 153). It is important to take note of the fact that in Sen's understanding, the constructive role of public reasoning and democracy, however, is not limited to identifying and responding to people's elementary economic needs. Public debates and discussions are also very influential in the 'construction' of values of redistribution, justice, respect and solidarity. As Sen expresses it: 'The practice of democracy gives citizens an opportunity to learn from one another, and helps society to form its values and priorities' (Sen 1999c: 10).

In some sense, the idea that public reasoning can and must play a vital role in the construction of values revisits Tocqueville's admiration for democracy. Tocqueville (1965) had argued that a democratic regime with its guarantee of equality of all before the law and opportunities for public debates and discussions has more possibilities for compassion and solidarity among citizens than forms of government that retain hierarchy and social classes. Moreover, even underlying Sen's own much-discussed thesis that 'there has never been a famine in a functioning multi-party democracy' is a process of solidarity and value-construction (Sen 2003: 33; Alexander 2005c). It is generally the case that the percentage of the potential victims of famines in a country or region is relatively small – often it is between 5-10 per cent of the total population. Strictly speaking, if this comparatively smaller percentage of population does not vote for the government, it need not fall. And yet, in a functioning democracy, why does famine pose a big threat to the government? This is because through public reasoning and solidarity other citizens will criticize and are most likely to vote against the government. The possibility of value-construction through public reasoning seems important in view of representing capabilities as political objectives and strengthening the legitimacy of the capability approach as a persuasive public and political conception. It also assumes a special significance in resolving disagreements that are likely to arise in a public deliberation about capabilities and their priorities.

b) Capabilities as Content of Public Reasoning

Perhaps some more light can be shed on the kind of public reasoning envisaged by capability theorists by linking public reasoning to what Rawls calls the 'criterion of reciprocity' expressed through the 'moral duty' or 'duty of civility' of giving an explanation to one another for the principles and policies one advocates or votes for. Public officials such as judges, legislators and government officers as well as ordinary citizens are in some sense morally obliged to support their political action with public reasoning (Rawls 1993: l-lvii, 213-219). As a further elaboration of this reason-giving duty, Sen adds tolerance and the willingness to learn from others as two essential features of public reasoning: 'The ideal of public reasoning is closely linked with two particular social practices that deserve specific attention: the tolerance of different points of view (along with acceptability of agreeing to disagree) and the encouragement of public discussion (along with endorsing the value of learning from others)' (Sen 2003: 31).

Again, somewhat similar to Rawls, Sen and other capability theorists argue that public reasoning particularly in the selection of relevant basic capabilities and prioritizing them for policy considerations is basically a 'political' exercise. Accordingly, public reasoning involved in the capability approach is independent of comprehensive doctrines. Inspired by the tenets of their religious or secular comprehensive doctrines, individuals may have 'private' reasons to believe and care about many things to be components of the good life and well-being. Yet since it is in the domain of the political that capability deliberations and decisions take place, individuals in their capacity as citizens ought to understand and accept the fact that not all of their private, non-public reasons and beliefs can be reflected and represented in public reasoning. Public reasoning in this sense might be partial and restrictive: some demands of citizens' comprehensive doctrines and non-public reason (particularly those that might cause other citizens' capability deprivations) might find themselves restricted or have only a limited role in arriving at political decisions.

Inevitably, disagreements and conflicts among the participants in deliberation are bound to arise. Sen says: 'I know of no value – not even motherhood ... – to which no one has ever objected' (Sen 1999c: 12). Disagreements for example might arise about the selection of relevant capabilities: what might to some seem as the most important and urgent, to others might turn out to be trivial and less urgent. Disagreements might also arise in the allocation of limited, and sometimes even scarce, public resources for the attainment of various capabilities. In the event of conflicts and disagreements, advocates of technical and aggregative models tend to resort to too easy a solution of seeking 'compromises' between different private interests. Sen, however, believes that some sort of rational agreement can be reached through public debates and discussions conducted in an atmosphere of mutual respect for the claims and opinions of the participants involved. Mutual respect does not mean that we ought to accept the claims of those with whom we disagree, but rather it requires an attitude of listening to what others say and that we justify our claims by reasons we truly believe all reasonable persons could endorse. As Gandhi for example had argued we can claim non-violence to be universally valuable, not because people everywhere accept and act according to this value, but rather that they have good reasons to see this as valuable (Sen 1999c: 12). Public reasoning is not to be envisaged as an effective decision-procedure intended to produce agreement. Rather, it is a special kind of 'communal' dynamics of arguments and counterarguments, dissent and disagreement, which deploys mutually agreed methods of justification, whether or not it results in agreement.

In a contrasting perspective, the content of public reasoning underlying the capability approach seems to be much more encompassing, and probably, also more demanding than that which supports political liberalism – not the least that of Rawls'. Rawls (1993: 223ff.) suggests that public reason in a liberal democracy should basically be steered by three things: basic liberties and opportunities that are found in constitutional democratic regimes; a special priority of basic liberties over other goods and perfectionist values; and an adequate measure of 'primary goods' to make effective use of their basic liberties and opportunities. Rawls does not seem to think that capabilities can be meaningfully included as part of the content of public reason. Or, as pointed out in Chapter 2, he at the most might assign a 'secondary' or 'auxiliary' role to capabilities insofar as the 'comprehensive' view involved in determining basic capabilities does not go against the content of public reason involved in political liberalism. For the capability theorists, however, a political theory should enlist not only fundamental civil and political rights but also the required basic capabilities as the content that would inform and shape public reasoning.

It should be emphasized that beyond a certain level of agreement as to the importance of public reasoning, not every capability theorist pursues the same direction of linking public reasoning with the capability approach. The first group of theorists are inclined to advocate a fully-fleshed out content-based approach where a set of basic capabilities are chosen beforehand from a particular world-view or comprehensive conception of the good life. As in the case of Nussbaum's version of the capability approach, public reasoning might also take the direction of being partly content-based and partly procedural – thus overcoming to some extent the problems connected with a purely content-based approach. It is content-based insofar as the universal list of (ten) basic capabilities serves as a set of political goals based on which legislators, policy makers and citizens can conduct their public discussions and deliberations. At the same time, since the list is 'open-ended' and the individual items on the list are defined at a very abstract level (parallel to the list of human rights), the list can be compatible with different reasonable religious and philosophical world-views and possesses a natural propensity to generate and facilitate further public discussion and deliberation. Robeyns (2003) is critical of the fact that Nussbaum endorses a definite list of capabilities. She therefore makes a detour of listing a set of 'criteria' (cultural sensitivity, methodological justification, etc.) for the selection of relevant capabilities. However, by using these criteria she also comes up with a list of capabilities for the purpose of analysing gender inequality in Western societies. Sen himself seems inclined to advocate a type of procedural approach without suggesting or endorsing any particular list of capabilities that would function as a predetermined content of public reasoning. Although Sen has repeatedly pointed out a number of basic capabilities (nutrition, health, education, self-respect and political participation) that would demand attention in any theory of social justice, he does not accept the idea that the capability approach should endorse one particular list that would function as the substantive content of public reasoning.

> The problem is not with listing important capabilities, but with insisting on a predetermined list of basic capabilities, chosen by theorists without any social discussion or public reasoning. To have such a fixed list, emanating entirely from pure theory, is to deny the possibility of fruitful public participation on what should be included and why. (Sen 2004b: 1)

In fact, for Sen, in view of its political legitimacy, the 'process' that generates a list of basic capabilities is as important as its 'outcome'. Therefore, instead of focusing on providing the most appropriate list of capabilities, it becomes imperative to search for fair and consistent democratic procedures of public reasoning that would generate the list of capabilities for different cultures and contexts.

7.4 Republicanism and the Capability Approach

As the above suggests, when social justice is understood as the realization of not just formal freedom and negative liberties, but of real freedom and effective opportunities, and when the determination of basic capabilities that ought to be realized is linked to democracy and public reasoning, it imposes a moral duty on the political community such as the state to create and maintain appropriate conditions and institutions. In particular, the state as a moral agent needs to ensure the provision of public goods and the distribution of material and social resources so that a maximum of conditions for the realization of basic capabilities for all citizens can be realized. This opens up immediately a very fundamental question concerning the legitimacy of state intervention. Generally, any form of coercion or interference is morally wrong. Yet in pursuing the aim of enhancing citizens' capability prospects and achieving equity, is the state justified in intervening in the lives of its citizens? If so, what kinds of state interventions are compatible with individual freedom? One standard liberal answer has been in the negative, particularly because freedom has been defined as the absence of interference from the state or fellow citizens. As the historian philosopher Quentin Skinner (1998) has illuminatingly shown, the 'liberal hegemony' in today's political philosophy and its preoccupation with freedom as non-interference can be traced back to the views of authoritarians (or 'royalists') in the mid-seventeenth century. These authoritarians not only advocated absolute power for the 'sovereign' and considered it as something inevitable for the attainment of individual liberty, but their political philosophy also advocated a rather negative role for the state and law.

> [T]here arose to prominence an associated view of the relationship between the power of the state and the liberty of its subjects. To be free as a member of a civil association, it was urged, is simply to be unimpeded from exercising your capacities in pursuit of your desired ends. One of the prime duties of the state is to prevent you from invading the rights of action of your fellow-citizens, a duty it discharges by imposing the coercive force of the law on everyone equally. But where law ends, liberty begins. Provided that you are neither physically nor coercively constrained from acting or forbearing from acting by the requirements of the law, you remain capable of exercising your powers at will and to that degree remain in possession of your civil liberty. (Skinner 1998: 5)

An emblematic version of this view, as analysed by Skinner, can be found in Hobbes. In *Leviathan*, Chapter 14, Hobbes writes: 'By LIBERTY is understood, according to the proper signification of the word, the absence of external Impediments: which impediments, may oft take away part of a mans power to do what he would' (Hobbes 1985: 189). In Chapter 21, he reiterates this view once again: 'A Free-Man, is he, that in those things, which by his strength and wit he is able to do, is not hindered to do what he has a will to do' (Hobbes 1985: 262). People, on this Hobbesian view, are hindered and made unfree only when they are *physically* coerced. Accordingly, when we say that someone has acted freely, this implies that he or she has done so without external restriction or hindrance. Conversely, when we say that someone lacks the freedom to act, this implies that an action within his or her power has been made impossible by some external force. It is not that Hobbes does not acknowledge the faculty of will in relation to human action, as we normally tend to do, but his 'materialist' (mechanistic) view of the world and human beings leads him to assign the will only a limited role: since the will is ultimately revealed in action, it is the action itself and the possible external restrictions to that action, that we have to be concerned about.

This way of looking at freedom – freedom literally understood as the absence of physical coercion – is also reflected in Hobbes' views about law. For Hobbes, law is always seen as an intrusion into people's lives, and therefore, the extent of people's liberty very much depends on what he calls the 'silence of the Law'. As long as there are no laws to which you must conform and obey, you remain in full possession of your freedom. 'In cases where the Sovereign has prescribed no rule', says Hobbes, 'there the Subject hath the liberty to do, or foreebeare according to his own discretion' (Hobbes 1985: 271). In short, Hobbes advocates the view that people remain free as subjects so long as they are neither physically nor legally coerced. Perhaps it is important to underscore that Hobbes is not a liberal, but he anticipates the modern liberal idea of freedom as non-interference by the state and its laws.

The capability theorists precisely challenge and reject such a narrow conception of freedom. For a capability theorist, freedom does not merely consist in the absence of interference, but the presence of required capacities and opportunities to live a life that one has reason to value. This implies that for a capability theorist certain qualified forms of intervention by the state and its laws should be tolerated and even considered necessary subject to the condition that such interventions are capabilities-promoting to everyone. It is important to take note of the fact that the capability theorists are not the only ones who seek to go beyond the liberal conception and look for alternatives. As identified and expounded in the writings of Skinner (1999) and Pettit (1997a), there has been a revival and renaissance of the republican political tradition with its emphasis on citizenship, public values and above all, a distinct notion of freedom as non-domination emerging in the 'neo-roman theory of free states' and in the slavery-versus-liberty discussion. Extending the theoretical framework of the capability approach in order to incorporate important elements associated with the republican tradition would not only offer conceptual resources to radicalize its critique of the liberal conception of freedom and justice, but also enable it to emerge as a convincing alternative to liberalism.

a) The Neo-roman Theory of Freedom

Skinner (1984; 1998) contrasts the liberal understanding of freedom as non-interference with the political thought in which freedom was associated not with absence of physical or legal coercion and intrusion, but rather with the classical ideal of the free state (*civitas libera*). Skinner calls this 'a neo-roman theory' of freedom.[7] It is 'neo-roman' because the elements embodied in this view could be traced back to ancient Roman legal and moral thought.[8] But they were at a later period revived and advocated by the defenders of 'republican *liberta*' in the Italian Renaissance, particularly by Machiavelli (Viroli 1998: Chapter 4). And they were also prominent in the writings of J. Harrington, A. Sydney and others in and after the period of the English Civil War and Commonwealth (Skinner 1994; 1998).

A distinctive feature that circumscribes this tradition, distinguishing it from its authoritarian competitors like Hobbes, is the intimate relationship between a 'free citizen' and 'a free state'. In the neo-roman tradition, individual citizen's freedom is always embedded in the context of what it means for a 'civil association' or a state to be free: only in a free state, is it possible for individuals to be free. Therefore, the advocates of this view, instead of focusing on individual freedom or rights, were primarily concerned about the freedom of the entire civil community or the state.

As Skinner (1998: 25ff.) suggests, a good way of understanding what the neo-roman theorists meant by a 'free state' is to look at the significance that the ancient metaphor of 'body politic' had for them.

> Just as individual human bodies are free... if and only if they are able to act or forbear from acting at will, so the bodies of nations and states are likewise free if and only if they are similarly unconstrained from using their powers according to their own wills in pursuit of their desired ends. Free states, like free persons, are thus defined by their capacity for

---

7   In some of his earlier writings (e.g. Skinner 1984), Skinner referred to this idea as a republican ideal. But in later writings he prefers to call this the neo-roman theory.

8   Perhaps it is interesting to note that the Romans had no exact parallel term for the Greek word *demokratia* – 'rule by the people'. But since they read the Greek philosophers they paraphrased the concept in Latin and introduced a new term *res publica* (republic, state, or the common good) which not only meant 'government of the free', but also involved legality (rule of law) and constitutionalism.

self-government. A free state is a community in which the actions of the body politic are determined by the will of the members as a whole. (Skinner 1998: 25-26)

From the standpoint of Hobbes or even some contemporary purely rights-based liberal political theories, focusing on the qualities of a 'free state' rather than on individual freedom' might seem wrong-headed. But a closer look reveals that it is not that individual freedom was considered unimportant in this way of thinking, but rather individual freedom, along with other benefits such as wealth and civic greatness, was considered to be a by-product assured to every member living in the free state. For instance, Machiavelli echoes such a view: he never uses the language of rights; instead he is content to talk about the enjoyment of individual freedom, along with wealth, prosperity, social recognition and civil honour, as one of the 'profits' or 'benefits' deriving from living under a well-ordered government. In addition, Machiavelli also explicitly states that it is only in lands and provinces which live as free states that individual citizens can hope to live a life of liberty (Viroli 1998: Ch. 4).

Furthermore, the idea of *res publica* (the common good) can also give some more indications about what the neo-roman theorists mean by a free state and about their affirmation that only a free state can engender individual liberty (Skinner 1998: 30ff.). A free state, these theorists point out, is a *res publica*. At the outset, it emerges that a *res publica* in the neo-roman tradition is not the aggregated common good of utilitarianism. Also, it turns out that a *res publica* advocated by the neo-roman thinkers is quite different from the Aristotelian presuppositions about the good life which were in different forms taken up by scholastic political philosophy. The neo-roman theorists, instead of proposing that there are one or more perfectionist goals and virtues we need to realize in order to count as truly free, suggest that different citizens will have different dispositions, and will accordingly value their liberty as the means to pursue their chosen goals. Therefore, in contrast to a utilitarian or teleological understanding of the common good, when the neo-roman theorists speak of a *res publica*, they specifically refer to a set of 'constitutional arrangements' under which it might be justifiably claimed that the *res* (the government) genuinely reflects the will and promotes the good of the *publica* (the community as a whole).

Since it is under a 'constitutional' regime that both the 'ruler(s)' and 'citizens' pursue the common good, the law assumes a central place. In fact, the law, for the neo-roman theorists, assumes a significance that in a way is just the opposite of what Hobbes and other authoritarians consider it to be. To Hobbes and others, as mentioned earlier, where the law ends, liberty begins. Put another way, the law protects our liberty by coercing *other* people; it helps me to draw a circle around myself and create a protective sphere into which others may not trespass, and simultaneously prevents me from interfering with others' freedom. In contrast, to the neo-roman theorists, the law preserves and engenders individual liberty. Machiavelli, for instance, says: 'it is hunger and poverty that make men industrious', whereas it is 'the law that makes them good' (quoted in Skinner 1984: 244). On a similar line, Machiavelli, along with others such as Sydney and Harrington, strongly believed that 'the empire of the law' is greater than any 'empire of men'. Accordingly, these theorists were keen to insist that the preservation of liberty by law is made possible not merely by coercing others, but also by directly coercing each one of us into acting in a particular way. The 'coercive' force of law is also used to force us out of our habitual pattern of self-interested behaviour and thereby ensure that the civic community or the state on which our liberty depends remains free (Skinner 1998: 45).

More importantly, the neo-roman theorists were keen to point out that the law creates and preserves individual liberty by ruling out 'arbitrary' use of power and domination, as in the conditions of slavery and servitude (Skinner 1998: 417). Insofar as there is no law against slavery, a slave remains obnoxious – a condition of perpetual subjugation and dependence, even when the master is benign, or the slave is so 'clever' that he can avoid being dominated. The slave, in other words, is at all times dependent on the good will of the master and remains vulnerable to his arbitrary exercise of power. Similarly, the neo-roman theorists point out that when people live under any form of government that allows for the exercise of prerogative or discretionary powers outside the law, they are in fact living as slaves.

b) Freedom as Non-Domination

Building on the historical precedence and legacy of the 'neo-roman' tradition, Pettit (1997a) advocates a 'republican'[9] political theory based on the conception of freedom as non-domination.[10] He argues that contemporary political philosophy has been so much centred on the idea of freedom as non-interference that it fails to take note of a number of conditions of unfreedom which can be present even in the absence of interference from others. As pointed out in the beginning of this chapter (§7.1), the capability theorists' grievance against a liberal mode of theorizing about

---

9   In the wake of Arendt's (1958) argument to revive the ancient Greek model of direct democracy that gives prominence to the political sphere over other spheres such as economics, family and civil society, republicanism has acquired a number of popular conceptions. Given the historical connections with the 'neo-roman' theory of freedom as non-domination, Pettit's republicanism, however, should be distinguished from 'populist' republican conceptions which consider 'active' and 'direct' democratic participation of the people as one of the highest goals of the political conception. And it should also be distinguished from some 'communitarian' republican conceptions that advocate that there should be shared ends and values among the members of the political community. See Pettit (1997a: 7-9).

10 Among contemporary political philosophers, Walzer too invokes the idea of non-domination as something very fundamental to social justice, but in a broader context of 'spheres' or 'realms' of social justice: 'The aim of political egalitarianism is a society *free from domination*' (Walzer 1983: xiii, my emphasis). In *Spheres of Justice* (1983), he defends a theory of 'complex equality' governed by a variety of distributive criteria such as desert, need and free exchange internal to each sphere. According to Walzer's theory of complex equality, the essence of social injustice is domination, when the goods of one social sphere influence the distributive patterns of another sphere – when, for instance, money buys votes and social status secures high-level jobs. Therefore, the key to social justice, Walzer argues, is not a single principle of distribution, or even a single set of principles, but rather a complex and interpretive social dialogue so that the goods are distributed in such a way that the distributive principle of one sphere does not dominate the distribution in another. This further corroborates our argument that the capability approach should extend its theoretical structure to address issues of domination.

social justice is that it tends to focus on people's negative freedom and pays very little attention to their real freedom reflected in their capability to achieve valuable functioning. Pettit, however, draws attention to those conditions of unfreedom that most varieties of liberalism overlook and the capability approach seems to address only indirectly. Taking note of these dominating conditions and looking for ways to overcome them are imperative for the realization of basic capabilities for all, especially for the poor and the weakest in society.

Quite reflective of the ancient theme of slavery that inspired the neo-roman theory of free states, the conditions of unfreedom that Pettit has in mind are the conditions where people have to live at the mercy of another, have to live in such a way that leaves them vulnerable and exposed to the arbitrary interference and imposition of the will of another. The husband who beats his wife at will and the wife in turn that does not have any possibility of redress; the employer who abuses or sacks the employee at his whim and suffers no sanctions whatsoever; the bureaucrats, tax officials and police who exercise power and intimidate individual citizens without following any procedure prescribed to them – all these enjoy high degrees of arbitrary power over those subject to them. The dominated individuals – the housewife, the employee and the public – in turn live a life of uncertainty and vulnerability, even when they are not actively coerced or obstructed by their dominators; the dominators still retain the *capacity* for interfering and of interfering on an *arbitrary* basis. Overcoming these conditions of unfreedom, Pettit points out, requires not just the absence of interference but also the absence of domination, and more particularly, security or immunity against domination.

Again, quite indicative of the neo-roman theorists' insistence on the necessity of a *res publica* and law for guaranteeing individual liberty, one essential way of achieving freedom as non-domination is 'constitutional provisions'. In the republican political conception that Pettit tries to revive and develop the conditions of freedom as non-domination can be obtained only when citizens through constitutional measures are secured against domination by another citizen, group or the state. Pettit says:

> The strategy of constitutional provision seeks to eliminate domination ... by introducing a constitutional authority – say a corporate, elective agent – to the situation. The authority will deprive other parties of the power of arbitrary interference and of the power of punishing that sort of interference. It will thereby eliminate domination of some parties by others and if it does not itself dominate those parties, then it will bring an end to domination. The reason that the constitutional authority will not itself dominate the parties involved, if it does not dominate them, is that the interference it practices has to track their interests according to their ideas; it is suitably responsive to the common good (Pettit 1997a: 67-68).

One important advantage of making freedom as non-domination hinge on laws and constitutional authority is that it promotes a common 'awareness' or 'vigilance' that is essential in eliminating dominating conditions and in building a polity of non-domination (Pettit 1997a: 70). In the republican political theory, freedom as non-domination is essentially a social ideal realized not through isolation and the absence of other people, but rather through the presence of other mutually interactive agents. This means that every member of the community shares in the public knowledge that they cannot be dominated and that they have recourse to systems of redress, if and when that happens. This also means that every individual has the necessary background conditions for living in 'tranquillity of spirit' and is able to enjoy the confidence of 'looking the other in the eye'. It is constitutional provision, more than any other private arrangements of immunity against domination, which makes this possible.

Furthermore, freedom as non-domination that is centred on constitutional arrangements is not hostile to interference *per se*; instead, it is only against those interferences carried out on an arbitrary basis and against those interferences that do not track the interests and ideas of those who are affected (Pettit 1997a: 65-66). In fact, freedom as non-domination tolerates and even promotes certain forms of 'non-dominating interferences' that are consistent with and maximize the conditions of non-domination for all. The parliament, the judge and the police officer, for instance, do interfere in the lives of the citizens when enacting, interpreting or implementing a piece of legislation. Yet their interference can hardly be considered as interference in the negative sense of the term. This is because their interference is mandated to take place non-arbitrarily within the framework of a *fair rule of law* and in a way that takes into account the well-being and interest of those with whom they interfere.

Finally, acceptable forms of non-dominating interference by the state, particularly those that take place within the law and those that track the citizens' ideas and interests assume special significance for redistribution in the name of social justice (Pettit 1997b: 125-127). This is because any form of redistribution always involves a degree of interference by the state. Even the most basic form of interference such as taxing some to give to others entails interference by depriving those who are taxed of a choice in how to use their money. But other more substantial forms of redistribution such as land ownership, education, self-respect and political offices require a greater degree of interference in the lives of citizens. In all these matters, if one's political conception were to embrace the ideal of freedom as non-interference, the tendency then would be to accept the *status quo* of inequalities. On the other hand, as in the case of Pettit's republican conception, if the political goal is to maximize the conditions of non-domination, then there is nothing inherently objectionable about non-dominating interferences for redistribution purposes.

When we confront the capability approach with the republican political theory many common features become evident. Both approaches are together in their critique of liberal theories that advocate a political conception based exclusively on freedom as non-interference. The capability approach and republicanism share the idea that non-interference, although necessary for freedom, is not sufficient to cover those important dimensions of freedom which might require focusing on people's capabilities and conditions of non-domination. Also, both approaches stress the importance of a 'civil community' or state for the achievement of individual freedom. It is impossible to think of citizens who are free apart from a state that is free. Indeed, a democratic state that is based on the rule of law and that tracks and promotes the capabilities of its citizens engenders individual liberty. Moreover both approaches also believe in the idea that certain qualified (non-arbitrary, non-dominating and capability-promoting) forms of interference by the state and law are quite consistent with freedom. For example, interventionist public policies in support of individual entitlements to food, health and education will have an important role in enhancing individual freedom (Sen 1988b: 289). Such qualified forms of interference in the lives of individuals might indeed be necessary to redistribute and to create the sort of public goods that are necessary in achieving the greatest possible condition for the realization of basic capabilities for all.

Despite these converging points, from the vantage point of republicanism, there is a lacuna, a missing element in the capability approach which characteristically receives direct attention and emphasis in the republican idea of freedom as non-domination. To put it more explicitly, when people are poor, illiterate, unhealthy and so on, and as a result, lack certain basic capabilities for leading a life of their choice, they are vulnerable and subject to certain forms of exploitation and domination. Consequently, any improvement in their basic capabilities' prospects can empower them to get rid of destitution and poverty; it can also give them the confidence necessary to resist any arbitrary interference and domination. This, however, seems to come short of a more socially radical ideal of freedom as non-domination. That is, while the capability approach largely focuses on whether someone is 'really free' and enjoys the required basic capabilities for leading the life they have reason to value, the republican theory goes further in order to inquire whether or not the life of 'real freedom' and the corresponding capabilities that the person enjoys are conditional on the favour or the goodwill of others.

Some supporters as well as critics of the capability approach have raised concerns over the lack of radicalism in the capability approach. Bagchi (2000), for example, points out that the capability approach mostly focuses on the ways in which institutions affect the exchange entitlements of individuals; it does not directly address the relationships of production and domination which restrict human capacities in serious ways. Bagchi writes:

> A very large proportion of the contradictions faced by the poor when they are exercising their choice can be attributed to competition and struggle for survival under existing capitalism. Competition is not simply a force external to a nation, an industry, a firm, or a household. It is something that leads to the redefining of national goals, sectoral composition of gross domestic product, and into the structures of firms, relations within the family and in short, into all human relationships. (Bagchi 2000: 4418)

Commenting specifically on Sen's work, Bagchi writes further:

> Sen has moved beyond the notion of what Marx would have called bourgeois right to that of broad human rights: for example, he wants, more resources to be put at the disposal of people who are disabled in any way. He has also gone beyond exchange transactions when he has enquired into entitlements within the family. But most of his analysis of the actual requirements of development is confined to the area of exchange entitlements. Sweatshop conditions under which a garment worker in Bangladesh or India works escape Sen's critical scrutiny except insofar as they might have a direct impact on her own health or the health and education of her children. But Sen's moral concerns would logically comprehend the garment worker's functioning as a fully capable human being. (Bagchi 2000: 4418)

Bagchi's point seems to make sense particularly because without directly addressing the power relationships in the household, workplaces and society at large, it might be difficult to counteract deeply embedded capability inequalities.[11] As Anderson has reminded us, a social philosopher has to continuously keep asking: 'What has happened to the concerns of the politically oppressed? What about inequality of race, gender, class, and caste?' (1999: 288).

A similar apprehension about the reach of the capability approach has been raised by feminists (Hill 2003; Phillips 1994) who find that certain socially entrenched forms of gender discrimination can be overcome not only by empowering women's capabilities, but also simultaneously ensuring that the enjoyment of these capabilities is not dependent on the favour and the goodwill of others – and particularly in this case on men in the family, work and society. Women's capability deprivation especially in traditional and gender-biased societies, these feminists point out, is a result of compound factors. While some are due to economic factors such as the lack of income and command over resources, others are, however, due to socio-cultural factors of a male-biased power relationship.

In a more fundamental way, conditions of dependence and relationships of domination between man and woman, between individuals with varying economic and social resources and between different groups in society can distort the process and outcome of public reasoning on which the capability approach as a political objective places so much importance. In a typical micro-level setting – village or town councils, for example – local landlords and elites tend to dominate, even when other participants are not so badly off in terms of basic capabilities of nutrition, education, health and so on. At more national or macro-level public discussions, it is the rich industrialists, the well-educated and well-placed in society, and the rich and powerful nations who tend to dominate and steer the course and outcome of public reasoning regarding people's capabilities and their priorities for public policies. As the general spirit of the capability approach literature seems to suggest, a substantial goal in all these power imbalances and asymmetries would be to enhance the educational, health, income-earning and professional capabilities of women, the poor and the underdogs of society – since the enhancement of their capabilities would eventually empower them to resist domination and subjugation by others. However, as republicanism urges, a more demanding goal might be to pay attention to the constitutional measures that would eliminate the possibilities of domination, without of course losing sight of capabilities that will enable an effective use of the conditions of non-domination. An extension of the capability approach along these lines would substantially enrich its theoretical base and help in achieving its objective of reducing capability inequalities.

---

11 Peter Evans makes a similar criticism of the capability approach. He writes: 'While Sen explicitly criticizes the choice-based utilitarianism of economics on grounds that its relation to individual well-being 'is not very robust, since it can be easily swayed by mental conditioning and adaptive attitudes', he does not explore the ways in which influences on 'mental conditioning' might systematically reflect the interests of those with greater economic clout and political power' (Evans 2002: 58).

7.5 Conclusion: Beyond Liberal Justice

Liberalism is a mansion with many different rooms (Vandevelde 2005). Reminiscent in some ways of Hobbes's view of political liberty and Berlin's definition of negative freedom, we have taken liberalism to advocate freedom as non-interference. But in advocating this ideal, it must be remembered that not all the liberals belong to the same camp. There are the 'right-of-centre' liberals who are content to establish non-interference as a formal, legal reality. Accordingly, what matters to them are some inviolable rights such as property rights and self-ownership rights, for example. When such liberals turn out be 'rights fetishists', merely concerned about legal and formal procedures, and are indifferent to how these make a difference to the actual lives of citizens, they might be placed on a par with the libertarians.

There are, however, 'left-of-centre' liberals who stress the need to make non-interference an effective value, not just a formal one. These, in addition to the value of non-interference also advocate goals such as equity, redistribution, recognition, participation and elimination of poverty, thus trying to arrive at some sort of equilibrium and harmony between freedom and other values. A good template for achieving this objective was opened up by Rawls's difference principle according to which social and economic inequalities are permitted only when they are intended to make the worst off in society as well off as possible. What is important to emphasize about this is that the moral judgement supporting the difference principle is not merely a judgement originating from charitable intentions to assist and help the poor, but a demand and principle of social justice. The underlying reason for this is that given the right conditions and institutions reasonable people in a political community would agree to share one another's fate. However efficiently and fairly we design the basic structure of society, there are likely to be both winners and losers in the social game and hence, justice demands that we pay attention to the lot of the worse off in society.

The capability theorists wish to extend and fully exploit this moral judgement by pressing the point that people can be made worse off by the basic structure of society not only in terms of primary goods, but also in terms of basic capabilities. When the capability shortfalls and deprivation that people face are things that they themselves have not asked for, a just society should address them as a claim of justice. Among other things, one way to substantiate this claim is to recognize broader arenas for 'the circumstances of justice' that motivate us to derive fairer principles and patterns of distribution. Inspired by Hume, Rawls for example, mentions objective as well as subjective circumstances: geographical territory, moderate scarcity, limited generosity, and different and conflicting conceptions of the good among individuals and associations. From the standpoint of the capability approach, it is imperative to add as part of the circumstances of justice the pervasive and undeniable human conditions of dependencies and vulnerabilities, exploitation and domination. It is also imperative to define the 'better off' and 'worse off' in society in terms of functionings and capabilities, what people are able to do and be.

Bibliography

a) Works by Amartya Sen

Sen, Amartya. 1970. *Collective Choice and Social Welfare*, San Fransisco: Holden-Day, Inc.

—— 1977. 'Rational Fools: A Critique of the Behavioural Foundations of Economic Theory', *Philosophy and Public Affairs*, 6, 317-344.

—— 1978. 'On Labour Theory of Value: Some Methodological Issues', *Cambridge Journal of Economics*, 2.

—— 1979. 'Utilitarianism and Welfarism', *The Journal of Philosophy*, 76/9, 463-489.

—— 1980. 'Equality of What?' in *Tanner Lectures on Human Values*, Vol. I, ed. S. McMurrin, Cambridge: Cambridge University Press, 197-220.

—— 1981. *Poverty and Famines: An Essay on Entitlement and Deprivation*, Oxford: Oxford University Press.

—— 1982a. *Choice, Welfare and Measurement*, Cambridge, MA: Harvard University Press.

—— 1982b. 'Rights and Agency', *Philosophy and Public Affairs*, 11/1, 3-39.

—— 1982c. 'The Right not to be Hungry' in *Contemporary Philosophy: A New Survey*, Vol. 2, The Hague: Martinus Nijhoff Publishers, 343-360.

—— 1984. *Resources, Values and Development*, Cambridge, MA: Harvard University Press.

—— 1985a. 'Well-being, Agency and Freedom', *Journal of Philosophy*, 32/4, 169-221.

—— 1985b. 'Rights as Goals' in *Equality and Discrimination: Essays in Freedom and Justice*, eds. S. Guest and A. Milne, Stuttgart: Franz Steiner Verlag Wiesbaden GMBH, 11-25.

—— 1985c. 'The Moral Standing of the Market', *Social Philosophy and Policy*, 2/2, 1-19.

—— 1986. 'Adam Smith's Prudence' in *Theory and Reality in Development*, eds. Sanjay Lall and Frances Stewart, London: The Macmillan Press, 28-37.

—— 1987a. *On Ethics and Economics*, New Delhi: Oxford University Press.

—— 1987b. *The Standard of Living*, Cambridge: Cambridge University Press.

—— 1987c. *Commodities and Capabilities*, New Delhi: Oxford University Press.

—— 1988a. 'Property and Hunger', *Economics and Philosophy*, 4, 57-68.

—— 1988b. 'Freedom of Choice: Concepts and Content', *European Economic Review*, 32, 269-294.

—— 1990. 'Justice: Means Versus Freedoms', *Philosophy and Public Affairs*, 19, 111-121.

—— 1992. *Inequality Reexamined*, Oxford: Oxford University Press.

—— 1993. 'Capability and Well-being' in *The Quality of Life*, eds. Martha Nussbaum and Amartya Sen, Oxford: Oxford University Press, 30-53.

—— 1995. 'Gender Inequality' in *Women, Culture and Development*, eds. M. Nussbaum and J. Glover, Oxford: Clarendon Press, 259-273.

—— 1997a. *On Economic Inequality*, Expanded Edition, Oxford: Clarendon Press.

—— 1997b. 'Inequality, Unemployment and Contemporary Europe', *International Labour Review*, 136/2, 155-172.

—— 1999a. *Development as Freedom*, Oxford: Oxford University Press.

—— 1999b. *Reason before Identity*, Oxford: Oxford University Press.

—— 1999c. 'Democracy as a Universal Value', *Journal of Democracy*, 10/3, 3-17.

—— 2000a. 'Consequential Evaluation and Practical Reason', *The Journal of Philosophy*, 97/9, 477-502.

—— 2000b. 'Work and Rights', *International Labour Review*, 139/2, 119-128.

—— 2002a. *Rationality and Freedom*, Cambridge, MA: Harvard University Press.

—— 2002b. 'Open and Closed Impartiality', *The Journal of Philosophy*, 94/9, 445-469.

—— 2003. 'Democracy and its Global Roots', *The New Republic* (October 6), 28-35.

—— 2004a. 'Elements of a Theory of Human Rights', *Philosophy and Public Affairs*, 32/4, 315-356.

—— 2004b. 'Continuing the Conversation', mimeo.

—— 2005. 'Why Exactly is Commitment Important for Rationality', *Economics and Philosophy*, 21/1, 5-14.

Sen, Amartya and Williams, B. 1982. 'Introduction', in *Utilitarianism and Beyond*, Cambridge: Cambridge University Press.

b) Works by Martha Nussbaum

Nussbaum, M.C. 1986. *The Fragility of Goodness* [Updated Edition, 2001], Cambridge: Cambridge University Press.

—— 1988a. 'Nature, Function, and Capability: Aristotle on Political Distribution', *Oxford Studies in Ancient Philosophy*, Oxford: Oxford University Press, 145-184.

—— 1988b. 'Non-Relative Virtues: An Aristotelian Approach', *Midwest Studies in Philosophy*, 13, 32-53.

—— 1990a. *Love's Knowledge: Essays on Philosophy and Literature,* Oxford: Oxford University Press.

—— 1990b. 'Aristotelian Social Democracy' in *Liberalism and the Good*, eds. B. B. Douglass et al., New York: Routledge, 203-252.

—— 1992. 'Human Functioning and Social Justice: In Defence of Aristotelian Essentialism', *Political Theory*, 20/2, 202-246.

—— 1994. *The Therapy of Desire*, Princeton: Princeton University Press.

—— 1995a. *Poetics of Justice*, Boston: Beacon Press.

—— 1995b. 'Human Capabilities, Female Human Beings' in *Women, Development and Culture*, eds. M. Nussbaum and J. Glover, Oxford: Clarendon Press, 61-104.

—— 1995c. 'Aristotle on Human Nature and the Foundations of Ethics' in *World, Mind and Ethics*, eds. J. Altham and R. Harrison, Cambridge: Cambridge University Press, 86-131.

—— 1996. 'Compassion: The Basic Social Emotion', *Social Philosophy and Policy*, 13, 27-58.

—— 1997a. 'Capabilities and Human Rights', *Fordham Law Review* (November), 273-300.

—— 1997b. *Cultivating Humanity*, Cambridge: Harvard University Press.

—— 2000a. *Women and Human Development*, Cambridge: Cambridge University Press.

—— 2000b. 'Aristotle, Politics and Human Capabilities', *Ethics*, 111, 102-140.

—— 2001a. *Upheavals of Thought*, Cambridge: Cambridge University Press.

—— 2001b. 'The Cost of Tragedy: Some Moral Limits of Cost-benefit Analysis' in *Cost-benefit Analysis: Legal, Economic and Philosophical Perspectives*, eds. M. D. Adler and E.A. Posner, Chicago: University of Chicago Press, 169-200.

—— 2001c. 'Comment' in J.J. Thomson, *Goodness and Advice*, ed. A. Gutmann, Princeton: Princeton University Press, 97-125.

—— 2002. 'Sex, Laws and Inequality: What India can Teach the US', *Daedalus* (Winter), 95-106.

—— 2004. *Hiding From Humanity: Disgust, Shame, and the Law*, Princeton: Princeton University Press.

—— 2006. *Frontiers of Justice: Disability, Nationality and Species Membership*, Cambridge, MA: Harvard University Press.

c) Other Works

Ackerly, B.A. 2000. *Political Theory and Feminist Social Criticism*, Cambridge: Cambridge University Press.

Alexander, J.M. 2003a. 'Capability Egalitarianism and Moral Selfhood', *Ethical Perspectives*, 10/1, 3-21.

—— 2003b. 'Inequality, Poverty and Affirmative Action: Contemporary Trends in India', Research Paper presented for the Conference 'Poverty, Inequality and Well-being', Helsinki: WIDER, United Nations University.

—— 2004. 'Capabilities, Human Rights and Moral Pluralism', *The International Journal of Human Rights*, 8/4, 451-469.

—— 2005a. 'Non-reductionist Naturalism: Nussbaum between Aristotle and Hume', *Res Publica: A Journal of Legal and Social Philosophy*, 11/2, 157-183.

—— 2005b. 'The Sen Difference', *Frontline* (February 25), 22/4, 4-12.

—— 2005c. 'Indian Democracy and Public Reasoning: An Interview with Amartya Sen', *Frontline* (February 25), 22/4, 13-20.

Alexander, J.M. and Vandevelde, A. 2006. 'Capitalism Recycled', *Frontline* (December 1), 23/23, 86-89.

Alkire, S. 2002. *Valuing Freedoms: Sen's Capability Approach and Poverty Reduction*, Oxford: Oxford University Press.

Anderson, E. 1993. *Value in Ethics and Economics*, Cambridge, MA: Harvard University Press.

—— 1999. 'What is the Point of Equality?', *Ethics*, 109, 287-337.

Annas, J. 1977. 'Mill and the Subjection of Women', *Philosophy*, 52 (April), 179-194.

—— 1993. *The Morality of Happiness*, Oxford: Oxford University Press.

—— 1996. 'Aristotle on Human Nature and Political Virtue', *The Review of Metaphysics*, 49 (June), 731-753.

Arendt, H. 1958. *The Human Condition*, Chicago: University of Chicago Press.

Aristotle. 1976. *Ethics*, Trans. J.A.K Thomson, London: Penguin Books.

—— 1992. *Politics*, Trans. T.A. Sinclair, London: Penguin Books.

—— 1991. *On Rhetoric*, ed. George A. Kennedy, Oxford: Oxford University Press.

Arneson, R. 1989. 'Equality and Equality of Opportunity for Welfare', *Philosophical Studies,* 56, 77-93.

—— 1990. 'Primary Goods Reconsidered', *Nous*, 24, 429-454.

—— 2000. 'Perfectionism and Politics', *Ethics*, 111, 37-63.

—— 2006. 'Distributive Justice and Basic Capability Equality' in *Capabilities Equality*, ed. Alexander Kaufman, New York: Routledge, 17-43.

Bagchi, A.K. 2000. 'Freedom and Development as End of Alienation?', *Economic and Political Weekly* (December 9), 4409-4420.

Baker, J. 1987. *Arguing for Equality*, London: Verso.

Baker, J. et al. 2004. *Equality: From Theory to Action*, Basingstoke: Palgrave Macmillan.

Barry, B. 1973. 'John Rawls and the Priority of Liberty', *Philosophy and Public Affairs*, 2, 274-290.

—— 1989. *Theories of Justice*, Berkeley: University of California Press.

—— 1991a. 'Tragic Choices' in *Liberty and Justice: Essays in Political Theory*, Vol.2, Oxford: Clarendon Press, 123-141.

—— 1991b. 'Chance, Choice and Justice' in *Liberty and Justice: Essays in Political Theory in Vol.2*, Oxford: Clarendon Press, 142-158.

Berlin, I. 1969. *Four Essays on Liberty*, Oxford: Oxford University Press.

Bentham, J. 1970. 'Of the Principle of Utility' in *The Collected Works of Jeremy Bentham*, eds. J.H. Burns and H.L.A. Hart, Athlone Press, 11-16.

Bojer, H. 2003. *Distributional Justice: Theory and Measurement*, New York: Routledge.

Boltanski, Luc. 1999. *Distant Suffering: Morality, Media and Politics*, Trans. G. Buchell, Cambridge: Cambridge University Press.

Broadie, S. 1991. *Ethics with Aristotle*, Oxford: Oxford University Press.

Chiappero-Martinetti, E. 2000. 'A Multidimensional Assessment of Human Well-being Based on Sen's Functioning Theory', *Revisita Internazionale di Scienza Soziale*, 108/2, 207-239.

Cohen, G.A. 1979. 'Capitalism, Freedom and the Proletariat' in *The Idea of Freedom: Essays Presented to Sir Isaiah Berlin*, ed. A. Ryan, Oxford: Oxford University Press.

—— 1989. 'On the Currency of Egalitarian Justice', *Ethics*, 99, 906-944.

—— 1993. 'Equality of What? On Utility, Goods and Capabilities' in *The Quality of Life*, eds. M. Nussbaum and A. Sen, Oxford: Oxford University Press, 9-29.

—— 2000. *If You are Egalitarian, How Come you are So Rich?* Cambridge: Harvard University Press.

Cooper, J. 1975. *Reason and Human Good in Aristotle*, Cambridge, MA: Harvard University Press.

Crocker, D.A. 1995. 'Functioning and Capability: The Foundations of Sen's and Nussbaum's Development Ethic' in *Women, Development and Culture*, eds. M. Nussbaum and J. Glover, Oxford: Clarendon Press, 153-198.

Daniels, N. 1990. 'Equality of What: Welfare, Resources, or Capabilities?', *Philosophy and Phenomenological Research*, 1 (Supplement, Fall), 273-296.

—— 2003. 'Rawls's Complex Egalitarianism' in *The Cambridge Companion to Rawls*, ed. S. Freeman, Cambridge: Cambridge University Press, 241-276.

De Dijn, H. 2003. 'Hume's Nonreductionist Philosophical Anthropology', *The Review of Metaphysics*, 56 (March), 587-603.

Deneulin, S. 2006. *The Capability Approach and the Praxis of Development*, Basingstoke: Palgrave Macmillan.

Denier, Yvonne. 2005. *Efficiency, Justice and Care: Philosophical Reflections on Scarcity in Health Care*, PhD Thesis, Institute of Philosophy, University of Leuven, Belgium.

Drèze, J. and Sen, A. 1989. *Hunger and Public Action*, Oxford: Clarendon Press.

—— 2002. *India: Development and Participation*, New Delhi: Oxford University Press.

Dworkin, R. 1975. 'Original Position' in *Reading Rawls*, ed. Norman Daniels, New York: Basic Books.

—— 1977. *Taking Rights Seriously*, London: Duckworth.

—— 1985a. 'Liberalism' in *A Matter of Principle*, Cambridge: Harvard University Press.

—— 1985b. 'Foundations of Liberal Equality' in *Equal Freedom*, ed. S. Darwall, Ann Arbor: Michigan University Press, 190-306.

—— 2000. *Sovereign Virtue*, Harvard: Harvard University Press.

Elster, J. 1982. 'Sour Grapes: Utilitarianism and the Genesis of Wants' in *Utilitarianism: for and Against*, eds. A. Sen and B. Williams, Cambridge: Cambridge University Press, 219-238.

—— 1986. 'The Market and the Forum: Three Varieties of Political Theory' in *Foundations in Social Choice Theory*, eds. J. Elster and A. Hylland, Cambridge: Cambridge University Press.

—— 1992. *Local Justice*, Cambridge: Cambridge University Press.

Evans, Peter. 2002. 'Collective Capabilities, Culture and Amartya Sen's Freedom as Development', *Studies in Comparative International Development*, 37/2, 54-60.

Fleurbaey, M. 2002. 'Development, Capabilities and Freedom', *Studies in Comparative International Development*, 37/2, 71-77.

Frank, R.H. 2001. 'Why is Cost-Benefit Analysis So Controversial?' in *Cost-benefit Analysis: Legal, Economic and Philosophical Perspectives*, eds. M.D. Adler and E.A. Posner, Chicago: University of Chicago Press, 77-94.

Frankfurt, H. 1987. 'Equality as a Moral Ideal', *Ethics*, 98, 21-43.

Fraser, N. 1997. *Justice Interruptus*, New York: Routledge.

Freeman, S. 2003. 'Introduction' in *The Cambridge Companion to Rawls*, ed. S. Freeman, Cambridge: Cambridge University Press, 1-61.

Friedman, M and Friedman, R. 1980. *Free to Choose*, London: Seckcr and Warburg.

Fukuda-Parr, S. 2003. 'The Human Development Paradigm: Operationalizing Sen's Ideas on Capabilities', *Feminist Economics*, 9/2-3, 301-317.

Glover, J. 1970. *Responsibility*, London: Routledge and Kegan Paul.

Goodin, R.E. 1995. *Utilitarianism as a Public Philosophy*, Cambridge: Cambridge University Press.

Gray, J. 1989. *Liberalisms: Essays in Political Philosophy*, London: Routledge.

Griswold, C.L. 1999. *Adam Smith and the Virtues of Enlightenment*, Cambridge: Cambridge University Press.

Hardie, W.F.R. 1968. *Aristotle's Ethical Theory*, Oxford: Clarendon Press.

Hare, R. M. 1981. *Moral Thinking*, Oxford: Clarendon Press.

—— 1997. *Sorting Out Ethics*, Oxford: Clarendon Press.

Harsanyi, John C. 1982. 'Morality and the Theory of Rational Behaviour' in *Utilitarianism: for and Against*, eds. A. Sen and B. Williams, Cambridge: Cambridge University Press.

Hart, H.L.A. 1975. 'Rawls on Liberty and its Priority' in *Reading Rawls*, ed. Norman Daniels, New York: Basic Books.

—— 1979. 'Between Utility and Rights', *Columbia Law Review*, 79/5, 826-846.

Hausman, D.M and McPherson, M.S. 1996. *Economic Analysis and Moral Philosophy*, Cambridge: Cambridge University Press.

Hill, M.T. 2003. 'Development as Empowerment', *Feminist Economics*, 9/2-3, 117-135.

Hobbes, T. 1985. *Leviathan*, ed. C.B. Macpherson, London: Penguin Books.

Hume, D. 1998. *An Enquiry Concerning the Principle of Morals*, ed. T.L. Beauchamp, Oxford: Oxford University Press.

—— 2000. *Treatise of Human Nature*, eds. D.F. Norton and M.J. Norton, Oxford: Oxford University Press.

Hurka, T. 2002. 'Capability, Functioning, and Perfectionism', *Apeiron*, 35/4, 137-162.

Irwin, T.H. 1980. 'The Metaphysical and Psychological Basis of Aristotle's Ethics' in *Essays in Aristotle's Ethics*, ed. A.O. Rorty, Berkeley: University of California Press, 35-54.

Jaggar, A.M. 2006. 'Reasoning About Well-Being: Nussbaum's Method of Justifying the Capabilities', *The Journal of Political Philosophy*, 14/3, 301-322.

Kant, I. 1997. *Groundwork of the Metaphysics of Morals*, ed. Mary Gregor, Cambridge: Cambridge University Press.

Kekes, J. 2003. *The Illusions of Egalitarianism*, New York: Cornell University Press.

Kittay, E.F. 2003. 'Human Dependency and Rawlsian Equality' in *John Rawls: Vol. III*, ed. C. Kukathas, London: Routledge, 167-211.

Korsgaard, C. 1993. 'Commentary' in *The Quality of Life*, eds. M.C. Nussbaum and A. Sen, Oxford: Clarendon Press, 54-61.

Kraut, R. 2002. *Aristotle: Political Philosophy*, Oxford: Oxford University Press.

Kukathas, C. and Pettit, P. 1990. *Rawls*, Cambridge: Polity Press.

Kuklys, W. 2005. *Amartya Sen's Capability Approach: Theoretical Insights and Empirical Applications*, New York: Springer.

Kymlicka, W. 1989. 'Liberal Individualism and Liberal Neutrality', *Ethics*, 99, 883-905.

—— 1990. *Contemporary Political Philosophy*, Oxford: Oxford University Press.

Locke, J. 2003. *Two Treatises of Government and A Letter Concerning Toleration*, ed. Ian Shapiro, New Haven: Yale University Press.

Lyons, D. 1977. 'Human Rights and the General Welfare', *Philosophy and Public Affairs*, 6/2, 113-129.

MacCallum, G.C. 1967. 'Negative and Positive Freedom', *Philosophical Review*, 74, 312-334.

McDowell, J. 1978. *The Law in Classical Athens*, London: Thames and Hudson.

—— 1998a. 'Some Issues in Aristotle's Moral Psychology' in *Mind, Value and Reality*, Cambridge, MA: Harvard University Press, 23-49.

—— 1998b. 'Two Sorts of Naturalism' in *Mind, Value and Reality*, Cambridge, MA: Harvard University Press, 167-197.

Menon, N. 2002. 'Universalism Without Foundations?', *Economy and Society* 31/1, 152-169.

Meyer, S. 1993. *Aristotle on Moral Responsibility*, Oxford: Blackwell.

Mill, J.S. 1965. *Principles of Political Economy*, Vols. 2 & 3 of *Collected Works*, ed. J.M. Robson, Toronto: University of Toronto Press.

—— 1974a. 'That the Ideally Best Form of Government is Representative Government', *Considerations on Representative Government*, Everyman's Library Edition, 136-151.

—— 1974b. 'On the Connection Between Justice and Utility', *Utilitarianism*, Everyman's Library Edition, 118-135.

—— 1980. *The Subjection of Women*, ed. Sue Mansfield, Crofts Classics Edition, Illinois: AHM Publishing Corporation.

—— 1995. *On Liberty*, eds D. Bromwich and G. Kateb, New Haven: Yale University Press.

Miller, David. 2001. *Principles of Social Justice*, Cambridge, MA: Harvard University Press.

Miller, F.D. 1995. *Nature, Justice and Rights in Aristotle's Politics*, Oxford: Clarendon Press.

Mulhall, S. and Swift, A. 2003. 'Rawls and Communitarianism' in *The Cambridge Companion to Rawls*, ed. S. Freeman, Cambridge: Cambridge University Press, 460-487.

Muller, J.Z. 1995. *Adam Smith in His Time and Ours: Designing the Decent Society*, Princeton: Princeton University Press.

Nagel, T. 2003. 'Rawls and Liberalism' in *The Cambridge Companion to Rawls*, ed. S. Freeman, Cambridge: Cambridge University Press, 62-85.

—— 2005. 'The Problem of Global Justice', *Philosophy and Public Affairs*, 33/2, 113-147.

Nozick, R. 1974. *Anarchy, State and Utopia*, New York: Basic Books.

Okin, S. 1989. *Justice, Gender and the Family*, New York: Basic Books.

Parfit, D. 1984. *Reasons and Persons*, Oxford: Oxford University Press.

—— 1995. 'Equality or Priority?', *The Lindley Lectures*, University of Kansas.

Pettit, P. and Brennan, G. 1986. 'Restrictive Consequentialism', *Australian Journal of Philosophy*, 64/4, 438-455.

—— 1987. 'Rights, Constraints and Trumps', *Analysis*, 46, 8-14.

—— 1988. 'The Consequentialist Can Recognize Rights', *The Philosophical Quarterly*, 38/150, 42-55.

—— 1991. 'Consequentialism' in *A Companion to Ethics*, ed. Peter Singer, Oxford: Basil Blackwell, 230-240.

—— 1993. 'Introduction' in *Consequentialism*, ed. Philip Pettit, Aldershot: Dartmouth Publishing Company, xiii-xix.

—— 1995. 'The Virtual Reality of Homo Economicus', *Monist*, 78/3, 308-330.

—— 1997a. *Republicanism: A Theory of Freedom and Government*, Oxford: Oxford University Press.

—— 1997b. 'Republican Political Theory' in *Political Theory*, ed. A. Vincent, Cambridge: Cambridge University Press, 112-131.

—— 1997c. 'The Consequentialist Perspective' in *Three Methods of Ethics*, eds. M. W. Marcia et al., Oxford: Blackwell, 92-174.

—— 2001. 'Capability and Freedom: A Defence of Sen', *Economics and Philosophy*, 17/1, 1-20.

Phillips, A. 1994. 'Dealing with Differences: A Politics of Ideas, or a Politics of Presence?', *Constellations*, 1, 74-91.

—— 2004. 'Defending Equality of Outcome', *The Journal of Political Philosophy*, 12/1, 1-19.

Plato. 2003. *Republic*, Trans. Desmond Lee, London: Penguin Books.

Pogge, T.W. 2002a. *World Poverty and Human Rights*, Cambridge: Polity Press.

—— 2002b. 'Can the Capability Approach be Justified?', *Philosophical Topics*, 30/2, 167-226.

Putnam, H. 2002. *The Collapse of the Fact/Value Dichotomy and Other Essays*, Cambridge, MA: Harvard University Press.

Rawls, J. 1971. *A Theory of Justice*, Oxford: Oxford University Press. [1999. Revised Edition, Cambridge, MA: Harvard University Press].

—— 1980. 'Kantian Constructivism in Moral Theory: The Dewey Lectures 1980', *The Journal of Philosophy*, 77/9, 515-572.

—— 1982. 'Social Unity and Primary Goods' in *Utilitarianism and Beyond*, eds. A. Sen and B. Williams, Cambridge: Cambridge University Press, 159-185.

—— 1985. 'Justice as Fairness: Political Not Metaphysical', *Philosophy and Public Affairs*, 14/3, 225-251.

—— 1993. *Political Liberalism*, New York: Columbia University Press.

—— 1999a. *Collected Papers*, ed. S. Freeman, Cambridge, MA: Harvard University Press.

—— 1999b. *The Law of Peoples*, Cambridge, MA: Harvard University Press.

—— 2001. *Justice as Fairness: A Restatement*, ed. Erin Kelley, Cambridge MA: Harvard University Press.

Raz, J. 1990. 'Facing Diversity: The Case of Epistemic Abstinence', *Philosophy and Public Affairs*, 19/1, 3-46.

Ricoeur, P. 1992. *Oneself as Another*, Trans. Kathleen Blamey, Chicago: University of Chicago Press.

—— 1996. 'Love and Justice', *The Hermeneutics of Action: Paul Ricoeur*, ed. R. Kearney, London: Sage Publications.

—— 2000. *The Just*, Chicago: University of Chicago Press.

Robeyns, I. 2001. 'Will a Basic Income do Justice to Women', *Analyse und Kritik*, 23/1, 88-105.

—— 2003. 'Sen's Capability Approach and Gender Inequality: Selecting Relevant Capabilities', *Feminist Economics*, 9/2-3, 61-92.

Roemer, J.E. 1988. *Free to Lose*, Cambridge, MA: Harvard University Press.

—— 1996. *Theories of Distributive Justice*, Cambridge: Harvard University Press.

—— 1999. 'Does Democracy Engender Justice?' in *Democracy's Value*, eds. I. Shapiro and C. Hacker-Cordon, Cambridge: Cambridge University Press.

Sandel, M. 1982. *Liberalism and the Limits of Justice*, Cambridge: Cambridge University Press.

Scanlon, T. 1975. 'Preference and Urgency', *The Journal of Philosophy*, 72/6, 655-669.

—— 2000. *What We Owe to Each Other*, Cambridge: Harvard University Press.

—— 2001. 'Sen and Consequentialism', *Economics and Philosophy*, 17, 39-50.

Scheffler, S. 1982. *The Rejection of Consequentialism*, Oxford: Clarendon Press.

—— 1988. 'Agent-centred Restrictions, Rationality and the Virtues' in *Consequentialism and its Critiques*, ed. S. Scheffler, Oxford: Clarendon Press.

Schokkaert, E. 1992. 'The Economics of Distributive Justice, Welfare and Freedom' in *Justice: Interdisciplinary Perspectives*, ed. Klaus R. Scherer, Cambridge: Cambridge University Press.

—— 1998. 'Mr. Fairmind is Post-welfarist: Opinions on Distributive Justice', *Discussion Paper Series*, Centre for Economic Studies, University of Leuven, Belgium.

Schokkaert, E. and Van Ootegem, L. 1990. 'Sen's Concept of the Living Standard Applied to the Belgian Unemployed', *Recherches Economiques de Louvain*, 56, 429-450.

Shue, H. 1980. *Basic Rights: Subsistence, Affluence and U.S. Foreign Policy*, Princeton: Princeton University Press.

Skinner, Q. 1984. 'The Paradoxes of Political Liberty' in *Tanner Lectures on Human Values*, Cambridge, MA: Harvard University Press, 227-250.

—— 1998. *Liberty Before Liberalism*, Cambridge: Cambridge University Press.

Slote, M. 1985. *Common-sense Morality and Consequentialism*, London: Routledge and Kegan Paul.

Smart, J.J.C. 1973. 'An Outline of a System of Utilitarian Ethics' in *Utilitarianism: for and Against*, Cambridge: Cambridge University Press.

Smith, A. 1976. *An Inquiry into the Nature and Causes of the Wealth of Nations*, 2 Volumes, eds R.H. Campell and A.S. Skinner, Oxford: Clarendon Press.

Steiner, H. 1990. 'Putting Rights in Their Place', *Recherches Economiques de Louvain*, 56/3-4, 391-408.

Subramanian, S. *Rights, Deprivation and Disparity*, New Delhi: Oxford University Press.

Sugden, Robert. 1993. 'Welfare, Resources and Capabilities: A Review of Inequality Reexamined', *Journal of Economic Literature*, 31, 1947-1962.

Tawney, R.H. 1952. *Equality*, London: Allen and Unwin.

Taylor, C. 1985a. 'Atomism' in *Philosophy and The Human Sciences: Philosophical Papers 2*, Cambridge: Cambridge University Press.

—— 1985b. 'What's Wrong with Negative Liberty' in *Philosophy and The Human Sciences: Philosophical Papers 2*, Cambridge: Cambridge University Press, 211-229.

—— 1993. 'Explanation and Practical Reason' in *The Quality of Life*, eds. M.C. Nussbaum and A. Sen, Oxford: Oxford University Press, 208-231.

—— 1995a. 'Irreducibly Social Goods' in *Philosophical Arguments*, Cambridge, MA: Harvard University Press.

—— 1995b. 'Cross-Purposes: The Liberal-Communitarian Debate' in *Philosophical Arguments*, Cambridge, MA: Harvard University Press.

—— 1995c. 'Liberal Politics and Public Sphere' in *Philosophical Arguments*, Cambridge, MA: Harvard University Press.

Tocqueville, A. de. 1965. *Democracy in America*, New York: Basic Books.

Vandevelde, A. 1994. 'Het intrestverbod bij Aristoteles' in *Intrest en Cultuur*, ed. L. Bouckaert, Leuven, Belgium: Acco, 37-58.

—— 2000. 'Reciprociteit en vertrouwen als gok en als sociaal kapitaal' in *Over Vertrouwen en bedrijf*, ed. A. Vandevelde, Leuven, Belgium: Acco, 13-26.

—— 2005. 'Beyond Liberalism', *Frontline* (February 25), 22/4, 18-19.

Van Parijs, P. 1995. *Real Freedom for All*, Oxford: Clarendon Press.

—— 2000. 'A Basic Income for All', *Boston Review*, 25/5, 1-16.

Viroli, M. 1998. *Machiavelli*, Oxford: Oxford University Press.

Waldron, J. 1986. 'Welfare and Images of Charity', *Philosophical Quarterly*, 36, 463-482.

—— 1988. *The Right to Private Property*, Oxford: Clarendon Press.

Walzer, M. 1973. 'Political Action: The Problem of Dirty Hands', *Philosophy and Public Affairs*, 2/2, 160-180.

—— 1983. *Spheres of Justice*, New York: Basic Books.

Williams, A. 2002. 'Dworkin on Capability', *Ethics*, 113, 23-39.

Williams, B. 1973. 'A Critique of Utilitarianism' in *Utilitarianism: For and Against*, Cambridge: Cambridge University Press.

—— 1981. *Moral Luck*, Cambridge: Cambridge University Press.

—— 1987. 'The Standard of Living: Interests and Capabilities' in A. Sen, *The Standard of Living*, Cambridge: Cambridge University Press.

Young, I. 2000. *Inclusion and Democracy*, Oxford: Oxford University Press.

Index